A Climber's Guide to the High Sierra

A guidebook is not a substitute for mountaineering skill, nor can it make climbing safe for those who do not practice the principles of safety. It is urged that inexperienced climbers avail themselves of the instruction and training given by the Sierra Club or other organizations before attempting difficult ascents.

Routes and Records for California Peaks

from Bond Pass to Army Pass

and for Rock Climbs

in Kings Canyon

A Climber's Guide
to the HIGH SIERRA

Edited by HERVEY H. VOGE

SIERRA CLUB · SAN FRANCISCO

The Sierra Club, founded in 1892 by John Muir, has devoted itself to the study and protection of national scenic resources, particularly those of mountain regions. Sierra Club publications are part of the nonprofit effort the club carries on as a public trust. Participation is invited in the program to enjoy and preserve wilderness, wildlife, forests, and streams.

Address: Mills Tower, San Francisco; 25 W. 45th, New York; Dupont Circle Building, Washington, D. C.

Contents

CONTENTS

Foreword

HERVEY VOGE'S labor of love should contribute greatly to the enjoyment of three of America's great national parks, Yosemite, Sequoia, and Kings Canyon, and of the John Muir Wilderness and adjoining national forest country, in all of which there are challenges to the mountaineer on every hand—spectacular and beautiful challenges. There are special rewards for those who forsake pavement and try trails instead, seeking out the untrammeled places, finding out what goes on there in a wilderness world man has chosen not to manage. The back country has a special allure for those who would forsake trails and try the routes instead, into the trailless canyons, to the high cirques, and up the arêtes and faces of the splendid peaks where the world seems new, still in the making, even raw at times, and extremely rugged.

Clearly, the roof country is not for everyone. There are some important prerequisites. This book can say where to go, but it cannot say who should go nor can it expound upon mountaineering technique. Here the rangers of the National Park Service and the U.S. Forest Service, with whom all climbers should register in the course of getting the required campfire permits, can be especially helpful. They have learned about the peaks the enjoyable way and the hard way, having climbed among the peaks for pleasure on the one hand and having accomplished heroic rescue work on the other. Many are well trained in appraising the experience a climber has and needs. In short, the rangers can be especially helpful to both bold and tentative novices. They can fairly judge whether you are equipped for a climb—mentally, physically, or with gadgets. And it helps them to know where to begin looking if you get into trouble.

On behalf of the Sierra Club I should like to thank Hervey Voge for accepting the double jeopardy of editing both the original and revised edition of the guidebook. It would try any friendship to ask a man to do either, let alone both. But it was a long friendship. I first encountered Dr. Voge in Humphreys Basin in 1933, when he was knapsacking south and I north. He talked me into joining the Sierra Club later that summer and we talked each other into a ten-week

"Survey of Sierra Routes and Records" the following summer—an effort that got me inextricably involved in committee work for the Sierra Club and in writing the beginnings of this book.

We left several improvised summit registers and found one—on Center Peak—in which there had been no entry between the original ascent and ours, forty years later. We developed an interest in the entire question of placing summit registers and safeguarding their contents. If other climbers should feel similarly inclined, I hope they will let the club know—about the condition of summit records, the need for new register boxes or books inside the boxes—and will bring in for the archives those records that seem to be of historic significance and are clearly in peril of loss. We will safeguard the originals and make photostats available for a subsequent ascent. We know that there is an added summit satisfaction in finding a few notes about who climbed before and how he felt—except perhaps for the "never again" entries that worry us about the coming descent. Perhaps this guidebook can assuage such worries, telling enough about the route down to help the descent, but never so much as to spoil it.

This book cannot be a substitute for training in mountaineering. Neither do we wish it to discourage people who have an age-old urge to get up on high places to see what they can see and to enjoy all the rewards associated with the fairly recent and very noble sport of mountain climbing. We would counsel that you remember the virtues of progressive training: ... you crawled before you walked and walked before you ran. It would be well to take your mountain pioneering in little nibbles rather than big leaps. Try the easy off-trail walks first, then the easy peaks, then the harder ones, always covering yourself with a good route of retreat and plenty of time to make it. And always heed the philosophy which the famous mountaineer, Norman Clyde, has passed on to many budding mountaineers: "The mountain will always be there tomorrow. Aim to be able to say the same of yourself."

One of the inalienable freedoms of the mountains is the freedom to turn back whenever the margin of safety seems to be getting too thin, to know that the mountain will still be there tomorrow. Exercise that freedom, we would urge, and the rest of the freedoms will be yours for a long time in one of the best of all possible mountain worlds.

DAVID BROWER, *Executive Director*
SIERRA CLUB

San Francisco, July 7, 1965

Preface

THIS VOLUME represents the culmination of an effort begun in 1933 when the Sierra Club Committee on Mountain Records started the collection of information on the ascents that had been made in the High Sierra. The project was soon enlarged with the ultimate aim of publishing a guidebook to Sierra climbs. Eight separate regions were described in a series of articles published in the *Sierra Club Bulletin* over the period 1937 to 1951, and these have now been corrected and combined with new material to make this volume. It is to be noted, however, that the project cannot be considered complete or final because many omissions have undoubtedly been made and there is certain to be additional material in the future as new generations of climbers seek out novel routes and unclimbed pinnacles. Therefore the compilers of this guide, now constituting the Sierra Club Mountaineering Committee, will welcome any additions or corrections. For omissions committed because of ignorance we can only offer our sincerest apologies, and shall gently suggest that in the future these climbs can be recorded if we are informed of them.

Mr. and Mrs. William Shand of Lancaster, Pennsylvania, have particularly aided this project through the William Shand Fund contributed in memory of their son, William Shand, Jr., who lost his life in an automobile accident en route to the Tetons in 1946. His parents' generosity has made possible the publication of the *Climber's Guide* in the present form.

Many members of the Sierra Club have contributed to the material in this guide. The patience and ingenuity of the authors of the various sections in correlating heterogeneous bits of information have been invaluable. Others who deserve special mention are: Arthur H. Blake, chairman of the Committee on Mountain Records during the period when many sections of the guide were compiled; David Brower, who throughout has contributed leadership and advice; Norman Clyde, who supplied much material in the region from Mammoth Pass to Kearsarge Pass from his personal notes; Richard M. Leonard, who in 1937 compiled the "Mountain Records of the Sierra Nevada," which listed all peaks and all known ascents (up to the first five); Gene Hammel and Allen P. Steck, who for successive periods organized and directed work on the guide; and Walter Starr, who had the "Mountain Records of the Sierra Nevada" and the climbing notes of Walter Starr, Jr., mimeographed for distribution to those who were active in climbing and might make further contributions.

Still others who have helped in various ways are: Kenneth Adam, Ansel Adams, Marjorie Borland, Chispa Chamberlain, Jack Davis, Glen Dawson, Betty De Coe, Marjorie Dunmire, Jules Eichorn, Joan Firey, Samuel W. French, Morgan Harris, Mary Houston, Elizabeth Klevesahl, Jim Koontz, Oscar Krupp, Norvill LaVene, R. G. Meisenheimer, L. Bruce Meyer, Howard Parker, Fernando Penalosa, Bill and Ellen Phillips, A. J. Reyman, William Rice, Ed Roper, Ned Robinson, Ruth Shapero, Jack Sturgeon, Denese Summitt, Chester Versteeg, Suzie Voge, Dale Webster, Laurie Williams, and Owen Williams. Among these A. J. Reyman and Chester Versteeg have been particularly active in climbing peaks for which no information was available and particularly helpful in sending in records from summit registers. The contributions of all are gratefully acknowledged.

Since it is hoped that revised editions of the guide will be published in the future, climbers are asked to send in additions and corrections. These should be addressed to the Mountaineering Committee, Sierra Club, Mills Tower, San Francisco.

Especially desired are records of first ascents and of new routes, either based on personal experience or copied from summit registers. We urge all climbers to carry pencils and notebooks so that details regarding routes and landmarks can be entered on the spot. For new routes, starting points, general orientation of route (compass direction from the summit), and a reasonable amount of detail are desirable. This will make identification of routes much more certain than it is in many of the descriptions in this guide.

There are still many minor peaks of the Sierra for which no records are available. For the most part these peaks have not even been listed here. Those who harbor a desire to tread rocks which have never before felt the presence of man may wish to seek out such peaks. Others will find the same satisfaction of pioneering in making new and perhaps more difficult routes on nonvirgin peaks.

H.H.V.

Berkeley, California, January 1954

Preface to the Second Edition

THIS SECOND EDITION is a thoroughly revised climber's guide, containing a great number of new routes. The Yosemite chapter has been removed and published as a separate book, *A Climber's Guide to Yosemite Valley*, by Steve Roper. New maps and some new illustrations have been added. More emphasis has been placed on knapsack routes because the book serves the needs of the cross-country hiker as well as the rock climber.

It is expected that at the next revision the Sierra will have to be covered by three or four books. To supply the information for these books, climbers are urged to send descriptions of climbs, comments, and corrections to the Sierra Club Mountaineering Committee. Sketches and marked photographs are especially desired.

As noted in the Preface to the first edition, many people have contributed to this book. The authors of the individual chapters are to be commended for their careful collection and organization of routes, names, peaks, and places. It is they who have written the book. Others who have helped by sending in information or in other ways are Dave Brower, Donald Clarke, Susana Cox, R. A. De Sota, Lewis Ellingham, William D. Engs, Karl Hufbauer, Don Lewis, Mike Loughman, Christine Mayne, A. J. Reyman, Steve Roper, Tom Ross, Andrew J. Smatko, Allen Steck, Chester Versteeg, Rhea Voge, Caroline Voge, Harry Weldon, and George W. Whitmore. Many others, too numerous to mention here, have sent in data regarding specific climbs or peaks.

With the growth of population in the west, mountain travel increases year after year. For the true wilderness feeling, cities, roads, and even trails must be left behind. The mountaineer finds real contact with nature on the peaks or cliffs, or in cross-country travel. It is hoped that this book will help him do so competently, joyfully, and reverently.

H.H.V.

Berkeley, June 1965

[xi]

William Shand, Jr.

WILLIAM SHAND, JR., was born October 5, 1918, in Lancaster, Pennsylvania, second son of William and Dorothy (Schaeffer) Shand. After attending Franklin and Marshall Academy and Phillips Academy, Andover, Massachusetts, from which he was graduated second in his class, he entered Princeton University with the class of 1940. His many achievements in college were climaxed by his graduation as valedictorian of the class, with highest honors in chemistry. After receiving the freshman First Honors Prize, Bill went on to win the Wood Legacy Prize, the McCay Prize in Chemistry, and a Phi Beta Kappa key in his junior year. He was a member of the Princeton Quadrangle Club and found time for the varsity cross-country squad and the varsity swimming team, the German Club, and the Experiment in International Living. It was during the summers of 1935, 1937, and 1938 in Europe with the latter organization that his interest in mountain climbing was aroused.

After graduation, Bill entered the Graduate School of the California Institute of Technology as a fellow in the department of chemistry. During the war, he performed research with the Office of Scientific Research and Development for the Army in Panama in 1944, and in the South Pacific and the Philippines in 1945. After the war, he returned to California Institute of Technology, where he received his Ph.D. in physical chemistry in June 1946. He was appointed an instructor in molecular physics at the University of California, Berkeley, on July 1, 1946.

An enthusiastic mountain climber, Bill was a member of the Sierra Club, The American Alpine Club, and the Swiss Alpine Club. In the summer of 1938, he climbed the thirteen highest peaks in Switzerland. He was a member of the party, headed by Bradford Washburn, which first scaled Mount Hayes in Alaska in 1941. With Dr. Ben Ferris, he later in the same year ascended a then unnamed peak near Mount Hayes, which had never before been climbed; later the peak was officially named Mount Shand in his memory. The Canadian government has similarly named a peak after him in the Coast Mountains of

British Columbia. Bill's unrealized ambition was to take part in an expedition to K-2, in the Himalaya.

In addition to his great enthusiasm for mountaineering, Bill showed an unusual ability in rock climbing. His friends in the Sierra Club report that he was a most capable rock climber during his years with the club and frequently undertook difficult ascents at Tahquitz Rock, in southern California, in Yosemite Valley, and in other places in the Sierra. His natural abilities and personality made him a popular leader in the rock climbing and mountaineering activities of the Southern California Chapter of the Sierra Club. Bill's favorite mountain was the Grand Teton in Wyoming, which he ascended several times. It was while driving alone to repeat an ascent of this peak that he met his death in a collision in Nevada on August 11, 1946.

Publication of this work was made possible through a gift to the Sierra Club from Bill's parents as a memorial to him, with the hope that many young climbers may benefit from the information contained herein.

The portrait by Raymond P. N. Neilson, reproduced in this volume, hangs in the William Shand, Jr., Memorial Library of the Chemistry Department of Franklin and Marshall College at Lancaster, Pennsylvania.

WILLIAM SHAND, JR., 1918–1946

Mount Winchell   *Ansel Adams*

The Climber's Sierra

North from Mount Ritter, Winter   *Robert L. Swift*

Mount Ritter and Banner Peak   *Philip Hyde*

Peaks above Purple Lake   *William Hail*

Mount McAdie   *Tom Ross*

On Northeast Buttress, North Palisade

Burt Turney

North Palisade

Tom Ross

Ragged Peak   *Ansel Adams*

Bergschrund, North Palisade.   Tom Ross

*East Face
of Mount Whitney*

Tom Ross

The Minarets. Philip Hyde

Arrow Peak.   Cedric Wright

The Three Teeth   *Ansel Adams*

Kearsarge Pinnacles
Ansel Adams

*East and South Faces
of Mount Mills
from Mount Abbot*

Tom Ross

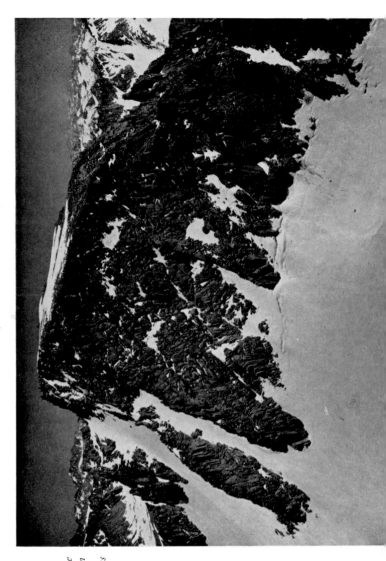

*North Face
of Mount Darwin*

Tom Ross

Mount Huxley   *Ansel Adams*

Introduction

M OUNTAINEERING in the Sierra Nevada of California is a sport
that offers an especially attractive combination of satisfactions.
There are many precipitous cliffs and jagged peaks to challenge the
climber, including many possible routes that have not yet been attempted. There is the High Sierra timberline country, an area un-
excelled in natural beauty, with thousands of streams and lakes, and a
parklike quality that often permits the climber to go cross country without need of a trail. There is a summer climate seldom rivaled in moun-
tainous areas, which nearly guarantees fair weather for both camping
and climbing. There is an unspoiled wilderness, yet any peak can be
reached in two days from the nearest roadhead. Lower down, in Yosemite Valley and elsewhere, there are readily accessible granite cliffs
where rock climbers can find routes as difficult and demanding as any
that have yet been ascended. Some idea of the Sierra terrain is given by
the photographs included in this volume, but the climber will have to
go out into the real mountains to experience the special Sierra charm.

It is the purpose of this guidebook to supply brief descriptions of the
routes of ascent for the High Sierra peaks and for certain cliffs in Kings
Canyon. An attempt has been made to include all novel ascents, and
thus the guide is also a compilation of mountain records. In this introduction something is said about the area covered, the general nature of
Sierra climbing, the classification system used, the method of describing
routes, and necessary safety precautions. For other information the
reader may wish to consult some of the books listed in the References
and Maps section at the end of this volume.

Area Covered

THE GENERAL area covered is the Sierra Nevada between Bond
Pass on the north and Army and Franklin passes on the south. Usually
only peaks above 10,000 feet elevation are included. Throughout, peaks
and climbs have been selected on the basis of interest to the climber
or because of their prominence in a region, rather than by definition
in terms of a minimum of so many hundreds of feet above the nearest
saddle. This choice has been arbitrary and has left out many small

[1]

peaks which may ultimately attract attention. On the other hand, the peaks included are quite numerous, and many are listed which can be very easily climbed.

The whole area is subdivided into sections marked off by the major passes across the Sierra Crest, as shown in Sketches 1 and 2. Dividing lines between sections follow water courses, with a few exceptions. Within sections there are certain areas which, because of their isolation or because of their accessibility from a single base, or because of unusual attractiveness for climbers, have come to be considered as units. Such, for instance, are the Sawtooth Ridge, the Palisades, and the Evolution Region. These areas are treated separately within the major sections. For each such area there are usually given a brief description, some history of the climbing, routes of access, information on campsites, a listing of passes and knapsack routes, and the routes and records for the peaks. In some sections general information for the individual areas is given only at the head.

Sketch maps are included for a few sections. These show certain features or routes not on the topographic maps of the U.S. Geological Survey, but are not intended as substitutes for the latter. Every climber will need the topographic maps to aid in identification of peaks and finding of routes. The Sierra region of interest has been completely mapped on a scale of 1:62,500 (15 Minute Series). These maps are listed in a table in the References and Maps section near the end of the book. Larger sheets made up of older maps show the areas of Sequoia and Kings Canyon, and Yosemite national parks. Climbers should be warned against possible errors in these older maps (1:125,000 series).

The guidebook is chiefly based on names and elevations shown on the new maps. For unnamed peaks the elevations serve as primary identification, being followed by the distance in miles from a nearby named feature. In some instances an exact elevation was given on the old maps, but none is shown on the new maps. Because of this, and because early records of the Sierra Club were based on the old maps, both new and old elevations are given for prominent unnamed peaks. Elevations from the old maps are designated "formerly." When an exact elevation is not given on a map, the elevation for the last contour line is written in the guide, followed by a plus sign to indicate the unknown additional elevation.

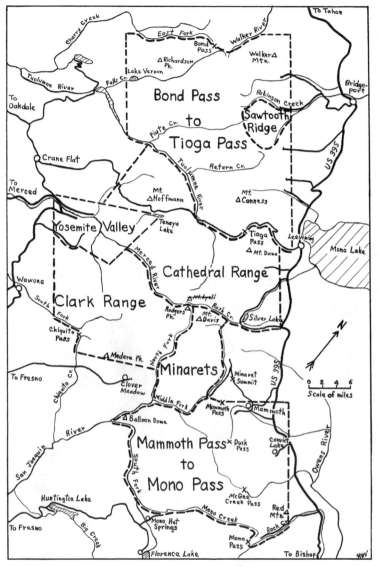

Sketch 1. Northern Areas.

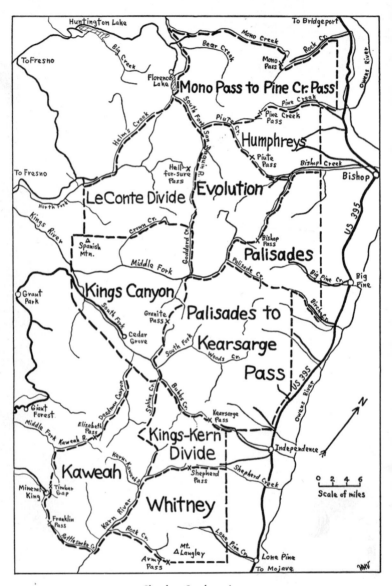

Sketch 2. Southern Areas

Sierra Camping and Climbing

CAMPING is the customary mode of habitation in the Sierra, although more civilized accommodations are available in the national parks and forests at a few places, and at a few pack stations. The climate in summer and fall is quite suitable for camping with a minimum of equipment, but a small tent or a large tarpaulin is advisable since rain can fall in spite of the fabled California climate. Wood for fires and trees for shelter are usually found up to about 11,000 feet; the knapsacker equipped with air mattress and primus stove can camp higher—even on the summits. The temperature at night in the summer is usually in the thirties or low forties at timberline, and ice on puddles is not uncommon. Daytime temperatures are usually much higher.

Campers are rarely bothered by animals in the High Sierra. In the national parks, when near popular centers, it is desirable to hang food out of the reach of bears at night. Otherwise the only likely thieves are small rodents or birds. Rattlesnakes are very infrequent above 8,000 feet but have been seen to 11,000 feet. Mosquitoes are the insects most apt to be troublesome; they are worst near moist meadows and just after the snow has melted. In early spring or late summer very few mosquitoes should be encountered. Often, if they are numerous, a camp a few hundred feet higher or lower will largely solve the problem. And the active climber, high up on the peaks, is never plagued by insects.

Access routes for the principal regions are described in the individual sections of the guide. The whole subject of trail routes is well reviewed in the *Guide to the John Muir Trail and the High Sierra Region,* by Walter A. Starr, Jr. (see References).

Climbing in the Sierra is largely rock climbing, although some steep snow and even ice may be encountered. The rock is chiefly granite and is quite firm compared to that of many mountains. This granite tends to fracture on planes at right angles, producing cubical or rectangular blocks and horizontal ledges well suited to climbing. Metamorphic rocks of various qualities are found in certain small regions, particularly in the Kaweahs, near Rae Lakes, the Black Divide, Convict Lake, and in the Minarets. With a few exceptions the metamorphic rocks are also fairly sound. Loose rock must be guarded against, however, and particularly in gullies or chutes will the climber meet loose rock which must be trod with care. The High Sierra peaks have been deeply carved by glaciers in the past. Steep glacial cirques, common on north and east sides, sometimes have overhanging upper edges or are bordered by sharp arêtes. Avalanche chutes cut by winter snow slides are the most notable additional characteristic of the peaks.

The easier routes up peaks are commonly chutes or ridges, since the faces are generally more difficult. In almost all ascents an approach must be made over intermediate terrain where one thousand feet or more of talus, broken shelves, snow slope or meadow are ascended. The actual climbing may then involve one to two thousand feet of rock, snow or ice. It is always interesting, while passing over the intermediate terrain, to choose the best route of approach, which will depend to some extent on the personal tastes of the climbers. In May or June the approach may be entirely over snowfields, while in August or September it is more likely to be over talus.

There are dozens of small glaciers remaining in the Sierra, but they are usually hidden under the northeast faces of peaks and are not major geographical features. Except for the bergschrunds that separate the moving glaciers from the rock and ice above, there are almost no crevasses of consequence. The hazards of the glaciers are largely those of steep ice and snow, although sometimes a certain amount of difficulty is met in crossing a bergschrund. The largest Sierra glacier, the Palisade Glacier, is quite flat, and may be crossed without difficulty. Steep snow is fairly frequent in the Sierra, especially early in the season, but the late-summer climber can often avoid all snow.

Annual and seasonal variations can cause a considerable variation in the difficulty of climbs. A chute which is ascended by easy rocks one summer may be filled with steep ice and snow in another year. Or a feasible snow slope may be replaced by a rather difficult rock climb. No attempt has been made in this Guide to judge all such variations and the climber should not be too surprised if a supposed class 3 climb actually turns out to be class 4 or 5.

Weather in the Sierra is quite dependable, and summer storms, when they occur at all, are usually mild. Furthermore, storms most often come in the afternoon. Thus a cloudless morning sky will sometimes be transformed by noon or mid-afternoon into a region of towering cumulus clouds and a little later lightning and rain may develop. Because of this it is well to start and finish a climb early in the day. Occasionally the thunderstorms are quite violent, and then the climber should take pains to remain well off summits and ridges, where lightning may strike. Chutes or couloirs are also to be avoided, for rain or hail can loosen dangerous barrages of falling rock. Since such storms are usually rather brief it is well to wait them out in some safe place rather than to try to proceed in spite of weather. In late May and in June there may be general storms of the type characteristic of the California winter climate. These will bring rain or snow in moderate amounts, but they will pass in a few days. July and August are normally fair except for summer thunderstorms. In September or October the first fall storms may be expected. These, like those of June, are usually brief and are followed by fair weather, so that foot travel in the High Sierra is often quite possible in September, October, and November. It sometimes happens, however, that quite heavy storms bringing much snow strike in the fall.

Equipment needed in the Sierra depends largely upon the type of climbing to be done. All climbers will want sturdy pants, a strong shirt, a sweater, windproof jacket, and a hat. Rock climbers will bring a 120-foot nylon climbing rope, a 200-foot Manila rappel rope, slings, pitons, carabiners, and a hammer. Those who go early in the season, or who visit the Palisades, the north face of Darwin, the Minarets, the Sawtooth Ridge, and other areas likely to require crossing steep snow and ice, will need ice axes and boots suitable for snow work. There is seldom enough hard snow or ice to justify carrying crampons. Footwear depends somewhat on individual taste. Formerly nails were used on snow and a change to light rubber-soled shoes was made for dry rock. At present, stout leather boots with rubber-cleated soles are the preferred all-around footwear. Those who plan to avoid snow can use sneakers or shoes with composition soles, but the Bramani, Vibram, or other lug-type cleated soles are generally better even if snow and wet rock are never crossed.

Safety Precautions

ESSENTIALLY, safety results from the judgment and competence of the climbers. Without these, rules or warnings are futile. Therefore it is most important that every climbing party should be aware of its abilities and limitations and should not attempt ascents beyond its power. The only safe way for a climber to develop ability and judgment is in prolonged practice climbing within a few feet of level ground or with an upper belay, and later on, in actual climbs with experienced persons. This guidebook is in no sense a substitute for such experience, and it is strongly urged that climbers limit themselves to class 1 or class 2 climbs until they have had opportunity to gain experience with competent climbers. Even on class 1 and class 2 climbs there are possible hazards, and all climbers are urged to refrain from attempting anything they are not confident of successfully completing. In mountaineering it is a sign of competence to retreat if the weather turns bad, if the party proves too weak, or if the route proves to be more difficult than expected. An adequate margin of safety should always be maintained.

The chief hazards in climbing are:

1. Falling off because of loss of balance or loss of grip.
2. Falling off because of loose rock, as when a handhold or foothold breaks.
3. Being struck by falling rock from above.
4. Slipping on steep snow or ice.
5. Being struck by or carried down by an avalanche of snow.

Hazard 1 is commonly recognized, and is the chief justification for the need of practice climbing. A competent leader knows his limits and is not at all likely to fall for these reasons.* In the event that a fall does occur, proper rope technique offers a strong secondary defense against serious injury.† Hazard 2 is a very real one and must be constantly guarded against. Especially dangerous is the rare but quite possible occasion when a large block, perhaps one to ten feet in size, is pulled loose by the leader. Many serious accidents have resulted from such an event. Falling rock, listed as hazard 3, may result from natural causes or from actions of a member of a climbing party. Natural rock falls are rather rare in the Sierra and do not constitute an intolerable risk except under certain circumstances, as in a chute when there is heavy rainfall or much melting snow and ice. On the other hand, knocking down of rocks by climbers is very common, and the hazard thereby created must be minimized by (a) avoiding whenever possible (and it usually is!) knocking or throwing down any rocks, (b) keeping the party spread out horizontally when this is feasible, or staying close together so that the velocity reached by a falling rock will be low, or staying in a sheltered spot while waiting or belaying, (c) calling out *rock!* whenever a rock is accidentally loosened, and (d) wearing a hard hat.

Snow or ice is chiefly dangerous because the climber may slip and slide onto rocks below, even though the snow is not especially steep. Since so much Sierra climbing is on rock, both footgear and experience are often ill-adapted to deal with this hazard. Furthermore it is not always possible to avoid crossing such slopes. When they are crossed good steps should be kicked or cut and the rope should be used for

* For an excellent discussion see the article by Morgan Harris, "Safety Last?" *SCB*, 1942, 65–74. Also available in reprint listed below.

† See "Belaying the Leader," by R. M. Leonard and Arnold Wexler, *SCB*, 1946, 68–90 (available as reprint).

belaying. Voluntary glissading has led to many accidents, and should not be undertaken hastily.

Snow avalanches are uncommon in the summer but they may occur when snow lies on smooth slabs or when there is a steep slope of wet snow. Warm afternoons are the most dangerous times. Experience is the prerequisite for judging the safety of a snow slope.

In the above paragraphs a few hints on safety have been given with the hope that they will help the users of this Guide to avoid trouble. These brief remarks are not intended to supply instruction, for, as noted elsewhere, this can best be obtained from organized groups. Those desiring information in print should consult one or more of the following:

Manual of Ski Mountaineering, David R. Brower, editor, Sierra Club, San Francisco, 1962. Three excellent chapters on climbing techniques are included.

Handbook of American Mountaineering, Kenneth A. Henderson, editor, Houghton Mifflin, Boston, 1942.

Mountaineers Handbook, published by The Mountaineers.

Mountaineering: The Freedom of the Hills, Harvey Manning, editor, The Mountaineers, 1960.

General safety rules—Safety comes primarily from a state of mind and cannot be insured by the blind observance of any number of commandments. A few rules, however, help to build safety consciousness. Some valuable ones are:

1. A climbing party of three or more is best. Two is tolerable if nearby support knows of the plans of the climbers. Solo mountaineering exposes the climber to very grave risks and may work unnecessary hardships on friends or would-be rescuers.

2. Climbers should at all times carry adequate clothing, food, and equipment.

3. The rope should be used on all exposed places. (This assumes a knowledge of rope management.) The leader should never refuse a belay if any member of the party requests it.

4. The party should be kept together. All must agree to obey the leader or the majority rule.

5. Climbers should never attempt anything beyond their ability and knowledge. Physical and mental condition at the time of the climb must be considered.

6. Judgment should not be swayed by desire when a retreat or an easier route is necessary. There is no climb that is worth the deliberate risk of life.

Route Descriptions

ROUTE DESCRIPTIONS in this Guide are mostly rather general and will require a considerable amount of route-finding ability from any climbers who follow them. In some, only the direction of approach is given, while in others, the entry merely constitutes a record that the peak has been climbed. For many climbs no more is needed, but in other descriptions, particularly for prominent peaks, ultimate further elaboration is desirable, and it is hoped that users will supply this.

Information has come from personal experience of the authors and their friends, from summit registers, from letters sent in to the Mountaineering Committee (formerly the Committee on Mountain Records), and from articles in the *Sierra Club Bulletin* and the Sierra Club Base Camps' mimeographed books. This information is incomplete and it is certain that many ascents worthy of record are not included. A climbing party may thus ascend a peak for which no record is available and still find a cairn on the summit. An effort has been made to limit the term "first ascent" to those cases where climbers stated that no cairn was found, but even this may be in error as cairns can be destroyed by storms or may not have been erected in the first place. Sardine cans and other human artifacts constitute fairly good proof of previous ascents and have been found when no cairns were evident. The priority of ascent of a new route up a peak is even harder to certify, and it is quite possible that some injustices have been done.

Conventions followed in describing routes should be mentioned. The basic location of a route is given by compass direction from the summit, for example, north face, west ridge, etc. Actions of the climber are stated for him as though he were advancing (usually toward the summit) in the general direction of the route; thus he may be told to turn left or right. For added certainty the compass bearing of his new line of advance is sometimes given. For example, directions may call for a traverse to the left (N). Since route descriptions are not detailed, they should not be taken too literally. If the description says: "Follow the west ridge to the summit," the climber should remember that the best route may actually involve a number of small deviations to one side or the other of the ridge, and that it is up to him to find these rather than to stick stubbornly to the ridge in difficult places. Actually on most routes a considerable number of variations will be possible, and many variations may be of about the same difficulty.

Times of ascent are given rather rarely. They should be considered as rough estimates, since the time for a given ascent will vary markedly, depending on the skill, speed, and condition of the party.

"Ducks" made up of two or three stones stacked vertically have been placed by various persons to mark routes on peaks and along knapsack routes. These are sometimes useful, but should usually be viewed with skepticism. Many ducks have little significance. Some may lead to poorer routes. The climber who encounters ducks does not usually know what the builder of the duck had in mind, and it is better for the climber to judge the situation himself than to follow blindly a series of ducks. Sometimes a duck is built to mark the right (or the wrong) chute for descent from a ridge. It is the feeling of the editor that climbers who know their business will rarely need a duck to find the return route. If a duck is built for such a purpose it is usually best to destroy it on return. The building of ducks, except in a few exceptional places, should probably be discouraged.

Terms commonly used in the guide have been roughly defined as follows:

Gully—the broadest and lowest angle of depression that grooves the mountainside.

Chute—steeper than a gully, and often subject to recurrent avalanches of rock or snow.

Couloir—a chute which has or is likely to have ice or snow.

Chimney—a steep, narrow chute with approximately parallel walls.

Crack—a narrow separation between rock faces varying from about one foot to two or three millimeters.

Face—a steep side of a mountain, which may vary from a slope of about 40° to a vertical cliff.

Slope—a side of a mountain gentler than a face.

Ridge—a high divide extending out from a peak.

Arête—a narrow, steep ridge.

Summit—the highest point of a peak.

Pass—the lowest or most convenient point at which a long ridge can be crossed.

Col—a high, steep pass. A rounded col is often called a saddle.

Notch—about the same as col.

Glacier—an ice deposit that moves slowly.

Bergschrund—a crack where a moving glacier draws away from fixed snow or rock at its head.

Classification of Climbs

SOME METHOD of classifying or rating climbs is essential in a guide-book. A great amount of thought and discussion has been given to this subject. At best a classification system which is simple enough to be used is certain to represent only a rough approximation of the truth when the effects of different seasons, different climbers, and different types of climbs are considered. The Sierra Club system involving classes 1–6 was first introduced in 1937, and was modified in 1939. This system served well for more than twenty years, and came into wide use throughout the country. But the development of climbing of the most difficult type, particularly in Yosemite Valley and at Tahquitz Rock, as well as certain other historical developments, have brought recent changes which are accepted by most western climbers. The three main changes are: 1) An emphasis on difficulty of free climbing, rather than on the equipment needed; 2) the complete sep-aration of artificial-aid climbs from free climbs; and 3) the addition of a Grade Number as a measure of time required by a competent party. To preserve historical continuity, the old classes 1–4 have been kept unchanged, and class 5 has been expanded in decimal fashion from 5.0 (easiest) to 5.9 (most difficult). The old class 6 has been replaced by classes A1–A5.

The complete description of the system is given below:

Class 1. Hiking. Any footgear is adequate.

Class 2. The terrain becomes rougher. Proper footgear, such as rub-ber-soled shoes is desirable. Hands are occasionally used for bal-ance.

Class 3. Handholds and footholds are used. The exposure or diffi-culty is such that many climbers may wish to be belayed.

Class 4. Ropes are needed for belays by almost all. Pitons may be desirable for anchoring belayers.

Class 5.0, 5.1...5.9. Increasingly difficult piton-protected climbing. May eventually expand to 5.10, 5.11, etc.

Class A1, A2...A5. Increasingly difficult artificial-aid climbing.

As a measure of the overall time required, the Grades I–VI are used. Here the Roman numeral distinguishes the grade from the Arabic class. As a general rule, the following times can be assigned to the various grades. They are the times taken by an average climbing team (but note that the climbers will have to be well above average to do the Grade V and Grade VI climbs that have been established in Yosemite Valley).

Grade I.   A few hours.

Grade II.   Half a day.

Grade III. Most of a day.

Grade IV. A full day, or somewhat more.

Grade V. Like IV, but limited to experts.

Grade VI. Several days.

A further discussion of rating systems is given in Roper's *A Climber's Guide to Yosemite Valley*. There, also, a comparison with the proposed National Climbing Classification System is presented. The latter is essentially the same as the system described above, except that classes 1–5.10 are compressed into classes 1–10, without decimal subdivision. This system has the difficulty, from the standpoint of the Sierra mountaineer, of converting the established class 3 to class 2, and the class 4 to class 3. To prevent confusion, we will make no further mention of the NCCS ratings in this book.

In the present book, as compared to the earlier edition, an effort has been made to give class numbers more conservatively, so that the interests of knapsackers and general mountaineers, rather than those of pure rock climbers, are served. This has meant raising many of the class numbers, both for peaks and for knapsack routes. Quite a few class 2's have now become class 3. It must be recognized, even so, that the class number is often a very rough indication, and that rating has been done by many different individuals. The climber should put his own judgment ahead of anything he reads in a book. If a class 2 climb proves to be difficult, he should recognize that it may have been incorrectly numbered in the first place—or he may be off route. A printed class number should never prevent a climber from turning back if the interests of safety demand this action.

Little use is made in this book of the decimal subdivision of the class 5 climbs. This neglect results mainly from ignorance, and can be corrected later if more information is forthcoming. Class 5 may mean anything from 5.0 to about 5.6.

As far as grade goes, most High Sierra peaks from normal camps are Grade III. The shorter climbs are Grade I or II. The more severe climbs, such as long class 4 and 5 climbs are Grade IV. The grade number is seldom given in this guide.

The climbing leader should use the information given by class number so that he may more capably judge the ascents he might wish to undertake and what equipment he will need. In the last analysis, however, it is the leader's judgment that will indicate to him which class a particular lead will be; that is to say, he will decide when to rope up and when to use pitons for protection or direct aid. His decisions will be influenced by weather and other seasonal variations, the capacities of his companions, and, of course, his own climbing skill and experience. It should be noted that greater climbing skill is often required for class 4 and class 5 ascents than for those of the class A category. No one should attempt a climb unless well equipped and with experience to meet the requirements for a safe ascent.

Explanation of Maps

THE MAPS were drawn by Harry and Vievedie Weldon. They are intended to supplement the U.S.G.S. Topographic Maps (15 Minute Series) for areas of major interest to climbers. They give names not found on the topographic maps, and they show feasible knapsack routes. Regarding these knapsack routes, it should be noted that they are not fixed geographic features like trails. Although rudimentary trails or ducked routes are sometimes present, at other times the hiker must choose his own path. The preferred way will not always be exactly as indicated on a map in this book, for it is often a matter of personal taste just where a stream is crossed or on which side a lake is passed. The marked knapsack routes should not be taken as gospel—they may occasionally be in error because of the incomplete information available to the authors of the guide. In general the knapsack routes are definitely not for pack animals, and many are suitable only for experienced mountain hikers. In some places much rough talus must be crossed, while in other places the climbing difficulty may be as high as class 3.

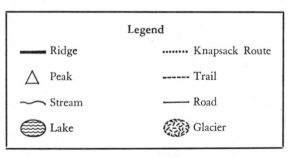

Bond Pass to Tioga Pass

NORTHWARD from Tioga Pass and Tuolumne Meadows peaks of the High Sierra diminish rapidly in elevation and, with a few notable exceptions, in ruggedness as well. Nevertheless this northern portion of Yosemite National Park, and the region to the east, contain much of interest to climbers. The Sawtooth Ridge, which is described as a separate area following these introductory remarks, is outstanding for its clean granite climbs and its accessibility from the east. The other peaks are scattered in a mountain area of quiet charm, and are listed in the second subdivision of this section.

Many of the peaks may be climbed without encountering technical difficulties, merely by following the routes dictated by an inspection of the topographic map or the mountain itself. There remain, however, a few summits which are best approached by specific routes; and there exist peaks which by virtue of their more impressive faces might bluff wary mountaineers out of enjoyable ascents. Maps for this area are Tower Peak, Matterhorn Peak, and Tuolumne Meadows.

APPROACHES AND CAMPSITES

The central part of the Bond Pass–Tioga Pass area is not often approached from the west, probably as a result of the distance which must be covered and the less exciting terrain which lies along the route. All three of the other directions provide easy and popular routes of entry.

From the north trails leading southward from the Sonora Pass highway start at Kennedy Meadow and at Leavitt Meadows. The Leavitt Meadows route follows the Walker River for several miles before trending southwest and crossing Dorothy Lake Pass. The Relief Valley Trail starts at Kennedy Meadow, and joins the other route at Dorothy Lake after entering the park by way of Bond Pass. Either trail may be hiked to its crossing of the park boundary in a matter of two days. A temporary mining road leads from the Sonora Pass road via Leavitt Lake to Snow Lake just north of Bond Pass. This road is closed to the public beyond Leavitt Lake. Campgrounds have been established at Kennedy and Leavitt meadows where stock is available.

The eastern approaches consist of secondary roads leading in to short, steep trails. Campsites and stock are available at some road ends, and in general trail systems lead into the park. The approaches to the Sawtooth Ridge are described separately for that area.

The southern routes start from the Tioga Pass road. From Tuolumne Meadows and Snow Flat, trails lead to Glen Aulin and thence northward. Or, from a point near White Wolf a trail descends into the Grand Canyon of the Tuolumne at Pate Valley; and then, after 3,500 vertical feet of switchbacks, leads north over easy country to Benson and Smedberg lakes.

The major trails in the northern Yosemite Sierra area are fairly well shown on the USGS sheet of Yosemite National Park, and several routes within the area are described in detail in Starr's *Guide to the John Muir Trail*. A few days of hiking on these trails should indicate to most hikers what sort of terrain difficulties may be encountered in the region and how the trail system will cope with them. Only a few passes reach heights of more than 10,000 feet, and the meadows and valley floors lie between the 6,000- and 9,000-foot levels. The trails are for the most part well constructed, and although they follow considered routes along the paths of least resistance, cross-country knapsack routes are often open to hikers not hindered by the limitations imposed by stock. It is well to seek advance information, however. The traveler who inspects the map and can imagine no reason for the lack of a direct trail connection between Waterwheel Falls and Matterhorn Canyon can quickly if not easily find the reason for the longer route followed by the trail. But hiking through some areas in which the contour lines indicate no topographic obstacles is neither unreasonable nor difficult even if no trails exist. For example, knapsack parties have often crossed from Matterhorn Canyon to Spiller Creek Canyon by the unnamed pass north of Whorl Mountain, bearing left on descending into Spiller Canyon. Hikers can also leave Spiller Creek by a pass north of Spiller Lake which leads to the plateau west of Camiaca Peak. These passes are easy class 3.

Campsites are plentiful throughout the area, particularly along lake shores (Tilden Lake, Benson Lake), and in the major canyons (Virginia Creek, Matterhorn Canyon), and only at the most popular campsites is a shortage of grass or wood likely.

The Sawtooth Ridge

RICHARD M. LEONARD (1937); HERVEY H. VOGE (1953, 1964)

THE SLENDER PINNACLES and narrow arêtes of the Sawtooth Ridge form a portion of the northeast boundary of Yosemite National Park. The main peaks are shown on the U.S. Geological Survey map (Matterhorn Peak Quadrangle) and on the map of the Yosemite National Park, but the accompanying Sketches 3 and 4 must be consulted for more complete detail and for names not shown on the official maps. Although the peaks are only from 11,400 to 12,281 feet in elevation, nevertheless they constitute one of the most interesting and difficult

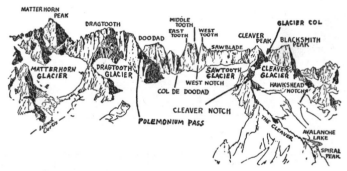

Sketch 3. The Sawtooth Ridge from the northeast.

climbing regions of the High Sierra. The rock is a firm white granite, often of a spiry formation. The northeast face of the ridge is severely undercut by recent glaciation, four small glaciers still remaining. The portion of the climbing that requires the use of the rope averages about 500 feet in height. In general climbing is more challenging from the northeast or glacier side, although the Three Teeth are difficult from all sides. This same northeast side is attractive for combined skiing and climbing in the spring, since it is easily accessible and the snow slopes are excellent.

The region may be reached from the south by good trail from Tuolumne Meadows to campsites below Whorl Mountain, in Matterhorn Canyon at 9,600 feet, and north of the Finger Peaks, in Slide

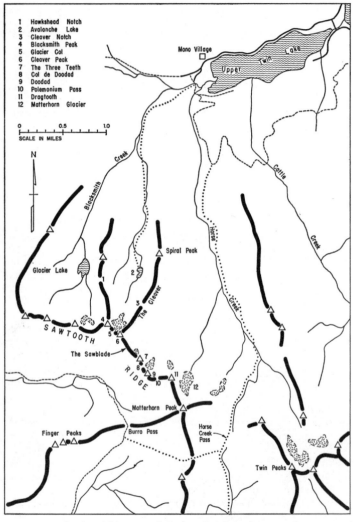

1	Hawkshead Notch
2	Avalanche Lake
3	Cleaver Notch
4	Blacksmith Peak
5	Glacier Col
6	Cleaver Peak
7	The Three Teeth
8	Col de Doodad
9	Doodad
10	Polemonium Pass
11	Dragtooth
12	Matterhorn Glacier

0   0.5   1.0
SCALE IN MILES

N

Mono Village

Upper Twin Lake

Cottle Creek

Blacksmith Creek

Glacier Lake

Spiral Peak

The Cleaver

Horse Creek

SAWTOOTH

The Sawblade

RIDGE

Matterhorn Peak

Finger Peaks

Burro Pass

Horse Creek Pass

Twin Peaks

Sketch 4. The Sawtooth Region. (See legend, page 14.)

Canyon, at 10,000 feet elevation. However, the peaks are more accessible from the north, via Bridgeport and Twin Lakes. By a climb from the road of 3,000 feet in three miles, without regular trail, a campsite can be reached at an altitude of 10,000 feet near a glacial lakelet on the east branch of Blacksmith Creek. Good camping is available on the west branch of the same creek. Campsites are also to be found on the headwaters of Horse Creek at somewhat higher elevations, and these sites are closer to the Three Teeth and the peaks to the southeast. There is a trail partway up Horse Creek.

Although Matterhorn Peak was climbed in 1899, most other points seemed too difficult until modern methods of rock climbing were introduced in the summer of 1931. With the application of a new technique all major points have now been ascended. There are, however, many fine new routes still to be made.

Principal Passes

Polemonium Pass. Class 3. This is the deep notch between the Doodad and the Dragtooth. The southwest side is class 2, and presents no difficulties. On the northeast a very broad, steep chute descends to the glacier. For 500 vertical feet the slope is 45° or over. When this is snow-covered in the spring and early summer it offers an attractive mountaineer's route for crossing the ridge, with steep snow the only problem. Later in the season bare ice and a bergschrund may make this northeast side more difficult.

Col de Doodad. East chimney, south to north. Class 4; 200-foot reserve rope required, ice axe useful. This pass was first used July 2, 1933, by Henry Beers, Bestor Robinson, and Richard M. Leonard. It is the most convenient route from Slide Canyon to the northeast face of the central portion of the ridge. The approach from Slide Canyon is up easy scree to the lowest and most prominent gap between the Three Teeth and the Doodad. The 45° couloir on the north is usually snow-filled in the upper half and is bare disintegrating granite in the lower parts. From the col, rappel down the snow 100 feet to a ledge. Traverse 10 feet horizontally left (NW) to the head of a dry disintegrating chimney. From there rappel 90 feet to a steel spike driven into a crack in the right (NE) wall at the head of a steep 60-foot drop in the glacier. A third rappel brings one to the head of the glacier.

Col de Doodad. West chimney, north to south. Class 3. From the northeast ascend a moderate 35° gully close against the East Tooth. Follow this gully left (SE) under an overhanging block to the crest of the ridge. Thence, drop to the right (SW) 30 feet over moderately hard climbing to a platform, then to the left (SE) to a chockstone at the head of a short steep chimney. Climb down this chimney to the scree gully on the south side of the Col de Doodad. This route is much easier from north to south than the East Chimney and is somewhat easier from south to north, but should be attempted in the latter direction only by those experienced in route finding as it is poorly defined from the Slide Canyon side.

Glacier Col. Class 2; ice axe advisable. The ascent of this pass between Cleaver Peak and Blacksmith Peak is over moderate scree and benches from Slide Canyon and 40° snow and glacier on the north. It is probably the least difficult pass across the Sawtooth Ridge.

Cleaver Notch. Class 2. First used July 2, 1933, on the first ascent of the Three Teeth. It is the most practical route across the exceedingly sharp arête of the Cleaver. The notch is crossed at its southern edge, only 30 feet above the glacial benches on either side.

Hawk's Head Notch. This notch is on the arête about 100 yards north of Blacksmith Peak just short of the sharp minor pinnacle with the overhanging summit known as the Hawk's Nest. The eastern approach is moderate, but on the west very difficult crack climbing may be required; details are not available.

Horse Creek Pass. Class 2. The low pass (10,640+) between Twin Peaks and Matterhorn Peak connects Horse Creek to Spiller Creek.

Routes on the Peaks (Northwest to Southeast)

Eocene Peak (11,581; 1 NW of Blacksmith Peak)

Class 3. First ascent July 16, 1932, by Herbert B. Blanks and Richard M. Leonard. A ropeless ascent may be made of the southwest slopes of this fragment of the ancient Eocene landscape. The final pinnacle rising 50 feet above the plateau may require ropes for inexperienced climbers.

Blacksmith Peak (11,760+)

Route 1. Southwest face. Class 3. First ascent July 3, 1933, by Bestor Robinson and Richard M. Leonard. Go up a prominent gully on the southwest face to its head among the four summit pinnacles. The highest is on the northwest end. The register is on the flat-topped pinnacle third from the highest.

Route 2. The north gully. Class 5; pitons required. First ascent September 8, 1936, by Bestor Robinson and Carl Jensen. From the base of the north arête ascend a steeply sloping ledge on the Cleaver Glacier side diagonally upward toward the south. About 200 feet above the talus the ledge ends against a vertical face. Traverse to the right (W) and protected by several pitons climb about 20 feet of face on small holds to the large north gully. Ascend this gully to its head among the summit pinnacles. On the first ascent (1933) the peak was traversed from south to north by rappelling from the lower end of the north gully.

Cleaver Peak (11,760+)

Route 1. Southwest face. Class 3. First ascent July 3, 1933, by Henry Beers and Oliver Kehrlein. From Glacier Col climb on to the southwest face and traverse diagonally upward to the left (N) to a broad depression on the northwest face. Follow this to the summit.

Route 2. Northeast face. Class 3. First ascent July 27, 1934, by Glen Dawson and Jack Riegelhuth. Go up a series of ledges and blocks on the northeast face to the arête of The Cleaver 50 feet north of the summit. Traverse the arête to the summit.

Route 3. South face. Class 5. Ascended August 6, 1950, by M. L. Wade and F. Chrisholm. Ascend a chute (easy class 4) facing Burro Pass until within about 150 feet of the notch separating Cleaver Peak from the Sawblade. Here a large block leans against Cleaver Peak. (By climbing under this block one reaches the notch southeast of Cleaver Peak.) Turn left at the lower side of the block and ascend the south side of Cleaver Peak. Several interesting fifth class pitches.

The Sawblade (11,600)

Traverse south to north. Class 4; rappel rope useful. First ascent July 25, 1934, by David R. Brower, Hervey Voge. From Slide Canyon the route proceeds up steep climbing to the notch just west of the tall pinnacle on the northwest arête of the West Tooth. An attempt to traverse this portion of the Sawblade to the West Tooth was blocked by the pinnacle which could not be turned. Descent was made to the northeast.

The Three Teeth (11,600+)

Route 1. Traverse northwest to southeast. Class 4; rappel rope required. First ascent July 2, 1933, by Henry Beers, Bestor Robinson, and Richard M. Leonard. (See "Three Teeth of Sawtooth Ridge," *SCB*, 1934, 31–33.) The route is up a series of ledges in a broad depression on the center of the northeast face of the West Tooth. Several variations are possible at the start. About one-third of the way up, traverse diagonally upward to the right (SW) to less difficult ledges leading upward to the Sawblade. Follow the arête back to the left (SE) to the tunnel beneath the summit block. Climb to the northwest out of the tunnel, and then up the northwest face of the block to the summit of the West Tooth.

From a point at the southeast end of the tunnel rappel 75 feet toward the Middle Tooth to a 3-foot ledge. Climb downward toward Slide Canyon 100 feet along steeply sloping ledges and cracks. Traverse back northeast to the West Notch. Ascend a chimney rising from the notch toward the summit of the Middle Tooth. Follow this chimney about 200 feet until easier face climbing appears on the left (NE). Traverse this face diagonally right (SE), cross the chimney about 50 feet below the summit, and then by good holds on the face to the right of the chimney climb to the summit of the Middle Tooth.

The route down to the East Notch follows a short chimney near the northeast end of the summit, then steep cracks to the head of the large chimney a short distance below the notch on the Slide Canyon side. Traverse southeast 75 feet along ledges on the Slide Canyon face of the East Tooth to a narrow steep chimney up the face. Climb the chimney to a chockstone, then traverse to the right (SE) a few feet on small holds out of the chimney to a parallel crack. Follow this crack to the summit of the East Tooth.

From the summit follow the Slide Canyon side of the southeast arête down over steep, exposed and very difficult climbing. About half-way down this arête a pinnacle about 20 feet high will be encountered. This can be passed by direct attack and a rappel down a steep chimney on the opposite (SE) side to less difficult climbing leading to the Col de Doodad. A better route is to turn right at the Pinnacle and descend the southwest face over progressively easier climbing to the Slide Canyon base of the Middle Tooth.

Route 2. Traverse southeast to northwest. Class 5. First ascent July 25, 1934, by Glen Dawson and Jack Riegelhuth. From a short distance below the Col de Doodad, on the Slide Canyon side, ascend the short chimney with the overhanging chockstone leading to the arête and the west chimney of the Col de Doodad. Follow the arête to the base of the tall pinnacle. Pass this on the left by crawling through a remarkable tunnel on the southwest, to more difficult climbing leading back to the southeast arête. Thence by Route 1 to the summit of the East Tooth.

A more obvious route is from the Slide Canyon base of the Middle Tooth to the tall pinnacle on the southeast arête of the East Tooth and thence to the summit.

Traverse the Middle Tooth by Route 1, thence to the base of the rappel on the West Tooth. The angle of the next 75 feet is about 80°, highly exposed. The holds are rather unsound. Protected by pitons, the ascent is made up thin cracks and narrow ledges to the tunnel, thence by Route 1 to the summit of the West Tooth. Route 1 may then be followed to the base on the northeast, or various routes hereinafter described may be used for rappelling the Slide Canyon face.

Route 3. The Middle Tooth from the north. Class 4; ice axe required. First ascent July 2, 1933, by Lewis F. Clark, Richard G. Johnson, Oliver Kehrlein, and Randolph May. From the northeast, ascend the steep snow couloir leading toward the West Notch. One hundred feet above a chockstone leave the snow and traverse diagonally back northeast on a ledge on the left (SE) wall. When snow is low some difficulty may be experienced in getting on the ledge. After traversing the ledge fairly well onto the face, ascend a prominent chimney and ledges upward to the right (SW) to a point on Route 1 in the chimney rising from the West Notch. Follow Route 1 to the summit.

Route 4. The West Tooth from the southwest. Class 5. First ascent July 23, 1941, by David R. Brower, L. Bruce Meyer, and Art Argiewicz. From the scree slope at the base of the West Notch, on the Slide Canyon side, begin climbing up the left (W) shoulder, working diagonally toward a ledge at the top of the lowest and first chimney. From this point a delicate fingertip traverse is necessary to cross the top of the chimney to another scree chute directly above the lower chimney. After ascending the chimney to about 30 feet below its mouth one must work back (SW) and to the left (W) over an easy ledge. After working over this ledge a short distance, ascend the chimney above by swinging around a flake to the left (W) and above the ledge and then using cross pressure in the chimney. At the top of this chimney work to the left (W) and then up the southwest face to the prominent vertical face of the West Tooth. From here the summit is reached as in the last part of Route 2.

Route 5. West Notch from the glacier. Class 4 to 5. In 1949 Oscar Cook, Joe Firey, Larry Taylor, and Jack Hansen ascended the couloir or chimney leading to the West Notch from the northeast. From the notch traverse directly out to the right on a hand ledge ending in a chimney which leads straight up to the end of the tunnel.

Rappel Routes. Class 5; 200-foot rappel rope required. By the use of many pitons nearly any route is probably possible. It is well, however, to mention certain routes that have actually been used. Slide Canyon can be reached from the northwest arête of the West Tooth near the junction with the Sawblade by a series of four rappels involving the use of one piton. It is also possible to rappel from the West Tooth toward the Middle Tooth by Route 1 and thence by three more rappels along the southeast buttress to Slide Canyon. The last rappel, from a piton on a ledge, is 105 feet, most of it overhanging. From the West Notch it is practicable to rappel the north chimney to the glacier, though the last rappel is about 125 feet. A successful rappel route from the Middle Tooth to Slide Canyon by the great southeast chimney from the East Notch has been followed. Another route down from the Middle Tooth, to the north base, proceeds from the lower end of the chimney on the northwest face, the upper part of which forms a portion of Route 3. About half of the last rappel is overhanging. A severe route, not recommended, goes down the north face of the East Tooth from the East Notch; it involves the use of pitons, and slings to sit in as one of the intermediate stances.

The Doodad (11,600+)

Route 1. South face. Class 4. First ascent July 7, 1934, by Kenneth May, Howard Twining. Several routes varying from difficult to very difficult, are possible up the south face to the 25-foot granite cube which forms the summit and which overhangs on all sides. The final climb is up a crack on the south side. On September 7, 1936, Carl Jensen made a traverse by descending the more difficult crack on the north.

Route 2. Northeast face. Class 5+. Ascend a gully which leads up from the northwest end of the Doodad massif and slants to the left (S). In general follow the gully, deviating to one side or another to pass chockstones, etc. Finally a hand traverse to the left leads to a series of large ledges from which the summit block can be reached. This can be climbed on north or south side. This route was climbed in July 1956 by James Derby, Peter Lipman, and Thomas Vaughan.

The Dragtooth (12,080+)

Route 1. Southwest face. Class 2. First ascent July 20, 1931, by Walter Brem, Glen Dawson, and Jules Eichorn. Nearly any portion of the south face will be found practicable.

Route 2. North face. Class 4. First ascent July 16, 1941, by J. C. Southard and Hervey Voge. From the Dragtooth Glacier ascend the steep snow slope below the north face to a point about 100 feet to the left (E) of the main chute that comes down the north face. This chute is just east of the massive northwest buttress. Leave the snow by ledges leading up to the left, and follow these ledges to a less prominent chute that lies about 200 feet east of the main chute. Climb this chute for about 200 feet and then cross over to the right to the main chute. Climb up the left (E) side of the main chute to within 100 feet of the summit ridge, and then ascend a 75-foot chimney which leads to the ridge about 50 feet northwest of the summit.

Route 3. Northeast buttress. Class 4. Ascended 1952 by Joe Firey, Norm Goldstein, Chuck Wharton, and John Orrenschall. From the Dragtooth Glacier proceed to the base of the buttress, and ascend it largely on the eastern flank. Higher up stay directly on the crest, which ends in a short chimney below the summit.

Matterhorn Peak (12,264)

Route 1. Southwest face. Class 2. First ascent 1899 by M. R. Dempster, J. S. Hutchinson, Lincoln Hutchinson, Charles A. Noble. This peak, the highest point of the Sawtooth Ridge, offers the most extensive view in the region. There is an easy route from near Burro Pass up the broad scree gully on the center of the southwest face.

Route 2. Northwest face. Class 3. First ascent July 20, 1931, by Walter Brem, Glen Dawson, and Jules Eichorn. Proceed from Matterhorn Canyon to the notch between the Dragtooth and the Matterhorn Peak, and climb up a gully, or the face, to the summit.

Route 3. Southeast face. Class 2. This face may be reached from upper Spiller Creek, or from Horse Creek via the pass between Twin Peaks and Matterhorn Peak.

Route 4. East Couloir. Class 3. Ascend the obvious couloir on the east side of the northeast ridge. From this one may climb to the east ridge and follow this to the easy southeast face.

Route 5. North arête. Class 5.5. First ascent September 1954 by Jerry Gallwas, Wally Kodis, and Don Wilson. From the glacier that lies between the Dragtooth and Matterhorn Peak, the steep, sharp north arête is seen to be truncated at the bottom, leaving a steep face. A platform above the truncation can be reached by starting to the left (E) of the face, and climbing three pitches. (Or, according to James Derby, Peter Lipman, and Thomas Vaughan [1956], the arête can be reached from the west side of the face by means of a large ledge and several fourth class leads.) From the platform, climb one pitch up the arête and then traverse onto the west face of the arête. A steep crack is climbed for 100 feet to a large ledge below the final 200 feet of a very sharp arête. From the large ledge traverse left (E) and ascend a chimney with a chockstone. Then follow a subsidiary ridge east of the arête proper. From the end of the ridge one pitch completes the climb.

Twin Peaks (12,240+)

Early records are not available. The saddle between the two peaks may be reached from the south, and both peaks may be readily climbed from this saddle. Class 2 to 3. The west peak is the higher.

Other peaks and ridges

There are many minor pinnacles and sharp ridges in the Sawtooth area that offer enjoyable climbing. These are not listed in detail. Many have been climbed, while others have yet to be visited. Worthy of mention are The Cleaver, including Spiral Peak at the lower end, the ridge running north of Blacksmith Peak, the ridge north of Eocene Peak, and the northeast side of the ridge between Twin Peaks and Matterhorn Peak.

Bond Pass to Tioga Pass—Other Peaks

ROBERT L. SWIFT and DAVID A. NELSON (1953);
HERVEY H. VOGE (1964)

Peaks of the Main Crest (North to South)

Forsyth Peak (11,180)

The first ascent was made by Rene Kast, Don Hersey, Paul Hersey, Al Teakle, Harry Tenney, Jr., Arthur Evans, and Leon Casou, on July 10, 1937. The original route led up from the south, but the west slope is also easy. Class 2. On August 23, 1953, LeRoy Johnson, Fred Schaub, and Ken Hondsinger climbed the north ridge from Dorothy Lake. Class 3.

Tower Peak (11,755)

The first ascent was made from the north "without any difficulty" in 1870 by C. F. Hoffmann, W. A. Goodyear, and Alfred Craven after earlier unsuccessful attempts by Goddard, King, and Gardiner. From the saddle northwest of the peak and directly above Mary Lake a ridge is followed to a staircase gully which leads to the summit. Class 3. Class 4 routes involving roped climbing have been made on the west face and on the side leading toward Craig Peak. The southeast chute into Stubblefield Canyon has been used for descent.

Ehrnbeck Peak (11,240)

First ascent on July 27, 1945, by A. J. Reyman. The climb was started from the saddle north of Wells Peak and the ridge between Stubblefield and Thompson canyons. Class 2. Another route is by the West Walker River and the northeast ridge. Class 3.

Hawksbeak Peak (11,120+; ¼ S of Kirkwood Lake)

No information is available.

Center Mountain (11,273)

First ascent in 1905 by members of the survey party who placed Boundary Mark No. 87. Second ascent was made on July 28, 1914, by Robert Batyer, Leland Day, Herman Sayers, and George Kenney. The easiest route is found on the south slope. Class 1.

Crown Point (11,346)

First ascent was made in 1905 by Geo. R. Davis, A. H. Sylvester, and Pearson Chapman of the USGS. It is an easy ascent from Snow Lake immediately to the south, or from Peeler Lake. Class 2.

Slide Mountain (11,040+)

Climbed by Norman Clyde in 1921. A trail leads over the top of the peak.

Camiaca Peak (11,739)

First ascent was made in 1917 by Walter L. Huber. The peak is accessible from Summit Lake near Virginia Pass. Class 2.

Peak 11,200+ (¼ S of Summit Lake)

No information is available.

Peak 12,126 (¾ N of Excelsior Mountain)

No information is available.

Excelsior Mountain (12,446)

Ascended by Howard Sloan on June 13, 1931, by way of the pass at the head of Virginia Creek.

Shepherd Crest (12,015)

First ascent was made by Herbert B. Blanks, Kenneth May, and Elliot Sawyer July 13, 1933, via one of the steep avalanche chutes from the south. Class 2. The class 3 northeast ridge was climbed by W. Ryland Hill and Charles W. Chesterman on July 5, 1941. (Interesting articles on "Little Lost Valley of Shepherd Crest" appear in *SCB,* 1933, 68–80, and 1949, 82–86.)

North Peak (12,242)

First ascent was made on June 26, 1937, by Bill Blanchard, Hubert North, and Gary Leech from Saddlebag Lake. Class 2.

Mount Conness (12,590)

This mountain was first climbed by Clarence King and James T. Gardiner on September 1, 1866. Many ascents have been made since then by various routes which are given below.

Route 1. Young Lakes. Class 2. This is the most popular route and is essentially that of the trail (not shown on the new topographic map). Follow the south fork of Conness Creek to a point just past a group of boggy ponds shown on the map as a lake. Then go north up the scree slopes to a valley on a large plateau, up this valley to the ridge above the glacier, and then west on this ridge via a trail to the summit. Route 1 may also be reached from the east, via the Carnegie Institute Experimental Station one mile SW of Saddlebag Lake. Go up the valley in a northwest direction toward Mt. Conness, staying on the north side of the valley. Climb to the east ridge of Conness, and cross from it to west side of the main divide, where the trail of Route 1 is joined. Class 2–3.

Route 2. McCabe Lakes. Class 3. From the saddle east of the upper-most lake follow the narrow crest southeasterly. Turn a shoulder to the southeast by traversing diagonally upward to the crest. Follow the crest southward to the top of the mountain.

Route 3. Glacier. Class 3. From southwest shore of Saddlebag Lake go up the glacier valley and cirque between the east ridges of Conness and North Peak to the glacier. Traverse the glacier in the direction of a pronounced depression in the east ridge of Conness, then climb up over steep slopes of loose rock to the ridge at the foot of the summit. Follow the trail from there to the summit.

Route 4. Northeast face. Class 5. Climbed in July 1958 by George

Harr, Lynn Grey, and Ray Van Aken. Climb over the glacier to a point almost directly below the summit. Go up a gully sloping to the left of a prominent buttress dividing the face. At the top of the gully traverse to the north, crossing the buttress. Several fourth class pitches lead to an overhang. A traverse is made to a suitable crack, and several more pitches lead to a notch about 200 feet north of the summit.

Route 5. Southwest face. Class A. First ascent July 14–15, 1959, by John Merriam and Donald Harmon. The route starts at the talus fan at the base of the cliff and proceeds up a network of cracks that divides the face and which lead up into the great gully draining the upper half of the face. It begins in a wide chimney, class 4, but soon involves smaller cracks and several bolts. From the great gully there are two exits; a class 5–A chimney leading directly to the summit, and a class 4 scramble up the gully to the southeast ridge just below the summit. Loose rock is a serious hazard on this climb.

Route 6. West face direct. Class A. First ascent in September, 1959, by Warren J. Harding, Glen Denny, and Herb Swedlund. This route is to the left (northwest) of Route 5. The ascent involved 3½ days of climbing, with 25 class 5 pitons, 85 class A pitons, and 15 class A bolts.

White Mountain (12,000 +)

Climbed in 1917 by Walter L. Huber. Class 2.

Peak 12,002 (¼ E of Skelton Lakes)

No information is available.

Gaylor Peak (11,004)

Class 1–2 from Tioga Pass.

Peaks West of the Crest (General North to South Order)

Bigelow Peak (10,539)

First ascent in 1927 by Allan M. Starr, Ralph Minor, and Sherman Chickering. The peak may be climbed from Bond Pass or by traversing from Kendrick Peak. Class 1.

Keyes Peak (10,670)

First ascent on September 1, 1942, by A. J. Reyman. An easy route may be found starting from Tilden Lake. Class 2.

Saurian Crest (11,095)

First ascent on September 7, 1938, by John Dyer. Long talus slopes extend to within a few feet of the summits, which require a short bit of scrambling. Class 3.

Michie Peak (10,035)

May be climbed from either Twin Lakes or Jack Main Canyon. Class 2.

Kendrick Peak (10,390)

First recorded ascent was made by A. J. Reyman July 25, 1945, who traversed south from Bond Pass via Bigelow Peak. A shorter and easier route starts from Jack Main Canyon. Class 2.

Craig Peak (11,090)

Though apparently climbed in July 1911 the first known ascent was that made by John Dyer in 1938. The peak is a class 2 traverse from either north or south, but reaching the northern ridge from Tower Peak involves class 3 climbing.

Wells Peak (11,118)

First ascent was made on July 27, 1945, by A. J. Reyman from the saddle between Wells and Ehrnbeck peaks by the north ridge. Class 2.

Snow Peak (10,950)

The first known ascent was made by John Dyer in 1938. The southern slope of the mountain is easily climbed from Tilden Lake. Class 2.

Acker Peak (11,015)

The first ascent was made July 28, 1945, by A. J. Reyman who climbed the east side from the saddle above Kerrick Meadow. Class 2.

Haystack Peak (10,015)

First ascent August 23, 1960, by H. F. Watty and three scouts. Class 1 from the east.

Chittenden Peak (9,685)

First ascent August 29, 1894, by Lt. N. F. McClure. The easiest route is from the east. Class 2.

Richardson Peak (9,884)

First ascent was made July 18, 1928, by Allan M. Starr and Ralph Minor. Class 2.

Price Peak (10,716)

The first ascent was made July 28, 1945, by A. J. Reyman on a traverse from Acker Peak and connecting ridges. Another route would be up the west slope from Thompson Canyon. Class 2.

Piute Mountain (10,541)

First ascent July 27, 1911, by Francis P. Farquhar, James Rennie, and Frank Bumstead. An easy ascent may be made by the Bear Valley trail. Class 2. A more difficult route would be by the north chute.

Finger Peaks (11,390)

First ascent on July 19, 1931, by Jules Eichorn, Glen Dawson, and Walter Brem, who climbed the east peak from the lake below Burro Pass. It is lower than the peak to the west, which was climbed later. The climb to the lower peak direct from the lake has several difficult pitches. Class 3. On July 25, 1934, the fingers were traversed from west to east by Lewis Clark, Allan MacRae, and Carl Scheerer.

Whorl Mountain (12,029)

From near the head of Matterhorn Canyon several practicable gullies lead to the main north-south ridge.

South Peak (11,975+). First ascent by J. W. Combs, R. W. Messer, and William T. Goldsborough July 23, 1911. Class 2–3.

North Peak (11,950+). First ascent by Ralph A. Chase and Sierra Club party July 17, 1921.

Middle Peak (12,050). First ascent by Herbert B. Blanks, Kenneth May, and Elliot Sawyer July 9, 1933, on a class 4 route.

Virginia Peak (12,001) (Formerly called Red Peak.)

First ascent by Kenneth May and Howard Twining July 3, 1934. Class 2–3 from west, southwest, or south.

Stanton Peak (11,695)

First ascent was made during a blizzard May 31, 1934, by Richard G. Johnson, Kenneth May, and Howard Twining. Class 2.

Suicide Ridge (*11,089*)

First ascent by Glen Dawson and John Cahill May 31, 1934. Class 2.

Grey Butte (*11,365*)

The first known ascent was made by Howard Twining in August 1934. A trail passes a short distance east of the peak. Class 2.

Bath Mountain (*10,558*)

Glen Dawson and John Cahill made the first ascent July 30, 1934.

Doghead Peak (*11,102*)

Climbed before 1911 by H. C. Bradley. A very good view is afforded from this peak which can be easily climbed by following up Wilson Creek. Class 2.

Quarry Peak (*11,161*)

First ascent in 1905–1909 by Geo. R. Davis, A. H. Sylvester, and Pearson Chapman of the USGS, who established a triangulation station atop the peak. Class 2.

Volunteer Peak (*10,479*)

First ascent was made in 1895 by Lts. H. C. Benson and McBride. An easy ascent can be made from the south. Class 2. Traverses may be made to or from West, Regulation, and Pettit peaks.

Regulation Peak (*10,560+*)

First known ascent was made in 1921 by R. A. Chase. The peak is an easy climb from the trail. Traverses may be made to the adjoining summits of West, Volunteer, and Pettit peaks. Class 2.

Pettit Peak (*10,788*)

Climbed by Lewis F. Clark and Virginia Greever on August 1, 1934, at which time a cairn was found indicating an earlier ascent. It is an easy traverse from Regulation Peak and can also be traversed from West Peak. Class 2.

West Peak (*10,480+*)

First known ascent July 17, 1931, by Kenneth May and Gus Smith. The peak is commonly approached by a traverse from Volunteer and Pettit peaks. Class 2.

Cold Mountain (*10,301*)

First recorded ascent by Glen Dawson and party in 1929. Class 2.

Sheep Peak (*11,840+*)

First ascent July 1, 1934, by Kenneth May and Howard Twining. Class 2.

Ragged Peak (*10,912*)

First ascent was made on July 6, 1863, by William H. Brewer and Charles Hoffmann. The usual route is by the saddle, west shoulder, through scree and talus to the top. Class 2. On August 25, 1939, Boynton Kaiser led a Sierra Club party up the northwest face. Class 4. A class 5 route was done up the east face of the north peak on August 16, 1953, by W. J. Harding, Ray Alcott, and Norah Straley.

Lembert Dome (*9,450*)

This is a very popular viewpoint. The first ascent is unrecorded.

Route 1. North slope. Class 1. The Dog Lake trail takes one practically to the summit.

Route 2. East or south slope. Class 2 and class 3.

Route 3. Northwest face. Class 4–5. First ascent by the northwest face was made in August 1951 by Dorothy Dern, Philip L. Dern, Alfred R. Dole, H. Stewart Kimball, and Richard Leonard. The route follows a wide class 2 ledge on the face climbing gradually to the south to a smooth, slightly overhanging buttress at the junction with the south face. One or two pitons are necessary at this point for protection in about fifteen feet of climbing to gentler slopes above. A variant was described by F. J. Meyers. Several hundred feet from the western edge of the northwest face ascend a ledge diagonally to the right (west) up steep slabs to the base of the vertical face where a large vertical slab has pulled away. Climb a 25-foot, class 4 cleft by chimney technique, and follow easy ledges to the right (west) to the west face above its steep portion.

Route 4. Direct west face. Class 5. Climbed by means of about four class 4–5 pitches in 1954 by W. J. Harding and Frank De Saussure.

Route 5. Northwest buttress. Class A. The poorly defined northwest buttress was climbed in July, 1953, by Frank Tarver and Gordon Petrequin.

Peaks East of the Crest (General North to South Order)

Walker Mountain (*11,563*)

No information is available.

Flatiron Butte (*11,360+*)

This butte has been climbed.

Hanna Mountain (*11,486*)

Ascended prior to 1948. A class 1 traverse from Flatiron Butte.

Eagle Peak (*11,845*)

First ascent in September 1905 by Geo. R. Davis, A. H. Sylvester, and Pearson Chapman, topographers of the USGS. Approaches are the same as for Hunewill and Robinson peaks. Class 2.

Grouse Mountain (*10,775*)

First ascent August 3, 1949, by A. J. Reyman by a class 1 route up the northwest couloir and west ridge. A class 3 ascent via the east face was made in August 1953 by LeRoy Johnson, Fred Schaub, and Ken Hondsinger.

Hunewill Peak (*11,680+*; *11,713*)

Formerly called Hennerville Peak because of a spelling error.

First recorded ascent was made in August 1946 by Ken Crowley, R. Dickey, Jr., Ken Hargreaves, and H. Watty, who climbed from Barney Lake. Class 2.

Victoria Peak (*11,732*)

First recorded ascent on September 8, 1946, by A. J. Reyman. The peak is one of the Buckeye Ridge group, all of which may be approached from either north or south. Class 2.

Robinson Peak (*10,806*)

Although circumstances of the first ascents are not known they were probably made by members of the 1905–1909 survey and by various sheepherders. The first recorded ascent was made August 22, 1946, by

K. Hargreaves, H. F. Watty, R. F. Dickey, Jr., and Ken Crowley from Twin Lakes. The northerly approach from Buckeye Creek and Eagle Creek would appear to be better. Class 2.

Cirque Mountain (10,714)

First ascent by A. J. Reyman, August 16, 1948. Class 1 up tree-covered west slope from Buckeye Pass.

Kettle Peak (11,010)

First ascent in August 1948 by William Dunmire and R. L. Swift from the pass between Big Slide and Little Slide canyons. Class 2.

Monument Ridge (11,778)

Though early ascents may have been made by prospectors, the first recorded ascent of the highest point was made by A. J. Reyman September 10, 1946. The ridge may be reached from West Lake or Green Lake or from Cattle Creek and Crater Crest. Class 2.

Gabbro Peak (10,960+)

This peak may be climbed from East Lake or the Virginia Pass trail. Class 2.

Page Peaks (10,880+)

The climb is a long pull over scree if started from the cirque west of East Lake or the gully between Page Peaks and Epidote Peak. The approach from Virginia Pass is shorter and may be preferred. Class 2.

Epidote Peak (10,880+)

Climbed by several Sierra Club members in 1917. Class 2.

Dunderberg Peak (12,374)

The first ascent was made in 1878 by Lt. M. M. Macomb and party of the Wheeler Survey. The peak is composed of steep, broken rock but presents no technical difficulties. Class 2. A spring ascent was made on April 10, 1936 by Robert Brinton and Walter Mosauer.

Black Mountain (11,760+)

First ascents in 1905-1909 by A. H. Sylvester, G. R. Davis and P. Chapman, topographers of the USGS. The second ascent was made by Howard Sloan on June 17, 1931, from Trumbull Lake via Cooney Lake and northeast slope. Class 2.

Mount Warren (*12,327*)

First ascent by Mr. Wackenreyder prior to 1868. Class 2.

Tioga Peak (*11,513*)

Climbed prior to 1939.

Leevining Peak (*11,691*)

Climbed prior to 1948. Class 2 up the southeast slope.

Mono Dome (*10,614*)

First recorded ascent August 7, 1948, by Ben Prusek, M. F. Dickson, and Chester Versteeg. Class 2 from the north.

Leevining Crags

This is a group of prominent pinnacles about ½ mile above the Tioga Road in Leevining Canyon. First ascents of a number of these were made August 20, 1954, by Cris Jesson, R. M. Dohrmann, and D. G. Harmon in class 4 climbing.

Tioga Pass to Mammoth Pass

THE SOUTHERN PORTION of Yosemite National Park, and the Mount Dana–Minarets Wilderness Area of the adjacent National Forests, which together make up the section from Tioga Pass to Mammoth Pass, constitute a very popular area for climbers because of the varied terrain and the ready accessibility. Good roads lead to Yosemite Valley, Tioga Pass, and Minaret Summit, on the boundaries of this section. Descriptions of history, trail approaches, and topography are given in the individual areas, which are arranged as follows:

Yosemite Valley. Climbs for this section are described in a separate guidebook published by the Sierra Club.*

The Cathedral Range and Eastward. This includes the Sierra Crest from Tioga Pass to Donohue Pass. The peaks are arranged in geographical order from northwest to southeast, first in the Cathedral Range and then in the Crest.

The Clark Range and Adjacent Peaks. This area also has been arranged in a general north-south order.

The Minarets and the Ritter Range. Here again a north-south description of the peaks is given.

It has been indicated in Sketch 1 that the Main Crest from Island Pass to Mammoth Pass is not considered in this guide. Since there is very little possibility for real climbing in this short section of the crest, this omission will not be regretted by many.

The Cathedral Range and Eastward

EDWARD S. ROBBINS and ALFRED W. BAXTER, JR. (1953); ELLEN PHILLIPS (1964)

BETWEEN MOUNT LYELL and the Tioga Road the Sierra Nevada has two crests: the Cathedral Range running in a northwesterly direction from Mount Lyell to Cathedral Peak, and to the east of this the

---

* *A Climber's Guide to Yosemite Valley,* by Steve Roper, Sierra Club, San Francisco, 1964.

higher true crest from Mount Lyell to Mount Dana. Almost all this area lies within the boundaries of Yosemite National Park and is easily accessible by good trails. Most of the peaks can be climbed in a single day from the Tioga Road. Maps for this area are the Tuolumne Meadows and Mono Craters quadrangles, plus small parts of Hetch-Hetchy Reservoir and Merced Peak.

The Cathedral Range forms the divide between the upper basins of two of the most spectacular river courses in the Sierra, the Tuolumne and the Merced. The general aspect of the range differs from that of other climbing areas in the High Sierra, for forests of lodgepole pine and mountain hemlock often extend high on the shoulders of the peaks, and an abundance of nearby lakes and subalpine meadows create a friendly sort of beauty when contrasted with the spectacular expanses of rock and ice found in the higher mountain areas to the south. The beautifully castellated peaks of the northern part of the range provide a number of short but popular rock climbs. While there are no large permanent snowfields, fine practice slopes for snow work can be found in early summer, around Budd Lake and elsewhere. This range is largely granite.

The main crest of the Sierra in this region is considerably higher than the Cathedral Range. In common with most peaks of the range, the main peaks have easy routes for ascent from the west. The first ascent of Mount Gibbs was on horseback. There are a few small glaciers on their northern and eastern sides, the best known being on Lyell, Dana, and Kuna. It was on the Maclure lobe of Lyell Glacier that John Muir made the measurements first proving the existence of glaciers in the Sierra. In the Mount Lyell region the rock is Half Dome quartz monzonite, but farther north much of the rock is volcanic and sedimentary; Parker, Dana, and Gibbs especially are composed of the original rock that once formed a thick roof over the Sierra.

History

This is one portion of the Sierra where the climbing history should mention the original Indian inhabitants. The Mono and Yosemite Indians had a trading area in the vicinity of Tuolumne Pass, and François E. Matthes found a bow high on the slopes of Parsons Peak. White men who first entered the area, under the leadership of Joseph Reddefield Walker in 1833, traveled along the western extension of the Cathedral Range. In 1863, the California Geological Survey, led by Josiah Dwight Whitney, made several ascents, including one of Mount Dana.

The group attempted to climb Mount Lyell, but they were stopped 600 feet short of the summit, which they regarded as inaccessible. Gold was found east of the crest in 1852, and several mines were established, one at the head of Bloody Canyon. Mining equipment was carried by pack train across the Mono Pass Trail until 1882, when the Tioga Road was opened by a private company.

All the main peaks of these areas have now been ascended, the last being those in the Echo Peak group and on Matthes Crest.

APPROACHES AND CAMPSITES

The Tioga Road, usually open from late May until November, makes this area easily accessible from east or west. For the backpacker, trails into the area include several from Yosemite Valley, including the Tenaya Lake Trail, the Sunrise and Soda Springs Trail by way of Little Yosemite, and the Merced Lake Trail combined with either the Babcock Lake Trail or the Vogelsang Pass Trail. From the south a trail leads from Agnew Meadow via Thousand Island Lake over Donohue Pass. From the east a trail may be followed from Walker Lake up Bloody Canyon and over Mono Pass. Another trail goes from Silver Lake up Rush Creek where it joins the Parker Pass Trail and, higher, the John Muir Trail, leading to Donohue Pass.

There are a lodge, a store, a garage, a ranger station, and a campground in Tuolumne Meadows. Fine camping areas may be found at Budd Lake, Cathedral Lake, the head of Lyell Fork of the Tuolumne, on the Lyell Fork of the Merced, Vogelsang Lake, and in many other places. Plans to camp at sites within the park other than those maintained by the Park Service, as well as all plans for climbing in the park, should be checked with the rangers in advance.

Peaks of the Cathedral Range (Northwest to Southeast)

Double Rock (9,872)

Both summits, on the rim of Tuolumne Canyon, were climbed on July 18, 1934, by Glen Dawson, Joel Hildebrand, Milton Hildebrand, Dorothy Morris, May Pridham, and David Parish.

Colby Mountain (9,631)

Climbed by John Muir in September 1871. The ascent is an easy walk from Ten Lakes Trail by the south ridge and affords a good view of Tuolumne Canyon. Class 1.

Mount Hoffmann (10,850)

The first ascent was made by J. D. Whitney, Wm. H. Brewer, and Chas. F. Hoffmann, members of the Whitney Survey, June 24, 1863.

Route 1. South slope. Class 2. The peak is easily climbed by south slopes after approaching from May Lake or from the Tioga Pass road further west.

Route 2. West slope. Class 3. Approach is from the north from a fork of Yosemite Creek. Ascend the west slope, which may contain a snowfield, and follow the southwest ridge to the summit.

Route 3. North face. Class 5+. Climbed by George Sessions and Merle Alley, July 1957. Ascend the snowfield to the base of a chimney 200 feet west of the overhanging summit block. The chimney is followed all the way to the ridge. Three overhangs present the greatest difficulty throughout 500 feet of class 5 climbing. The first ascent took nine hours and 20 pitons.

Hoffmann Thumb. The first ascent of the western pinnacle was made by Jules Eichorn October 16, 1932. The route lies on the face away from the summit of the main peak and consists of a single pitch on steep loose rock. Class 5. On July 20, 1934, Muir Dawson made the first ascent of the upper side of the pinnacle, using an upper belay. Another route on the side facing the summit of Hoffmann was climbed by Jim Baird and Tom Emery in 1951. Class 4. A class 5 climb of the west face of the Thumb was made in 1956 by Ray Van Aken and Mel Creusere.

Hoffmann Turret. Class A. At the end of the low northwest ridge of Hoffmann there is a sharp, turret-like pinnacle. A first ascent of the northeast face of this turret was made in August 1958 by Jerry Gray, George Ewing, and Les Overstreet. The route begins to the west of a gently sloping buttress of the turret, in the western of two jam cracks fifteen feet apart, and leads to a large V-shaped opening. Using a 150-foot rope, proceed up the base of the V to an open crack that permits a hand traverse across the left slope of the V to the upper of three steps. Proceed to the right around a buttress and horizontally across a friction pitch to a difficult open chimney. From the top of the chimney easy scrambling leads to the summit. About six hours.

Tuolumne Peak (10,845)

Climbed prior to 1932.

Polly Dome (9,810)

Probably climbed by John Muir in August 1869 (see "My First Summer in the Sierra"). Climbed in June 1896 by Theodore S. Solomons with four girls.

Fairview Dome (9,731)

First ascent July 4, 1863, by H. Brewer and C. F. Hoffmann.
Route 1. East face. Class 3.
Route 2. North face. Class A. Climbed by Chuck Pratt and Wally Reed in August 1958. The route consists of a series of disjointed cracks in the center of the face. The cracks lead to a wide, crescent-shaped ledge halfway up the face. Fourth and fifth class pitches above the ledge lead to the summit. Time: 14 hours; two bolts for direct aid.
Routes 3 and 4. North face. Class A. Two other north face routes on Fairview Dome were climbed by Wally Reed and Glen Denny in 1962 (*SCB*, December 1963, p. 110).

Daff Dome (9,153)

The name is an abbreviation of "Dome across from Fairview." A class 5.7 crack that extends nearly all the way up the west face was climbed in July 1963 by Wally Reed and Frank Sacherer. The crack is over 400 feet long.

Tenaya Peak (10,301)

The south slopes are class 2 and have been climbed on skis.

Cathedral Peak (10,940)

The first ascent was made by John Muir in September 1869, probably by Route 1.
Route 1. East slope and northwest face. Class 3 except for the summit pitch, which is class 4. Three fourths of a mile north of Budd Lake on the Budd Creek Trail, go west and ascend a broad talus slope to a shallow notch on the ridge north of the summit. Descend on the west side of this notch and follow a series of ledges to the broken rock north of the ridge between the summit and the west peak. Climb a series of ledges to a sloping ledge just below the summit block. From here traverse eastward to a mantelshelf and climb to the summit.
Route 2. West face. Class 3 with one class 4 pitch. Leave the Sunrise Trail from a point about a half mile north of Lower Cathedral Lake and climb talus and slabs of the west face to a point just north of the notch on the ridge between the summit and the west peak. Scramble

up over blocks and slabs to the sloping ledge just below the summit
block. Follow Route 1 to the summit.

Route 3. South face. Class 4. From the south ascend the talus chute
toward the main chimney to the west of the summit, as high as possible. Then traverse to the left to the base of the chimney proper. Ascend the chimney for about 125 feet, then traverse to the right and
upwards to a ledge just below the crest and east of the west peak.
Climb to the ridge and follow Route 1 to the summit.

Route 4. Southeast buttress. Class 5. First ascent by Charles Wilts and
Spencer Austin. Follow the broad southeast buttress of Cathedral Peak.
The climb is long as well as difficult in comparison with other climbs
in this area, involving almost 500 feet on 60° to 70° slabs. Other routes
on the south face and the southeast buttress offer the most interesting
possibilities for new routes of class 5 to A difficulty on Cathedral Peak.

Route 5. Northeast face. Class 5. Climbed by Frank Tarver and Gordon Petrequin July 1953. Start about 100 yards to the right of the
lowest point on the northeast side of the southeast buttress. Ascend to
the ridge which rises on the left and follow it to the summit.

Route 6. North face. Class 5. Climbed by Wally Reed and Cathy
Warne, July 1961. This is a short (175 foot) climb that starts in a
broad, chimney-like depression, about eight feet wide, with an overhanging rock at the top. The route finishes at the notch to the left
of the summit block.

Route 7. South face. Class 5.6. Climbed July 1962 by Wally Reed and
Don Harmon. Viewed from the south, a prominent crack about six
inches wide extends downward about 50 feet just to the right of the
summit ridge. A further crack system below this extends in a nearly
straight line to the ground. Climb up following these cracks, sometimes climbing on the face near the cracks. About 300 feet of class 5
climbing is required.

Eichorn's Pinnacle (the prominent pinnacle below and west of Cathedral's west peak). Class 4. First ascent July 24, 1931, by Glen Dawson
and Jules Eichorn. From the notch between the pinnacle and the west
peak, descend a short distance on the north, traverse out onto the side
facing Cathedral Lake, and climb to the top.

Cockscomb Peak (11,040+)

First ascent by Lipman and Chamberlain in 1914. Second ascent by
Jules Eichorn and Glen Dawson in 1931, by the west face. There are
various class 4 and 5 routes.

West face. Class 4. From the northwest corner of the peak ascend on the west face to a large flat ledge exposed to the east. From here traverse to the south by the west face to a wide cleft. The summit is the knife-edge east of this cleft which is a few inches higher than the large block to the west. Alternative: From the large flat ledge climb a prominent crack to a fingertip traverse left to the notch (class 5).

Unicorn Peak (10,880+)

From the north, this peak appears to be a single spire on a ridge; however there are three pinnacles, of which the north one is the true summit. There are many possible routes on the west face, and the poorly defined north arête, many of class 5 difficulty. The first ascent was by the northeast face by Francis P. Farquhar and James Rennie in 1911. Twenty years later, with Farquhar, Robert L. M. Underhill introduced the use of modern rope management to the Sierra on the north face.

For a class 3 route from Elizabeth Lake, ascend to the notch between the north and middle pinnacles and follow the arête to the summit.

Echo Ridge (11,120+)

This is the prominent summit between the Cockscomb and Echo Peaks.

Route 1. West ridge. Class 2. From Budd Lake go up to the col between Echo Ridge and Echo Peaks, and from there scramble east to the summit.

Route 2. North face and east ridge. Class 4. First ascent by Joe Firey, Peter Hoessly, Ron Hahn, and Ed Robbins in 1949. From the east end of Budd Lake ascend talus to the base of the eastern chimney on the cliff at the base of the north face. Two or three pitches lead onto the broad east ridge. Ascend to and traverse the ridge from this point, or proceed along the north face (class 3) to a notch, cross to the south face and traverse west until beneath the peak at the north end of the ridge, and then scramble to the top. Some of the rock on the north face is rather rotten.

Echo Peaks (11,040+)

This group of pinnacles west of Echo Ridge can be approached from Budd Lake or Upper Cathedral Lake. The numbering is indicated on Sketch 5, which lists the most prominent nine.

Peak 1. Route 1. East face. Class 3. First ascent on August 4, 1936, Owen L. Williams. Ascend the center of the east face to the notch between Peaks 1 and 2 and follow the ridge north to the summit.

Route 2. West face. Class 4. Ascend the west face to the notch between Peaks 1 and 2, and follow the east side of the ridge to the summit.

Peak 2. East face. Class 3. Ascend the east face to the notch between Peaks 1 and 2. Follow the ridge south to the summit.

Peak 3. This, the highest of the Echo Peaks, was climbed July 7, 1931, by Norman Clyde and Carl Sharsmith.

Route 1. East face. Class 4. Ascend the gully on the east face to the

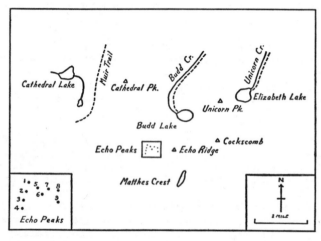

Sketch 5. Cathedral Peak Area.

notch between Peaks 2 and 3. Follow the ridge south to the summit.

Route 2. West face. Class 3. Ascend the west face to the notch between Peaks 2 and 3. Follow the ridge south to the summit.

Peak 4. First ascent by Owen L. Williams and Ethyl Mae Hill, August 6, 1936.

Route 1. Class 4. From the summit of Peak 3, descend the east side of the ridge between Peaks 3 and 4 to a point about 30 feet below the notch. From here climb the northeast face directly to the summit.

Route 2. Class 4. Climb from the left of a prominent row of shrubs at the base of the northeast face, directly to the summit.

Peak 5. Class 3. Ascend the north ridge.

Peak 6. Class 3. Ascend vague northeast ridge.

Peak 7. Class 3. Ascend northeast ridge.

Peak 8. Class 3. Ascend north face.

Peak 9. Class 5. First ascent by Charles Wilts and Spencer Austin. Descend from notch west of Peaks 8 and 9 until the south face can be easily reached, traverse out on the south face and go straight up to an overhang. Traverse east and up and back west to the arête. Then go along the arête to the summit.

Matthes Crest (*10,880+*)

First ascent by Jules Eichorn, Glen Dawson, and Walter Brem on July 26, 1931. This is the spectacular knife edge on the south slope of Echo Ridge. In the past it has borne other names since it has also been known as Echo Ridge, and Echo Crest. The present name, in honor of François C. Matthes, the geologist, was made official in 1946. The north peak is the higher.

Route 1. East face. Class 5. Climbed by Donald Harmon and Robert Dohrmann in July 1954. Ascend the east face, directly below the highest summit, climbing slabs to a short, open chimney below the summit block.

Route 2. South arête. Class 5. First ascent by Charles and Ellen Wilts in June 1947. Ascend the south arête above a group of pines and traverse along the ridge.

Route 3. North pinnacle. Class 4. Ascend the north arête and then go out on the east face and climb to the summit.

Tresidder Peak (*10,560+*)

This cockscomb was ascended prior to 1948. The south peak is the highest.

Route 1. Class 4. Approach up the south arête. Near the top traverse north on the west face, then up the face to the south summit. The peak on the north end of the ridge is class 3.

Columbia Finger (*10,320+*)

A cockscomb; first ascent July 22, 1921, by William H. Staniels, Donald E. Tripp, and B. H. Bochmer.

Route 1. West face. Class 3. Ascend the easy ridge north of the pinnacle and climb the west face.

Johnson Peak (*11,070*)

First ascent in 1933 by H. B. Blanks. This peak can be climbed easily from Elizabeth Lake.

Rafferty Peak (11,120+)

First ascent by Edward W. Hernden. Second class by talus and ledges from the col at the head of the middle fork of Rafferty Creek.

Peak 11,282 (1 SW of Rafferty Peak)

First ascent in 1931 by Julie Mortimer, Alice Carter, and Eleanor Smith. Class 2 from Booth Lake, the largest in the group of small lakes between Fletcher and Emeric creeks, southwest of Tuolumne Pass.

Fletcher Peak (11,408)

Route 1. Southwest slope. Class 2. Ascend from the north end of Vogelsang Lake through brush, scree, and talus to the summit.

Route 2. Northwest couloir. Class 4. Climbed August 1959 by Ronald Smith and Bob Happle. Proceed east from Vogelsang High Sierra Camp to the couloir, ascend on the right side of the ice, and higher up traverse back and forth until a large crack is reached. Climb this, go to the left to a small group of trees, and then proceed up the southwest slope to the summit.

Vogelsang Peak (11,516)

Ascended before 1923 by F. E. Matthes. Class 2. From Vogelsang Lake climb to the saddle between the main peak and the north peak, then south to the summit.

Parsons Peak (12,080+)

First ascent by Marion Randall Parsons before 1931. The ascent can be made either from the head of Ireland Creek or from the Bernice Lake area south of Vogelsang Pass. Class 2.

Simmons Peak (12,503)

First ascent in 1931 by Sierra Club members. Class 2 from upper Bernice Lake.

Mount Florence (12,561)

First ascent by Theodore S. Solomons and F. W. Reed, August 1897.

Route 1. West slope. Class 2. From southeast of Washburn Lake follow the stream toward Mount Florence. Scramble over shale and weather-beaten rock to the summit. Alternatively, one may leave the Isberg Pass Trail south of Lewis Creek, where it crosses a ridge at

9,600 feet, and proceed eastward to the northwest ridge or the west slope of Mount Florence. Class 2.

Mount Maclure (12,960+)

First ascent by Willard D. Johnson in 1883.

Route 1. East ridge. Class 3. From the col between Mounts Lyell and Maclure ascend the talus and ledges to the summit.

Route 2. South face. Class 3. First ascent by a Sierra Club party led by Ted Waller, 1934. From Hutching Creek ascend on the left side of the prominent gully on the south face and then traverse east to the ridge. Follow the ridge to the summit.

Route 3. Northwest ridge. Class 4. First ascent by Al Steck and George Steck. From the pass between Simmons Peak and Mount Maclure follow the ridge to the summit.

Peak 12,358 (¾ SW of Maclure)

First ascent July 1934 by Julie Mortimer and May Pridham.

Peak 12,720+ (¾ SW of Mt. Lyell)

A probable first ascent was made in July 1955 by George W. Whitmore. From Hutching Creek basin ascend southeastward to the pass between 12,720+ and Peak 12,132. From the pass make an ascending traverse of the southeast slope of the peak. Class 2.

Peak 12,132 (2 SW of Mt. Lyell)

Probable first ascent in July 1955 by George W. Whitmore. Class 2 via the northeast ridge from the pass between Peak 12,720+ and 12,132.

Peaks on and near the Main Crest

Mount Dana (13,053)

First ascent June 28, 1863, by W. H. Brewer and C. F. Hoffmann, who found the view so impressive that J. D. Whitney climbed the peak the next day.

Route 1. Class 1. From the Tioga Road many easy routes are available up the west and south slopes.

Route 2. Glacier route. Class 3. Ascend over the glacier on the north side of Mount Dana to the prominent couloir that heads just east of the summit (ice axe necessary), or climb the rock east of the couloir.

Route 3. Northeast wall. Class 3. Proceed up Glacier Canyon to a point 500 feet from the glacier. Climb the wall to the west and follow the northwest ridge to the summit. Climbed in August 1949 by F. J. Meyers and party.

Mount Gibbs *(12,764)*

The first ascent was on horseback, August 31, 1864, by W. H. Brewer and F. L. Olmsted *(père)*. The ascent from any direction except the east is class 1.

Mount Lewis *(12,296)*

No records. The ascent from Mono Pass at the northwest is class 1.

Kuna Peak *(12,960+)*

First ascent in 1919 by Walter L. Huber. Third class routes may be selected on the northwestern side.

Kuna Crest *(12,207)*

This is the long ridge extending in a northwesterly direction from Kuna Peak and forming the east wall of Lyell Canyon. First ascent by Water L. Huber in 1909. Class 3 routes may be selected on either the east or west side.

Mammoth Peak *(12,117)*

This is the high point at the north end of Kuna Crest. First ascent by Walter L. Huber in 1902. Careful inspection will reveal many class 2 and 3 routes.

Parker Peak *(12,861)*

First ascent by Norman Clyde in 1914. It may be easily climbed from the Parker Pass Trail where it passes between Parker and Koip peaks. Class 1.

Koip Peak *(12,979)*

First ascent by Chester Versteeg in 1912. May be readily climbed from the Parker Pass Trail where it passes between Parker and Koip peaks. Class 2.

Mount Wood *(12,637)*

First ascent in 1928 by persons unknown. Second ascent in 1937 by

Don McGeein from the highway between Silver and Grant lakes. Class 2.

Koip Crest (12,000+ to 12,668)

Koip Crest extends south from Koip Peak to Blacktop Peak and then southeast from Blacktop Peak. On the northern section of the crest there are nine pinnacles. The first traverse, by George Templeton and Milton Hildebrand on August 9, 1939, took 12 hours. Class 4.

On the southern section (southeast of Blacktop) there are seven pinnacles; the largest and highest is the round one at the northwest end joining the Eocene plateau of Blacktop. This pinnacle is class 2 from Blacktop, class 3 from the southeast arête. From the southwest it is possible to make a class 5 climb up the most prominent chimney on the southwest face of the highest summit. This chimney strikes the ridge just east of the summit. The first ascent of this last route was made by Richard M. Leonard and Jim Koontz August 1950.

Blacktop Peak (12,710)

No records except for the traverse of Koip Crest (above). Class 2 by the southeast slope, from Gem Pass.

Donohue Peak (12,023)

First ascent in 1895 by Sergeant Donohue, U.S. Cavalry, on horseback. The northwest face affords class 1 and class 2 routes. The southwest ridge can be followed from Donohue Pass (class 2–3). The view from the peak is quite good.

Mount Lyell (13,114)

The highest peak in Yosemite National Park was described as an "inaccessible pinnacle" by the first party to attempt it, Wm. H. Brewer and Charles F. Hoffmann in 1863. It was first climbed by John B. Tileston, August 29, 1871. The first winter ascent was on March 2, 1936, by David R. Brower, Lewis F. Clark, Boynton S. Kaiser, Einar Nilsson, and Bestor Robinson, who skied up the Merced Canyon from Yosemite Valley via Bernice Lake and crossed the north ridge of Maclure to Lyell Glacier (4 days).

Route 1. North glacier and north face. Class 2 to 3. This is the easiest and most popular route; however, it requires careful judgment. A rope should be carried, especially if there are inexperienced people in the party. The difficulty may vary considerably with the season, depending on the amount and condition of the snow or ice. Ascend the talus and

the west end of the glacier to the notch between Mount Lyell and
Mount Maclure. From here climb toward the summit of Lyell along
sloping class 2 ledges somewhat above the snow, but below the rock
face. After a rather short distance on these ledges, ascend a narrow,
steep crack at 65° to the arête (class 2 to 3). Then ascend the arête to
the summit (see Sketch 6).

Sketch 6. Mounts Lyell and Maclure from the northeast,
showing Route 1 on each.

It is also possible to climb to the summit slopes up ledges or chutes
a little farther east, but this will necessitate climbing rather steep snow
above the glacier. Nevertheless it is a popular route, and may be
reached from rather high on the Donohue Pass trail by walking to the
moraine below the east lobe of the glacier, crossing the moraine
through a saddle, climbing directly up the face of the glacier, crossing
the bergschrund, and proceeding westward along the base of the cliff
above the glacier until a series of ledges is found by means of which
the easy summit plateau can be reached.

Route 2. North glacier and east arête. Class 3. From the base of the
glacier, climb to the col east of Lyell, crossing the upper snowfield as
soon as possible. Ascend the east arête to the summit.

Route 3. Lyell-Maclure col from the south. Class 3. From the head
of Hutching Creek ascend the obvious gully to the col between Maclure
and Lyell and follow the west ridge or Route 1 to the summit.

Route 4. Southwest ridge. Class 4. Climbed by George Whitmore in

July 1955. From the head of Hutching Creek climb eastward to the col between Peak 12,720+ (¾ SW of Lyell) and Lyell. Follow the southwest ridge until it merges with the south face. Several hundred feet of high-angle climbing on good rock lead to the crest about 100 feet west of the summit.

Route 5. South face. Class 4. From the Lyell Fork of the Merced ascend the talus chute directly to the summit. Care must be taken on the loose rock in the upper portion of the gully.

Route 6. West face. Class 5. First ascent August 1963 by Les Wilson, Dennis Schmitt, Tim Gerson, and Peter Haan. From the cirque at the head of Hutching Creek the west face of Mount Lyell is seen as a wide, steep face culminating in a vertical nose. The route starts directly beneath the nose in a decaying chimney and goes up and somewhat to the left, finishing a little northwest of the nose.

The Clark Range and Adjacent Peaks

RICHARD M. LEONARD (1953); HERVEY H. VOGE (1964)

THE CLARK RANGE early attracted the attention of geologists, to-pographers, and mountaineers because of the commanding position of its peaks, standing as they do near the center of the granite wilderness of the headwaters of the Merced River. Clarence King wrote of its principal peak:

"From every commanding eminence around the Yosemite no distant object rises with more inspiring greatness than the obelisk of Mount Clark . . . its slender needlelike summit had long fired us with ambition. . . . There was in our hope of scaling this point something more than mere desire to master a difficult peak. It was a station of great topographical value, the apex of many triangles, and, more than all, would command a grander view of the Merced region than any other summit."

Accordingly, after he had spent the summer of 1864 surveying the Yosemite Grant, the new park that had just been granted by the Federal Government to California, King started out on November 11, 1864, with Richard D. Cotter, and reached a fine camp near timberline in the cirque between Clark and Gray Peak just to the south. There a violent early winter storm nearly trapped them in a foot and a half of new snow. Their escape provides a fine tale of early mountaineering. More prudently, his next attempt was made in warm weather, July 12, 1866, with James Terry Gardiner. They made the ascent by a thrilling route along the southeast arête from the same cirque at the head of Gray Creek.

GEOLOGY

The Clark Range is a remnant of the ancient, folded, metamorphic mountains of Appalachian type that reached an elevation of approximately half that of the present range about 130 million years ago. The northwest-southeast trend of these peaks is roughly at right angles to the great southwest slope of the Sierra granite block, which was uptilted only ten million years ago. Remnants of the ancient metamorphic rocks can still be found in the quartzite of "Quartz Peak," just north of Mount Clark, and in the ancient metamorphic lavas similar to those of the Ritter Range which give the dark color to Merced Peak and explain its earlier name, "Black Mountain."

Mount Clark is composed of a very firm granite rather free of master joints, and would probably have become a dome except that it was severely glaciated on three sides. The absence of the black iron-bearing minerals gives Mount Clark an exceptionally light appearance. Gray and Red peaks, as the names indicate, are strangely different. Their granites are similar to the white granite of Mount Hoffmann, but on Red Peak the black iron-bearing minerals seen in Gray Peak are weathered to an iron rust that colors the granite brilliantly. On Gray Peak these minerals are still predominantly black. Merced Peak is composed of extremely hard metamorphic lavas approximately 190 million years old, similar to those that form the sharp crest of Mount Ritter and the Minarets. The mixture of red and white granite and the black rocks of Merced Peak combine with brilliant blue lakes and bright green meadows to form a bowl at Ottoway Lakes that is one of the most colorful in the Sierra.

APPROACHES AND CAMPSITES

The peaks of the range are easily accessible by fine trails and open benches on all sides. The easiest route is from Glacier Point or Mono Meadow to the point where the trail crosses the Clark Fork of Illilouette Creek, where there is fine camping and scattered animal feed. There are many additional campsites above the trail along the west slope of the range, with a particularly fine spot on the trail at Ottoway Lake; and across Red Peak Pass there are good campsites by a series of fine lakes at timberline on the Merced Peak Fork of the Merced

River. Mount Clark can also be reached from the Nevada Fall Trail by the old army trail to Starr King Meadow, or from Merced Lake Ranger Station up the other end of this early trail on Gray Peak Fork of the Merced River. The trail has not been maintained for sixty years and therefore can be considered as only an indication of a feasible route.

The southern peaks of the range are easily accessible from the road-head at Clover Meadow Ranger Station, in Sierra National Forest, reached from the Bass Lake junction of the Fresno-Wawona Road. There are four passes, each crossed by good trails, which bring one into the southern portion of the Clark Range and its adjacent peaks.

The Clark Range is shown on the Merced Peak Quadrangle map.

Peaks of the Clark Range

Mount Clark (11,522)

Route 1. Southeast arête. Class 3. First ascent July 12, 1866, by Clarence King and James T. Gardiner. A thrilling account of this climb is given by King in *Mountaineering in the Sierra Nevada.* Although a rope is not normally used on this route, one should be available. The sharp southeast arête can be reached without difficulty from either west or east. On the arête, King's thrilling gaps in the knife-edge will still be found, and it is at those points that a rope is welcome protection. Approach from Merced Lake: Cross over logs at the confluence of the Merced River and Gray Peak Fork and proceed up fishing trail along Gray Peak Fork to the upper basin (above the waterfall) and, keeping to the right, follow to a small creek (8,400 feet) running from Mount Clark into the Gray Peak Fork. Follow this watercourse to the lakes and thence to foot of Mount Clark over fairly open and gradual slopes. One can also proceed directly south from Merced Lake.

Route 2. Northeast face. Class 3. Although Mount Clark was a popular climb with at least four ascents before 1893, it was not until the solo ascent by Francis P. Farquhar on July 4, 1916, that the easiest route was clearly described. He climbed from Merced Lake, and observed, on reaching the head of the snowfield on the northeast face, that a series of broad ledges on the north edge of the face provided a simple route to the summit.

Route 3. Northwest arête. Class 4–5. In October 1934, Neil Ruge and Douglas Olds pioneered this difficult route, which is unmistakable to one with class-4 training and equipment. It consists of 1,500 feet of roped climbing on sound granite.

Route 4. North face. Class 5.6. Climbed in September 1958 by Henry Kendall, Herb Swedlund, Hobey DeStaebler, and Tom Frost. From the cirque north of the peak cross the ice (step cutting needed) and reach the rock somewhat to the left of the summit. Continue up until a ledge allows a traverse to the right directly under the face. Two class-4 rock pitches lead directly upward to the right member of a pair of vertical chimneys (class 5.6), and a succeeding class-5.4 lead ends on the northwest ridge.

Winter ascent. Class 4. In February 1937 Ken Adam, Ken Davis, Hervey Voge, and David Brower made the ascent from the southwest, ending via the southeast ridge.

Gray Peak (11,574)

Class 2. In 1920 Ansel Adams placed a Sierra Club cylinder type register on the summit. The best route is up the broad southwest slope of the Illilouette Basin. From the Gray Peak Fork side, an ascent would be considerably more difficult.

Red Peak (11,699)

Class 2 to 3. Presumably climbed by the California Geological Survey in 1870. In 1910 S. L. Foster made a solo ascent and found a cairn. In 1920 Ansel Adams placed a Sierra Club cylinder type register. This peak has some steep cliffs on the north. The easiest route is via the canyon to the north of the three summits, or via the crest of this summit ridge. The cliff face is very difficult.

Ottoway Peak (11,440+)

Class 2. The first recorded ascent was made by Ansel Adams on September 16, 1934, when scouting the route for the present trail, just a half-mile to the west. The route from the summit of the trail is easily ascertained.

Merced Peak (11,726)

The highest peak of the Clark Range was an early favorite as a climbing objective. In 1870 the California Geological Survey wrote that "All these points [of the Clark Range] except Gray Peak have been climbed by the Survey." In 1878 the peak was again occupied, this time by the Wheeler Survey party under Lieutenant M. M. Macomb. On July 29, 1897, Robert M. Price, his wife, F. W. Reede, and Theodore S. Solomons, placed Sierra Club Register number 56 on the summit. Fifty-two years later the tube was still there, though the records were missing. In 1871 the glacier in the cirque below the north face was found by Muir and described in detail in 1875 as the first living glacier to be found in the Sierra Nevada. His drawing of the great icicles in the bergschrund "12 to 14 feet wide" is a fascinating bit of recent Sierran geological history. The glacial milk in the lakelet below the cirque in 1949 prompted Alfred R. Dole and Richard M. Leonard to reëxplore the glacier. Ice was still present in good quantity, but they felt the glacier, one of the lowest glaciers in the Sierra, should probably be classed as "fossil" or inactive.

The early accounts do not give the route of climb.

Route 1. Northeast arête. Class 2. On a traverse of the peak in August, 1949, Alfred R. Dole, Stewart and Elizabeth Kimball, and Richard M. Leonard found the northeast arête the easiest. It is reached from fine camping on lower Ottoway Lake by following up the canyon to the class-2 pass between Ottoway and Merced peaks, and ascending the blocks of talus, keeping to the ridge crest to lessen danger from loose blocks.

Route 2. West arête. Class 3. This route is a half-mile in length and contains several steep pitches that require detours on the south slope down onto smooth 50° slabs of very hard ancient metamorphic lava. Traversed in August 1949 by Dole, the Kimballs, and Leonard.

Peaks on the Merced–San Joaquin Divide

Rodgers Peak (12,978)

Class 3. This peak was known in early literature as "Kellogg Peak." The first recorded ascent was made on August 5, 1897, by Robert M. Price, who climbed from the Lyell Fork of the Merced. Captain N. F. McClure made an early ascent, and in 1924 Ansel Adams placed a Sierra Club cylinder type register. The best route is from the east (Rush Creek Basin). It can be climbed from the upper canyon of the Lyell Fork of the Merced, but is more difficult from that side. It can also be climbed (class 2) from the north fork of the San Joaquin River.

The ascent from Rush Creek may be made by way of the large upper Davis Lake. From this lake proceed to a saddle on the main divide, just northwest of point 11,627. Contour northwest on the southwest side of the ridge for about 400 yards, drop down obliquely about 400 feet in elevation to a small lake, continue westward into a cirque, then turn due south and climb to the top of the southeast ridge of

Rodgers Peak, which can be followed to the summit. Class 2 except for some class 3 near the top of the southeast ridge.

Peak 12,560+ (0.7 S of Rodgers)

Class 2. Climbed July 10, 1924, by Ansel Adams, Cedric Wright, and Willard Grinnell.

Electra Peak (12,442)

Class 2. Ascents were made by Norman Clyde in 1914 and 1919, and one by Ansel Adams in 1931. Ted Waller led a Sierra Club High Trip party of eight to the summit on July 12, 1934. From the upper Lyell Fork of the Merced, climb to the ridge north of the summit, and thence southward to the summit. The south slope is quite easy.

Mount Ansel Adams (11,760+; 1 NE of Foerster Peak)

Class 3. First ascent July 11, 1934, by Glen Dawson, Jack Riegelhuth, and Neil Ruge. From the Lyell Fork meadows on the Merced River this is the most spectacular and beautiful peak in sight. Two days after the first ascent, Ruge led to the summit a Sierra Club High Trip party which proposed the name "Mount Ansel Adams." The route ascends a prominent gully to the south of the peak, thence to the summit over the south face.

Peak 12,000+ (½ E of Foerster Peak)

Climbed July 13, 1934, by Marjory Bridge, Helen LeConte, and Louise Hildebrand.

Foerster Peak (12,058)

Class 2. Norman Clyde led a knapsack party in 1914, Robert Owen made an ascent on July 13, 1929, and three ascents were made on successive days by the Sierra Club High Trip in July 1934. The best route is on the southern slope. The west face is dangerous owing to rotten rock. The west side of the north ridge provides a class 2–3 approach, ascended by George Whitmore, July 1954.

Peak 11,535 (1 S of Foerster Peak)

Climbed July 13, 1929, by Robert Owen.

Long Mountain (11,502)

Class 2. Ansel Adams made an ascent in August, 1922. The best route is from the south.

Isberg Peak (10,996)

Class 1. The first recorded ascent was made April 20, 1924, by Ansel Adams. It is an easy ascent from the upper basin of the Triple Peak Fork of the Merced.

Post Peak (11,009)

Class 1. The first recorded ascent was by Ansel Adams. It was climbed September 7, 1930, by Walter A. Starr, Jr., who described it as "A fine vantage point from which to get a fine view of the upper Merced and San Joaquin region." A branch of the old Isberg Pass Trail passes within a few hundred feet of the summit. The route is obvious.

Triple Divide Peak (11,607)

Class 2. The peak splits two forks of the Merced from the East Fork of Granite Creek, a tributary of the San Joaquin. It affords a fine view. It was climbed by Norman Clyde in 1920. Ansel Adams, Elizabeth Adams, and F. C. Holman placed a Sierra Club cylinder type register in 1922. The best route is from the upper valley of Triple Peak Fork. The summit should be approached from the northeast.

Peak 11,261 (¾ SW of Triple Divide Peak)

Climbed August 3, 1934, by Edwin L. Garthwaite, Jed Garthwaite, and Jean Scupham.

Peak 10,823 (1.5 SW of Triple Divide Peak)

Class 2. Climbed in August 1934 by Edwin L. Garthwaite, Jed Garthwaite, and Jean Scupham.

Gale Peak (10,693)

Class 2. The first recorded ascent was made in 1920 by Lawrence Fley, Freeman Jones, and Thomas Jones. The peak is well situated at the head of the beautiful Chain Lakes, almost at the southernmost boundary of the park, and can be climbed easily by ascending the ridge dividing the Chain Lakes from Breeze Lake to the north.

Sing Peak (10,552)

No record is available.

Redtop (9,977)

This peak, on the south boundary of Yosemite, was at one time known as "Madera Peak" (*which see*). William Frederick Badè made an ascent prior to 1919.

Peaks East of the Divide

Sadler Peak (*10,567*)

No record is available. Probably class 1.

Madera Peak (*10,509*)

This is the approved name for the "Black Peak" of earlier editions of the topographic map. The peak is the southernmost high point of the northwest-southeast ancient ridge that formed the Clark Range. Class 2. Mr. and Mrs. Garthwaite, their 7-year-old son Jed, and Mrs. Hermina Daulton made the ascent in August, 1931. They "found a cairn but no records." The Brewer Survey reports an ascent on August 19, 1864, but they were probably referring to Merced Peak, 7 miles to the north, which at that time was known as "Black Peak" owing to its dark volcanic rock. The peak may be ascended from the upper basin of the Black Peak fork of Granite Creek. An easier ascent can be made over the west slopes.

The Minarets and the Ritter Range

WALTER A. STARR* (1938); ALLEN STECK (1964)

THE SIERRA CREST south of Island Pass surrenders its Alpine summits and scenic attractions to the Ritter Range, whose peaks rise two to three thousand feet higher to the west. The Ritter Range is a remnant of an ancient mountain system and, as François Matthes writes, "when you climb Mount Ritter you climb the core of one of the ancestral mountains that were formed more than a hundred million years before the present Sierra Nevada was uplifted."

Geologically the Ritter Range is composed of dark mottled rocks representing ancient lavas, highly metamorphosed, associated with a complex of dark igneous rocks. This tough rock has resisted the forces of erosion through the ages, which accounts for the height of the range.

* Assisted by Jules Eichorn, Glen Dawson, William Rice, Ansel Adams, and the climbing notes of Walter A. Starr, Jr. Later revision by Louis Elliott (1953).

The joint planes generally are vertical, or at high angles, with north-westerly trends. This structure causes the almost vertical faces and knife-edge ridges which are characteristic of the range. Caution is called for in climbing because of the danger of loose blocks or slabs which may pull away from the faces.

The chutes in the Minarets, as in other parts of the Sierra, constitute convenient routes of approach. But the systems of chutes are often complex, and many carry difficult chockstones. Most of these chutes contain loose rock, and rock-fall danger is high. However, the rock on the faces and ridges is generally sound, though hand-holds, which are usually plentiful and of adequate size, should be tested carefully.

Many of the ledges slope downwards, and exposure is often considerable. There are a great many possible routes up almost any of the Minarets when combinations of chutes, ridges, and ledges are considered. The rocks are very hard and many have sharp edges that approximate right angles and will cut hands or ropes unless care is taken. It is difficult to round the edges of some of these rocks with a hammer, and hence padding is sometimes desirable for a rappel point.

The John Muir Trail passes east of the range close to its base. Here lie several lakes, famed for their beauty—Thousand Island, Garnet, Ediza, Shadow, Iceberg, Cecile, and Minaret. The nearest approaches by road are Silver Lake, Agnew Meadow, and Devil's Postpile. Good campsites will be found above the western end of Lake Ediza (9,280+) and on the meadows of Shadow Creek above Shadow Lake (8,800). More exposed campsites may be found at Garnet Lake (9,700), and Thousand Island Lake (9,834). There are good campsites on upper Minaret Creek (9,000–9,500), and between Lake Ediza and Iceberg Lake from which to approach the southern end of the Minarets. For detailed information concerning approaches and trails see Starr's *Guide to the John Muir Trail and the High Sierra Region*. The map for this area is the Devil's Postpile quadrangle.

Mount Davis is the most northerly peak of the range and Iron Mountain the most southerly. Sketch 7 presents a map of the region. Although peaks of this range have been climbed for many years, no pinnacle of the Minarets was climbed until 1922. Since 1931, by application of sound rock-climbing methods, the difficulty and danger have been greatly lessened, and most of these pinnacles have been ascended. This region offers some of the finest climbing in the Sierra Nevada, and it is also endowed with unusual grandeur, beauty, and fascination.

Banner and Ritter are twin peaks, connected by a saddle. To the east a cliff drops off from the saddle. Sloping northwestward from the

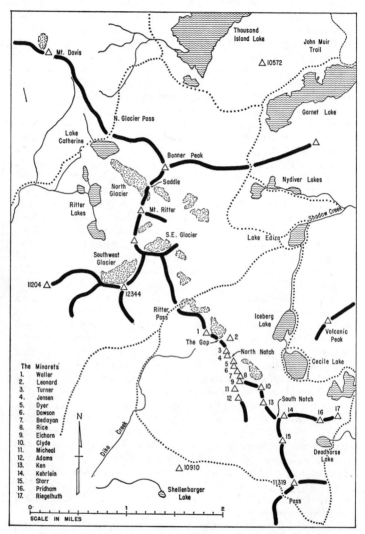

The Minarets
1. Waller
2. Leonard
3. Turner
4. Jensen
5. Dyer
6. Dawson
7. Bedayan
8. Rice
9. Eichorn
10. Clyde
11. Micheal
12. Adams
13. Ken
14. Kehrlein
15. Starr
16. Pridham
17. Riegelhuth

Mt. Davis

Thousand Island Lake

John Muir Trail

△ 10572

N. Glacier Pass

Lake Catherine

Garnet Lake

Banner Peak

Saddle

North Glacier

Nydiver Lakes

Ritter Lakes

△ Mt. Ritter

Shadow Creek

S.E. Glacier

Lake Ediza

Southwest Glacier

11204 △

△ 12344

Ritter Pass

Iceberg Lake

Volcanic Peak

1
The Gap   △ 2
3
4   North Notch
5
6   Cecile Lake
7
8
9
11 △   △ 10
12   △ 13   South Notch
14   16   17
△ 15

Deadhorse Lake

N

Dike Creek

△ 10910

11319

Pass

Shellenbarger Lake

0   1   2
SCALE IN MILES

Sketch 7. The Ritter Range and the Minarets. (See legend, page 14.)

saddle, North Glacier covers the floor of the chasm between the two peaks, flowing down to Lake Catherine. Half a mile south of this lake and lapping the western base of Ritter lies Ritter Lake. Beyond and somewhat above, another lakelet is fed by Southwest Glacier which fills a rugged amphitheater on the north side of a bold jagged spur extending southwesterly from the summit of Ritter. The highest point on this arête might be regarded as the western summit of Ritter. On the southeast side of Ritter, draining into Lake Ediza, Southeast Glacier slopes steeply down, enclosed in an amphitheater bounded on the north by the face of the peak and on the south by pinnacles extending downward from the crest of a spur which dips southeastward from the summit to a saddle. South of this saddle the knife-edge ridges of the Minarets, crowned with many pinnacles, split the sky. At its southern end the ridge forks into two groups of minarets, the eastern dominated by Clyde Minaret and the western by Michael Minaret, the two highest pinnacles. Between them a remarkable amphitheater is formed by their sheer walls, in which lies a small ice lake. Several small, steep glaciers lie along the sloping walls of the eastern base of the Minarets.

An ice axe is necessary and crampons may be helpful for ascents over the glaciers east of mounts Banner and Ritter and of the Minarets.

Principal Passes

The Ritter Range may be approached from the North Fork of the San Joaquin River on its western side, but by far the nearest and most interesting approaches are from the trails leading to its eastern side. To cross the range several passes are available.

Glacier Lake Pass, east to west. Class 2. From the head of Thousand Island Lake ascend to the saddle between Banner Peak and Mount Davis, keeping to the side of the basin toward Davis. North Glacier Lake (Lake Catherine) lies on the saddle. Easy rocky slopes are met on the west side.

Banner-Ritter Saddle, east to west (*12,000+*). Class 3; ice axe needed. From Lake Ediza, or Garnet Lake, ascend to the basin lying east of the cliff between Banner and Ritter. Climb the cliff to the saddle, keeping to the right of black stains made by water courses near the middle of the cliff, and following a series of zigzag ledges. From the saddle descend on the north side of the glacier to the east end of Lake Catherine.

Ritter Pass, east to west. Class 2. From Lake Ediza ascend the cliff southwest of the lake to the saddle between Ritter and Waller Minaret. Easy, rocky slopes lie on the west side.

The Gap, east to west. Class 2; ice axe usually needed. From Lake Ediza climb the cliff or chimneys below the gap south of Waller Minaret, and ascend the small glacier to the gap. Steep talus slopes are on the west side.

North Notch, east to west. Class 3; ice axe useful (seasonal). From Lake Ediza ascend southwest up the stream which enters the head of the lake to an easy ridge leading toward the notch (lowest point) between Jensen and Dawson minarets. There is a nice ledge leading up from the north into the chute. Climb the chute past one small chockstone to the notch. This is the shortest route to the west side of the highest minarets from Lake Ediza. Rough steep talus slopes extend along the west base of the Minarets.

South Notch, east to west. Class 2 to 3 (seasonal); ice axe needed. To approach from Minaret Lake, ascend the stream entering the lake to a bench above the southwest end of Cecile Lake. To approach from Lake Ediza, ascend the stream on the south side of the lake to Iceberg Lake. Traverse on the east side and climb up to Cecile Lake. Traverse on the west side of this to a bench above the southwest end.

From the southwest end of Cecile Lake ascend the steep slope (snow conditions seasonal) to the col or notch between Kehrlein Minaret and Ken Minaret, which rise just south of Clyde Minaret. A prominent pinnacle stands above the north side of the notch. Traverse west from the notch into Minaret Amphitheater which contains a small ice lake. Ascend to the col on the southeast side of Michael Minaret and descend a chute (class 4) to the base (western side) of that minaret. To reach this point by the long route (class 1) from the amphitheater, circle Adams Minaret to the south and west and then cross a spur ridge to the north, keeping well to the west to avoid difficult chutes on the north side of the spur.

Beck Lakes Pass, south to north. Class 1. From the northwest side of Upper Beck Lake ascend northwest up talus, rocks, and snowslopes to a saddle. Cross the basin at the head of Iron Creek and cross a spur ridge extending southwest from Adams Minaret at a low point to the head of Dike Creek. Or, ascend to the upper end of Iron Creek into Minaret Amphitheater and proceed as from the South Notch. There is a trail from Devil's Postpile to Lower Beck Lake.

Routes on the Peaks (North to South)

Mount Davis (12,311)

First Ascent August 28, 1891, by Milton F. Davis.

Route 1. Southeast slope. Class 1. From Thousand Island Lake proceed to the low pass between Davis and Banner (Glacier Lake Pass) and climb up toward the summit, staying on the southwest side of the sharp ridge. The slope to be traversed is quite gentle and leads up to the easy southeast slopes of the peak. This route may also be reached by traversing southwest from Island Pass and passing through a notch in the ridge southeast of the summit. This variation requires careful route finding across the high shoulder above Thousand Island Lake.

Route 2. Northeast buttress. Class 4. Ascended by Hervey Voge and Virginia Romain, August 20, 1950. The northeast buttress rises above a slope of snow or ice somewhat east of the main north buttress. Ascend the east side of the northeast buttress, climb an open chute to the ridge of the buttress, follow this to the broad slopes southeast of the summit, and walk up these to the top.

Route 3. North buttress. Class 4. Ascended by Jim Koontz and Sarah Haynes, August 20, 1950. Climb up between the main north buttress and the glacier to the west, and when the rocks become easier go up the rocks to the top of the buttress which is followed almost directly to the summit.

Banner Peak (12,945)

Route 1. North glacier and southwest slope. Class 2. First ascent, August 26, 1883, by Willard D. Johnson and John Miller. From Thousand Island Lake, ascend to the east end of Lake Catherine (see Glacier Lake Pass), climb the rocks to the north edge of the glacier lying between Banner and Ritter, and ascend the glacier on that side to the saddle at its head, just short of the east cliff. Thence ascend steep talus slopes and easy rocks to the summit.

Route 2. East cliff and southwest slope. Class 3. From Lake Ediza, or Garnet Lake, climb to the saddle between Banner and Ritter, thence to summit as on Route 1 (see Banner-Ritter Saddle).

Route 3. Southeast face. Class 5. Ascent July 6, 1946, by Charles Wilts and Harry Sutherland, who went up approximately the middle of the southeast face as viewed from near Lake Ediza. Start in the first couloir right of a deep chimney, ascend to a point where it is necessary to cross left into another couloir rising from the chimney, and then continue diagonally right and up a nearly vertical face to a balcony which usually has a small snowfield. Traverse right about 100 feet and go straight up to reach the top about 100 yards left of the summit.

Route 4. East face. Class 4. First ascent August 3, 1931, by Jules M. Eichorn and Robert L. M. Underhill. From Garnet Lake start up the chimney to the left of the buttress to the south of Banner Glacier. Leave the chimney and take to the ridge north of the chimney leading up from the buttress. Climb the ridge until an overhang makes the ridge look impossible. Traverse diagonally right upward about 80 feet along a rather smooth wall, and then climb broad steep chutes or faces to the summit.

Route 5. East face direct. Grade III. Class 5.6. First ascent August 1961 by Allen Steck and Floyd Burnette. Ascend to upper slope of Banner Glacier and climb onto the wall about 40 feet to the right of a prominent couloir (a snow tongue leads into the base of this couloir) that leads up to the southeast buttress and Route 4. The snow tongue is roughly in the summit fall-line. Climb up through steep rock (blocky) for two leads (5.6). Move up several leads, keeping to the right, until the route is apparent leading directly upwards to the summit crest, 200 feet north of the summit. Delightful face climbing is found over much of this route, which is class 4 except for two leads.

Route 6. Northwest shoulder. Class 4. First recorded ascent by Sarah Haynes and Jim Koontz in August 1950. Ascend north side of shoulder, then climb to the summit over the plateau.

Winter ascent. March 1, 1939, by Chester L. Errett, Bob Brinton, and Lloyd Warner.

Mount Ritter (*13,157*)

Route 1. North glacier and north face. Class 3. First ascent October 1872 by John Muir (*The Mountains of California*, 1894, 52–73). From Thousand Island Lake proceed as on Route 1 for Banner Peak to the saddle between Banner and Ritter. Ascend the snowfield to the right hand or west chute of two chutes leading up the north wall of Ritter. From the top of the chute cross a ridge to the left into the head of the left hand chute to a wide ledge leading diagonally left to the arête. Thence follow the arête west to summit.

Route 2. East cliff and north face. Class 3. From Lake Ediza or Garnet Lake proceed as on Route 2 for Banner Peak, to the saddle between Banner and Ritter, and thence to the top as in Route 1.

Route 3. East face. Class 4–5. First ascent September 1961 by Nick Clinch and Thomas Hornbein. A large scar will be seen on the east face. Approach this scar by ascending a ledge that traverses up and to the right from where Route 5 skirts around the Southeast Glacier under the east face.

Route 4. Glacier Lake pass. Ritter Lake. West slope. Class 2. First ascent August 20, 1892, by Theodore S. Solomons. From Thousand Island Lake proceed to Lake Catherine (see Glacier Lake Pass). Thence proceed around the west side of the mountain to Ritter Lake. Climb the west slope (various routes) to the main ridge, and there go left toward the summit.

Route 5. Southeast glacier, south side. Class 3; ice axe useful. First ascent, June 28, 1928, by Norman Clyde. From Lake Ediza proceed to the base of the cliffs slightly to the left (S) of the lower end of the glacier. Climb the cliff to the left of the lowest of the pinnacles on the south side of the glacier. Pass through a gap above the lowest pinnacle onto the glacier. Continue up on the south side of the glacier, keeping left of an ice ridge which extends from the lower to the upper part of the glacier, until a crevasse renders further travel upward on the glacier impossible. Leave the south side of the glacier, climb over the ridge and descend across the glacier (use ice axe for safety) to its extreme northwest edge, whence ascend easy rocks and talus slope to the summit.

Route 6. Southeast glacier, north side. Class 2 to 3 (seasonal); ice axe may be needed when snow is high on the north side of the glacier. Evidently this was John Muir's route of descent in October 1872. It is the easiest route from Lake Ediza. First known ascent August 3, 1931, by Sierra Club party led by Lewis Clark and Ernest Dawson. From Lake Ediza proceed to the snout of the glacier and below it to its north side, and thence up talus at the base of the south cliff of Ritter along the north side of the glacier to a chute which leads up (N) to the talus slope extending northwest to the summit.

Route 7. Northeast buttress. Class 3 to 4. Ascent August 7, 1941, by Art Argiewicz and Lorin Trubschenk. This buttress rises 2,000 feet from the cirque enclosed by Banner and Ritter to the summit ridge, and is east of the prominent snow ledge on the north face as viewed from Garnet Lake. Proceed directly up the buttress on firm angular rock and over debris-covered ledges.

Pinnacles (highest pinnacle, 12,300). Class 3. First ascent of highest pinnacle August 4, 1936, by Richard M. Jones and William Rice. From Lake Ediza proceed as on Route 4 for Ritter to the lowest pinnacle. After crossing through the gap above, contour west a short distance and climb the highest pinnacle by one of several possible routes.

Ritter, southwest spur. There have been no recorded ascents of the several summits on the arête.

Winter ascent. An ascent was made in February 1952 by George Bloom, Bob Swift, and Floyd Burnette, who used Route 4.

THE MINARETS

These are listed from north to south, and the identifying numerals correspond to those on the accompanying Sketches 7, 8, and 9. The Minarets have been named after the climbers who made the first ascents, with one or two exceptions.

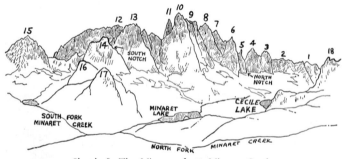

Sketch 8. The Minarets from Minaret Creek.

1. Waller	7. Bedayan	13. Ken
2. Leonard	8. Rice	14. Kehrlein
3. Turner	9. Eichorn	15. Starr
4. Jensen	10. Clyde	16. Pridham
5. Dyer	11. Michael	17. Riegelhuth
6. Dawson	12. Adams	18. Volcanic Pk.

No. 1. Waller Minaret (11,711)

Route 1. Class 4–5. First ascent August 1934 by **Ted Waller** and Jules M. Eichorn. This minaret is the summit of the ridge between the Gap and Ritter Pass. From the crest of the Gap follow the south end of the Waller ridge down and east for approximately 150 feet where a ledge will be found running east and then around a buttress and northerly on the east face. Rope up and follow this ledge. About one pitch along the ledge, work diagonally up the east face, aiming to reach the arête just above the vertical wall rising from the Gap. One or two pitons may be needed for protection in this section. Walk north up the chute dividing the arête for about 150 feet, until stopped by the high-angle, smooth south face of a large tower or step. This 180-foot face may be climbed directly by following a series of cracks and small footholds up the center. Pitons will probably be desired on this high-angle, airy

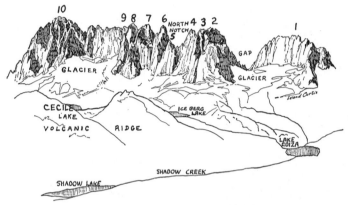

Sketch 9. East Face of the Minarets from Shadow Creek.

1. Waller
2. Leonard
3. Turner
4. Jensen
5. Dyer
6. Dawson
7. Bedayan
8. Rice
9. Eichorn
10. Clyde

series of pitches. Scramble north along this step, crossing over to the west side. Descend 20 feet, traverse around top of steep couloir and around a rib on west face. From here go diagonally right directly toward summit via one more step on ridge. Descent may be effected by the same route providing a 300-foot rappel rope is available. An ascent from the north and east may be easier.

Route 2. East face. Class 5. First known ascent July 1961 by Dick Long and Bob Hill. The route begins at the base of the wall directly below the summit. Ascend over good rock for 7 or 8 leads until the ridge is reached just south of the summit.

Winter ascent. December 29, 1963, by Dick Long, Jim Wilson, Dave Beck, and George Bloom.

No. 2. Leonard Minaret (11,600)

Route 1. Southeast rock chimney. Class 4. First ascent August 4, 1932, by Richard M. Leonard and H. B. Blanks. From Lake Ediza proceed on the route toward North Notch. From the benches above (W) of Iceberg Lake, Leonard Minaret will be seen on the right as a sharp spire, being the abrupt termination of a narrow arête projecting east at right angles to the main crest. A prominent (and sometimes snow-filled) chimney will be noted on the right center of the terminus of the arête. The best route on this face is up a less prominent rock chimney left (S) of the snow chimney, to a conspicuous ledge on the northeast face of the arête at the head of the snow chimney. Climb this face diagonally to the left (SE) to the crest, thence along the arête east to the cairn and register above the terminus.

Route 2. Traverse west to east. Class 4. First ascent August 19, 1933, by Norman Clyde. From the Gap climb up the ridge of the minaret, and traverse the arête east to the cairn and register at the east end.

Route 3. South face. Class 4. Ascent September 3, 1964, by Don Wilson and Bob Weyman.

No. 3. Turner Minaret (11,600)

A party of three led by Ed Turner made a first ascent of the Minaret north of Jensen Minaret on July 14, 1938.

No. 4. Jensen Minaret (11,760)

First ascent by Carl P. Jensen and Howard Gates June 1937. A new route was used in climbing Jensen Minaret by Spencer Austin, Dan Bannerman, and Charles Wilts July 27, 1943. From the Shadow Creek Basin, two prominent cracks or chimneys can be seen immediately to the right of the Minaret. The right-hand chimney was ascended to a sharp saddle on the main ridge. The arête was then followed to the left to the summit. Minimum class 5 (1 or 2 pitons).

No. 5. Dyer Minaret (11,680)

Route 1. Northwest face. Class 5. First ascent by William A. Horsfall and John Dyer in 1948. The pinnacle is just north of Dawson Minaret and is quite prominent when viewed from Cecile Lake. Approach from North Notch and ascend the final face in one lead from a small notch to the west.

Route 2. East face. Class 5.7. First ascent by John Doisey and Allen Steck August 1962. From North Notch traverse south to base of east ridge of the pinnacle. Ascend 110 feet (5.7) from large sloping platform to belay ledge on east face. Climb another 130 feet to summit. Take rappel slings.

No. 6. Dawson Minaret (11,920)

Class 4. First ascent August 16, 1933, by Glen Dawson, Jules Eichorn, and Richard Jones. From North Notch work along the west side of the first little minaret to the south, and traverse around it into the next chute. Then climb directly toward the summit up a broken face, work to the right to a prominent shelf on the ridge, and cross the head of the next chute to the final south face, where an open chimney leads to the summit. The final south face can also be reached from the west via the chute that heads just under this face, a chockstone being by-passed by a ridge to the left.

No. 7. Bedayan Minaret (12,080)

Route 1. Class 3. First ascent August 11, 1936, by Torcom Bedayan and William Rice. Traverse from Rice Minaret to the next minaret north. Another route was made August 25, 1950, by Hervey Voge and L. Bruce Meyer. From the west climb the chute that heads north of Bedayan Minaret, entering the chute by a ledge at the right (S) base, and about 100 yards from the top cross over to the next chute south and climb the south face.

Route 2. Northeast face. Class 4. First ascent July 6, 1963, by Rich Gnagy and Barbara Lilley. Start at the high point of the glacier between the watercourse seen descending the middle of the northeast face and the deep couloir leading up to Dawson-Bedayan notch. Ascend 100 feet on a series of ledges, gradually working left. A short traverse up and left leads to a sloping "sidewalk" ledge which is followed left to the watercourse. Ascend the right side of the watercourse (2 pitches) to a steep 200 foot snowfield (seasonal). Three hundred feet of class 3 and 4 climbing above the snowfield leads to the summit ridge, which is followed west to the summit.

Route 3. East couloir. Class 4. It is possible to ascend this couloir to the notch between Bedayan and Dawson minarets, thence via standard routes to either of the above mentioned summits. Extreme danger from loose rock. Several large chockstones must be climbed.

No. 8. Rice Minaret (12,160+)

Class 4. First ascent August 11, 1936, by William Rice and Torcom Bedayan. Ascend Starr's Chute, as on the start of Route 3 for Michael Minaret, and climb the minaret north of the head of this chute. An ascent from the chute to the northwest was made August 25, 1950, by Hervey Voge and L. Bruce Meyer, who crossed over from the chute southwest of Dawson Minaret.

No. 9. Eichorn Minaret (12,255)

Route 1. Class 3. First ascent July 31, 1931, by Jules Eichorn, Glen Dawson, and Walter Brem. This minaret is at the junction where the minaret ridge divides into east and west spurs. The east spur goes to Clyde Minaret, while the other turns south to Michael Minaret. Eichorn Minaret may therefore be reached by traverses along the arête from either Clyde or Michael minarets, or may be climbed directly up either Eichorn's Chute or Starr's Chute (see Michael Minaret).

Route 2. East face. Class 5. First ascent in 1955 by Jim Gorin and others.

No. 10. Clyde Minaret (12,281)

Route 1. Glacier. Class 4; ice axe needed. First ascent June 27, 1928, by Norman Clyde. From Minaret Lake or Lake Ediza proceed to the northwest end of Cecile Lake and then climb around the base of the minaret to the glacier. Ascend the glacier to near its head, and cross over to rocks (seasonal difficulty of bergschrund must be considered). Climb rocks diagonally left across a series of broad chutes and slight ridges to just below the summit, thence up a chimney to the summit arête. The summit is then about 30 yards to the left along the toothed arête. Variations are possible.

Route 2. Rock route. Easy class 4. First ascent July 26, 1929, by Glen Dawson, John Nixon, and William A. Horsfall. A variation of Route 1 and a preferable route. From the northwest end of Cecile Lake traverse upward to the first chute south of the glacier. This chute may be entered by a ledge from the lower part of the glacier, or via a chimney directly under the chute, or, better, by an easy ledge that starts about 100 yards southeast of the chimney. Ascend the chute to near its head and climb diagonally left to the summit as on Route 1.

Route 3. East face. Class 4. First ascent, August 8, 1932, by Walter A. Starr, Jr. From the southwest end of Cecile Lake, turn into the amphitheater below the minaret. On the right side of the cirque are three high points. Work up a ledge in red rock into a narrow chute. The chute comes out on a ledge running across the east face of the minaret. Proceed up along the ledge to a second chimney and climb the chimney until progress becomes impossible. Diagonal to the right up ledges, ridges, and chimneys to the arête north of the summit, and thence to the top.

Route 4. From Amphitheater Lake. Class 3. From east side of lake ascend to ridge some 300 feet north of Clyde Minaret, and follow ridge south to summit. A winter ascent of this route was made January 2, 1948, by Bill Long, Jim Wilson, and Allen Steck.

Variation: It is possible to ascend the gully between Clyde and Ken Minaret from the east. Class 3, except rope and axe will be useful on the hard snow at the base of the chute. Approach as per Route 5, but stay on snow and continue up into the chute.

Route 5. South face. Grade IV. Class 5.8. First ascent June 22, 1963, by Dick Long, John Evans, Chuck Wilts, and Allen Steck. Best approach is from Minaret Lake or a bivouac at south rim of Cecile Lake. Ascend snowfield to base of south face. Climb up and left, still on snow, until a moderate ascending traverse on rock (5.6) can be made out onto the face. Move right (class 4) 100 feet to a belay ledge past a large flake. Ascend 4 leads (150-foot rope—5.6) to a large ledge west (left) of Hidden Chimney. Move right 30 feet to base of Hidden Chimney and ascend to small belay ledge (5.7). Then 150 feet of face climbing (1–5.8 move) brings one to the base of a prominent 250-foot dihedral near the top of the south face. Ascend 90 feet (5.8) to belay ledge, and then make an improbable lead, traversing left for 40 feet, then climbing directly up for another 110 feet (5.6) to a large ledge. Watch out for loose blocks. One hundred fifty feet of face climbing (5.7) leads to the top of the face, thence class 3 to the summit. The rock is quite sound over most of this route.

No. 11. Michael Minaret (12,240)

Route 1. Michael's Chute. Class 4. First ascent September 6, 1923, by Charles W. Michael. From Lake Ediza or Minaret Lake proceed via North or South Notch to the west base of Michael Minaret. Climb the deep, narrow chute leading to the skyline directly north of the main pinnacle. From 200 to 300 feet up the chute, large stones are encountered. A third wedged boulder can be surmounted by a series of projections starting about 30 feet below the boulder. These projections bring one to a ledge leading back into the chute above the boulder. A less difficult route is by a shoulder stand over the "ladder with the lower rungs missing" nearer the huge boulder. Continue up the chute to the Portal at its top between Michael Minaret and two large spires. From the Portal follow a ledge going east on the minaret away from the chute and then work back up steep, difficult, exposed rocks to the summit. It is also possible but very difficult to work directly up from the Portal to the summit.

Route 2. Eichorn's Chute. Class 4. First ascent August 16, 1933, by Glen Dawson, Jules Eichorn, and Richard M. Jones. Go up the first chute north of Michael's Chute, meeting Route 3 near the top of the chute.

Route 3. Starr's Chute. Class 4. First ascent August 3, 1933, by Walter A. Starr, Jr. Go up the second chute north of Michael's Chute to a point about 300 feet below the main crest. There cross to the right into a branch chute leading up the south side of Eichorn Minaret. When near the head of this chute cross right into the head of Eichorn's Chute, thence cross a ridge of rock into Michael's Chute, just below the two spires. Thence follow Route 1 to the summit. This seems to be the best mountaineering route to the Portal.

Route 4. Clyde's Ledge. Class 4. First ascent August 25, 1933, by Norman Clyde. From the southwest base of Michael's Minaret ascend the cliff to a ledge which leads around into Michael's Chute at a point just above the 40-foot drop over the big chockstone. Continue up as on Route 1.

Route 5. Amphitheater Chute. Class 4. First ascent August 31, 1958, by Michael Sherrick and Wally Tinsley. From Lake Ediza or Minaret Lake proceed to Amphitheater Lake via South Notch. Ascend prominent chute at north end of the lake. Keep to the right side of the chute all the way to the notch between Michael and Eichorn minarets. There are several feet of difficult climbing to get around a large chockstone. Cross the notch and work down and west to reach the Portal, thence via Route 1 to the summit.

Route 6. South face. Grade III, class 5.7. One direct-aid sling used. First ascent August 13, 1962, by John Dorsey, George Steck, and Allen Steck. From Adams Minaret col, climb up an obvious chimney system for three leads. Move up two more leads keeping right toward a small notch in the southeast ridge. Climb another two leads (class 4) to the summit.

Winter ascent. December 29, 1963, by Dick Long, Jim Wilson, George Bloom, and George Marks via Route 3.

No. 12. Adams Minaret (12,000)

Class 3. First ascent July 15, 1937, by Ansel Adams and Rondal Partridge. From the col on the southeast side of Michael Minaret above the Minaret Amphitheater (which may be reached via South Notch; see Passes), climb cliffs south of col to a small peak. Thence proceed southeast along the crest to the summit of the minaret.

No. 13. Ken Minaret (11,760)

Route 1. Class 3. First ascent by W. Kenneth Davis and Kenneth D. Adam, September 5, 1938, via northeast face. Descent via west face was class 3.

Route 2. South ridge. Class 5. First ascent by Chuck and Ellen Wilts and Ray Van Aken on Labor Day, 1958. From the South Notch, traverse over toward the Amphitheater, heading for the notch just to the north of a prominent tower. Do not ascend directly to the notch but keep on west face, eventually reaching, after several leads, the top of the cliff rising above the notch. Turn the next step to the east (class 5). Several more pitches lead directly up the ridge to the tower below the big step. Rappel from piton to notch below the big step. Then traverse onto the east face up to the top of the big step (class 5). Easy climbing leads to the summit.

No. 14. Kehrlein Minaret (11,440)

On July 13, 1938, Oliver Kehrlein, Dick Cahill, Jim Harkins, and Fred Holmes climbed this point. It was first ascended August 23, 1933, by Norman Clyde, but is named after Kehrlein to avoid duplication.

Route 1. West side. Class 4. From the South Notch work up the south side of the ridge, then cross to the north, and traverse across a slab leading onto the northwest face. Climb up the face, working to the left and then parallel to the ridge.

Route 2. North face. Class 4. First ascent August 1941 by Fred Hudson and R. Olson. Broken ledges lead to the summit from Cecile Lake.

Route 3. East ridge. Class 5. First ascent September 3, 1961, by Charles Wilts and Ray Van Aken. The base of the ridge may be reached by climbing the gully west of Riegelhuth Minaret (from either north or south) and traversing over Pridham Minaret (class 2) to the notch between the latter and Kehrlein Minaret. This notch may also be reached from the south (class 2). The east ridge is a mixture of class 2, 3, and 4 with class 5 leads on the faces of the steps. Some rappels may be made in descending the west sides of the towers on the ridge. Descend the north side of the east summit and traverse the north face below the spire between the summits. Gain the notch between this spire and the west (higher) summit by a difficult class 5 pitch.

No. 15. *Starr Minaret* (*11,512*)

Route 1. Class 2. First ascent, July 14, 1937, by W. A. Starr, Ansel Adams, and Rondal Partridge. From South Notch traverse south to the northwest base of the minaret and climb a rocky slope to the summit.

Route 2. East face. Class 5. First ascent September 1960 by Charles Wilts and Ray Van Aken. From Deadhorse Lake ascend to the base of the face, keeping to the south side of the cirque. The face is mostly class 3, with a few class 4 pitches. The summit pitch is steep (2 pitons for protection). Allow about 5 hours for the climb.

No. 16. *Pridham Minaret* (*10,960*)

Class 2 from the east. Ascended July 4, 1938, by May Pridham and Mary Van Velsen.

No. 17. *Riegelhuth Minaret* (*10,560*)

Route 1. Ascended for the first time July 13, 1938, by Jack Riegelhuth, Charlotte Mauk, Josephine Allen, and Bill Leovey. Class 4 by the west face from the divide between Pridham and Riegelhuth.

Route 2. Northeast face. Class 4. First recorded ascent August 6, 1955, by David Tonkin and Lito Tejada Flores from Minaret Lake. Ascend several pitches to a prominent diagonal gully in the middle of the face. Follow the gully toward the notch between the summit and a tower to the east, thence north to the summit. About ten pitches.

No. 18. *Volcanic Ridge* (*11,501*)

West Peak. Class 3. First recorded ascent August 13, 1933, by Craig Barbash and Howard Gates. From the northwest end of Minaret Lake ascend to the saddle north of the lake and climb rocks to the summit west of the saddle. Or, from Lake Ediza, climb the shoulder of Volcanic Ridge just east of the lower end of the stream flowing down from Iceberg Lake and traverse the north ridge to the summit. There is a sweeping panorama of the Ritter Range from here.

Peak 11,110 (2 SW of Minarets)

An apparent first ascent of this peak was made July 13, 1938, by Oliver Kehrlein, John Cahill, Jim Harkins, Fred Holmes, Frank Aitken, and Edwin Koskinen.

Iron Mountain (11,149)

Route 1. South slope. Class 1. From the Devil's Postpile trail, just west of Cargyle Meadow, an old trail works north up the south slope to a point just west of the summit.

Route 2. East face. Class 3; ice axe useful. From Ashley Lake, which lies at the east base of the peak, ascend directly up the long snow tongue from the head of the lake, or by way of the spur on the south side of the lake, to the crest. Traverse the ridge north to the summit. A trail leads to Ashley Lake from Devil's Postpile.

Other Pinnacles

There are many minor pinnacles in the Minaret area that are not detailed here. Several pinnacles on the ridge between Deadhorse Lake and Beck Lakes were climbed by members of a Sierra Club Base Camp trip. The unnamed spire north of South Notch was climbed by the northwest face in 1959 by Ray Van Aken and Ernst Bauer (class 5). There are no records regarding the many pinnacles on the southwest ridges of Mount Ritter.

Mammoth Pass to Piute Pass

THE NORTH-CENTRAL section of the High Sierra, from Mammoth Pass to Piute Pass, is a colorful area containing many beautiful lakes and fine peaks. The climbing is not quite so challenging as in certain other areas, but there is still much to satisfy the mountaineer. The northern portion, near Mammoth Lakes and Convict Lake, contains dark volcanic rock and reddish metamorphic rock, and hence is a region where the colors of the landscape contrast markedly with those seen in most other parts of the Sierra.

Mount Humphreys, near Piute Pass, is the oustanding peak in this section; it stands tall and isolated on the crest of the Sierra, with distinctive terra-cotta-colored rocks forming its summit. Mount Humphreys is one of the more difficult peaks of the Sierra. Nearby the Piute Crags offer fine rock climbing. Another good climbing region is that around Mount Abbott, where there are sixteen peaks over 13,000 feet within a circle of 4.5 miles radius. In the area near Convict Lake challenging rock climbs may be made from camps at the roadhead.

APPROACHES AND CAMPSITES

The most convenient approaches are from the east side. A fine road leads to the Mammoth Lakes, close to Duck Pass, which may be crossed to reach the Muir Trail. Another road leads to Convict Lake, under the slopes of Laurel Mountain and Mount Morrison. A trail goes from the McGee Creek road barrier (3 miles from U.S. 395) over McGee Creek Pass just south of Red Slate Mountain. Little Lakes Valley is reached by a road up Rock Creek which ends at 10,000, and is a good place from which to climb Mount Morgan, Mount Abbot, or Bear Creek Spire. Another road goes up Pine Creek (to 7,000) from Round Valley and may be used to approach Pine Creek Pass or Granite Park. A private upper section of this road, not open to the public, leads to a tungsten mine high on Morgan Creek. Finally, there is a road up Bishop Creek to North Lake (9,300) where the trail to Piute Pass starts.

From the west the only practicable approach to the peaks of the Mammoth-Piute section is by way of the road from Huntington Lake over Kaiser Pass, which may be followed to Florence Lake or to Lake Thomas A. Edison. From Florence Lake (boat service) a trail leads up the South Fork of the San Joaquin to Selden Pass or on to Piute Creek and Humphreys Basin or French Canyon. From Lake Thomas A. Edison one may travel to Bear Creek, the Mono Recesses, or Silver Pass.

In this part of the Sierra trees adequate to supply firewood and shelter for camping grow up to an elevation beyond 11,000 feet (there is an albicaulis pine at 12,700 feet on Mount Stanford). There are hundreds of attractive places where knapsackers can camp, and an abundance of places suitable for those with stock. Some rocky canyons or uplands at about 11,000 feet are devoid of timber, however. For example, the environs of Lake Italy (11,154) are barren, and those desiring a fire will do well to camp below the lake about half a mile.

There are many possible mountaineering and knapsack passes in this region. A few of the more useful ones are noted under the individual areas. With the aid of the new topographic maps and some experience, climbers should be able to pick out other passes to suit their needs.

SUBDIVISION INTO AREAS

The section from Mammoth Pass to Piute Pass is divided into the following areas:

Mammoth Pass to Mono Pass. This includes the peaks near Red Slate Mountain, those around Convict Lake, the Silver Divide, and the peaks around Pioneer Basin.

Mono Pass to Pine Creek Pass. This includes Mills, Abbot, and Bear Creek Spire on the Sierra Crest, the Mono Divide, peaks of the Bear Creek drainage, and the Mount Morgan (south) peaks east of Rock Creek.

Mount Humphreys Region. This is the area from Pine Creek Pass to Piute Pass.

The arrangement of peaks within an area is first from north to south along the main ridge, and then roughly from north to south, first on the west side of the ridge and then on the east side.

Mammoth Pass to Mono Pass

GEORGE BLOOM and JOHN D. MENDENHALL (1953);
HERVEY H. VOGE (1964)

THIS COLORFUL AREA may be approached from the north by the
John Muir Trail or Duck Pass, from the south by way of Mono Creek,
and from the east along Convict Creek, McGee Creek, Hilton Creek, or
Rock Creek. The Muir Trail traverses the area from north to south,
crossing Silver Pass before dropping down to Mono Creek. Maps are
Mount Morrison and Mount Abbot, plus portions of Devil's Postpile
and Kaiser Peak.

Much of the climbing in this area has been centered around Convict
Lake, which is dominated by Mount Morrison, and is notable for the
maroon, black, cardinal, buff, and grey colors of the surrounding peaks.
Here the north face of Mount Morrison and the east cliffs of Laurel
Mountain provide imposing routes that are only a few miles from the
end of Convict Lake road. Some of the history of this region is of
interest, since it includes an appealing Indian legend, blazing guns, and
bodies swinging from gallows.

According to tales of the Indians, once there was no Convict Lake.
Little Pot-sa-wa-gees—spirits with the faces of Indian babies and fish-
like bodies—lived in the stream. Hi-na-nu, roughly the Indian version
of our Adam, strove to net them as they fled upstream. Desperate, they
appealed to the Great Spirit to save them. He created the lake known
to the Indians as Wit-sa-nap, our Convict Lake, and the little spirits
were saved.

In 1871, convicts escaped from Carson City and headed south, mur-
dering and looting. A posse led by Robert Morrison closed with them
at Monte Diablo (now Convict) Creek, and both Morrison and an
Indian aide, Mono Jim, were slain. Western justice was swift; the convicts were captured a few days later, and several were lynched.

PRINCIPAL PASSES

Trails cross Duck, Silver, and Goodale passes, as well as a pass between
Bloody and Laurel mountains connecting Convict and Laurel creeks.
A trail crosses the crest at McGee Creek Pass, just south of Red Slate
Mountain.

Climbers or knapsackers may cross from Lake Dorothy on Convict Creek over the crest to Purple Lake or Lake Viginia by passing just north of Peak 12,277 to Franklin Lake. Another knapsack pass lies one-half mile northeast of McGee Pass and leads from the head of McGee Creek to Lake Dorothy. Both these routes are class 2.

A scenic route from Mono Creek to the headwaters of Fish Creek passes just west of Red and White Mountain; it is reached by a trail that starts up Laurel Canyon on the west side, crosses to the east of the stream in the basin, and leads to lakes around which a way is picked to the pass between Red and White Mountain and Peak 12,238. Class 2.

Hopkins Pass leads from Upper Hopkins Lake to McGee Creek. Follow Hopkins Creek from the point where the trail to Lower Hopkins Lake crosses, switching from side to side several times. Go east of Upper Hopkins Lake to the pass. Class 1–2.

Pioneer Basin is connected with the Mono Creek trail by several small trails. At the first lake, branch trails lead up the west side to Lakes 2, 2A, and 3, and up the center to Lakes 3, 4, and 5. Walking through the basin off trail is generally easy. The saddle west of Mount Stanford can be crossed by a knapsack route (class 3) leading to McGee Creek. The saddle northwest of Mount Huntington can be crossed from Pioneer Basin Lake 4A to upper Hilton Creek (class 2–3).

Half-Moon Pass crosses the Sierra Crest just east of Golden Lake on the headwaters of Mono Creek, and is a good knapsacking shortcut that bypasses tedious Mono Pass. It is class 2 with a very short class 3 section. From the east side the pass is reached by going west up a small canyon just behind the Rock Creek Pack Station on the bench west of Rock Creek Lake.

Peaks of the Main Crest

Peak 11,772 (1 NE of Duck Lake; formerly 11,765)

Climbed by the southeast ridge by Don Lewis, September 1954. Class 2.

Peak 12,052 (1.7 W of Bloody Mountain; formerly 12,059)

First ascent August 18, 1924, by E. S. Wallace, E. E. Wix, and Bill Dye. Class 2 from the west.

Peak, 11,975 (1 SW of Bloody Mountain; formerly 12,003)

Peak 12,277 (1 SW of Lake Dorothy; formerly 12,292)

Ascended July 17, 1934, by David Brower. Class 2 from the north.

Red Slate Mountain (13,163)

First ascent possibly by J. T. Gardiner in 1864, although he may not have reached the summit. The peak is class 1 or 2 from any direction but northwest. The McGee Creek trail is a good approach; so is Convict Creek. The southwest ridge, from upper Fish Creek, is another good route. The upper portions are quite steep, and care should be taken if snow is present.

Red and White Mountain (12,850)

First ascent in 1902 by J. S. Hutchinson, Lincoln Hutchinson, C. A. Noble.

Route 1. Southwest face. Class 2. From Mono Creek ascend Laurel Canyon (opposite Second Recess) passing to the west of the large lake near the head. Ascend the large chute at the southwest side of the peak; then follow the ridge a short distance to the summit.

Route 2. West ridge. Class 3. Climb the west ridge from the saddle between Red and White Mountain and Peak 12,238.

Route 3. Northeast ridge. The McGee Creek trail is a good approach to the mountain according to Norman Clyde who climbed it by the northeast face and ridge in 1928.

Route 4. Southeast face. Class 2–3.

Mount Crocker (12,457)

First known ascent August 25, 1929, by Nazario Sparrea, a Basque shepherd. Class 1 by south or east ridges.

Mount Stanford (12,851)

First ascent 1907–1909 by George R. Davis, C. F. Urquhart, R. B. Marshall, and L. F. Biggs, surveyors of the Goddard Quadrangle. Class 2. A good approach is from the McGee Creek Trail. It may also be ascended readily from Pioneer Basin via the west ridge or southern gullies; or via the east slope from Hilton Creek Lakes.

Peak 12,309 (1 NW of Mount Huntington; formerly 12,333)

Ascended July 14, 1934, by David Brower, Norman Clyde, and

Hervey Voge en route from Mount Huntington to Mount Stanford. Class 2.

Mount Huntington (12,405)

First ascent July 14, 1934, by David Brower, Norman Clyde, and Hervey Voge. Class 2 by the southwest ridge, from Pioneer Basin. Class 3 by the south ridge. Class 3 from the northwest.

Mount Starr (12,870)

First ascent July 16, 1896, by W. A. Starr and Allen L. Chickering. *Route 1. West slope.* Class 2. From Mono Pass climb tedious unstable talus to the east of the pass to a broad, sandy false summit. Two hundred yards from the false summit is a pinnacle which is higher.
Route 2. East slope. Class 2. From Mosquito Flat Campgrounds on Rock Creek ascend the chute under the permanent snowfield visible on the northeast face of the north ridge.

Peaks West of the Crest

Peak 11,787 (1 SE of Duck Lake; formerly 11,783)

Peak 12,354 (1.3 NE of Lake Virginia; formerly 12,375)

Peak 11,915 (0.7 E of Lake Virginia; formerly 11,920)

Balloon Dome (6,881)

Climbed prior to 1954. Class 3 from the saddle south of the dome.

Double Peak (10,644)

Pincushion Peak (9,819)

Saddle Mountain (11,192)

First ascent prior to 1922 by François Matthes.

Peak 11,483 (1 SE of Sharktooth Lake; formerly 11,500)

First ascent July 1, 1951, by A. J. Reyman. A class 2 traverse up the southwest ridge.

Peak 11,639 (1 S of Sharktooth Lake; formerly 11,630)

First ascent prior to 1951. Class 2 from the south. Formerly called Sharktooth peak on 1:125,000 series map.

Sharktooth Peak (10,720)

The peak is adjacent to Big Margaret Lake on the 1953 Kaiser Peak Quadrangle, 1:62,500 series. (See above, Peak 11,639.)

Silver Peak (11,878)

First ascent prior to 1937. The climb from Margaret Lakes is class 2, via west or south slopes.

Peak 11,476 (1 SE of Silver Peak)

Ascended July 2, 1951, by A. J. Reyman. Class 2 by the northwest ridge.

Peak 11,554 (1.5 S of Silver Peak; formerly 11,551)

Ascended August 8, 1937, by Ed and Jed Garthwaite and Malcolm Smith.

Graveyard Peak (11,520+)

First known ascent September 8, 1935, by William Stewart and David Parish. Class 2–3 from the east or northeast. The easiest ascent of the summit pile is from the northeast side. The Bench Mark is south of, and lower than, the summit.

Peak 11,336 (1.5 E of Graveyard Peak; formerly 11,334)

First ascent September 15, 1945, by G. I. Beckwith and F. X. Wieland. Class 2 by the south slope.

Peak 11,363 (1.2 SW of Silver Pass; formerly 11,365)

First ascent on July 9, 1947, by William Bade and Andy Anderson. Class 2 by the southwest slope.

Peak 11,428 (0.3 W of Silver Pass; formerly 11,469)

First ascent unknown. There are three summits, the middle being highest. They were traversed by Owen Williams, August 17, 1937.

Peak 11,516 (1 S of Silver Pass; formerly 11,527)

Climbed by Owen Williams via north arête, August 17, 1937.

Peak 12,221 (0.7 E. of Silver Pass; formerly 12,211)

The southeast and southwest sides are class 2 scree and boulders.

Mount Izaak Walton (11,840+)

Route 1. Class 3. Follow the northwest ridge to the summit. One or two touchy points may be encountered near the top. Other, more difficult, routes have been made, including one from the south involving a short, class 4 overhanging pitch.

Peak 11,680+ (1.7 W of Red and White Mountain; formerly 11,678)

Peak 12,238 (0.7 SW of Red and White Mountain; formerly 12,225)

Ascended August 14, 1952, by G. A. Daum, G. F. Hurley, and J. M. Schnitzler. Class 2 by a choice of routes from upper Fish Creek or from the saddle to the east.

Peak 11,919 (1.7 W of Mount Hopkins; formerly 11,915)

First ascent prior to 1958. Class 2 by the south slope.

Peak 12,067 (1.6 SW of Mount Hopkins; formerly 12,040)

First ascent on July 11, 1902, by Lincoln Hutchinson and J. S. Hutchinson. Class 2 by the southwest ridge or by the north ridge.

Peak 12,178 (2 SW of Mount Hopkins)

First ascent August 26, 1958, by A. J. Reyman. Class 2 up the north slope.

Peak 11,669 (1.3 SE of Mott Lake; formerly 11,660)

Climbed July 11, 1947, by Wallace Hayes. Class 2 from the east by way of Laurel Canyon.

Peak 12,408 (1 N of Mount Hopkins)

First ascent July 5, 1950, by T. H. Hasheim, Elly Hinreiner, and Jean Campbell. Class 2 by western or southwest slopes from Hopkins Basin.

Mount Hopkins (12,302)

First ascent July 16, 1934, by David Brower, Norman Clyde, and Hervey Voge.

Route 1. From the east. Class 1. A good sand climb from Pioneer Basin.

Route 2. From the west. Class 2. From Hopkins Creek the route is similar to the eastern route, except for a rock cliff which can be avoided. Mount Hopkins may also be climbed by the south slope from the base of the Third Recess.

Peaks East of the Crest

Mammoth Rock (9,200+)

Probably climbed very early by miners from the mining camp just below.

Crystal Crag (10,364)

Probably climbed before 1900 by prospectors.

Route 1. South arête. Class 2. From Crystal Lake ascend to the saddle south of the crag and follow the arête to the summit, avoiding difficulties by staying well below the ridge top on the east side.

Route 2. From the west. Class 3. Several routes are possible from Crystal Lake.

Route 3. Northeast face. Class 4. Climbed August 11, 1936, by Owen Williams.

Peak 11,728 (2 N of Duck Lake; formerly 11,641)

Peak 11,382 (1.7 W of Laurel Mountain; formerly 11,389)

Peak 12,400+ (0.8 E of Red Slate Mountain)

First ascent August 29, 1952, by A. J. Reyman. A class 3 ascent by the northwest ridge from the saddle east of Red Slate Mountain. This is a shaly and loose rock knife-edge and care must be taken in making the ascent.

Peak 12,320+ (1.2 E of Red Slate Mountain; formerly 12,309)

Ascended July 17, 1934, by David Brower and Hervey Voge. Class 2 via western saddle.

Bloody Mountain (12,544)

First known ascent July 3, 1928, by Norman Clyde. From the south or southwest the climb is tedious, on rubbly slate. Class 2. May be climbed from Laurel Creek via the north slope and NNE ridge. (Also class 2.)

Laurel Mountain (11,812)

First recorded ascent September 25, 1926, by Norman Clyde. The east wall of Laurel offers a variety of unexplored routes starting only 500 feet above the end of the road.

Route 1. North ridge. Class 1. First ascent unknown. From the upper end of Convict Lake ascend brushy slopes to the ridge crest. Turn south and proceed across a small cirque to the summit.

Route 2. Northeast trough. Class 2. First ascent in 1925 by John D. Mendenhall. From the upper end of Convict Lake climb directly to the summit.

Route 3. Northeast gully. Class 4. First ascent September 7, 1930, by James M. Van Patten and John D. Mendenhall. Midway between the northeast trough and the arête that splits the east cliffs rises a steep gully. The base is easily reached from the Convict Gorge trail. The lower thousand feet are enjoyable climbing, with firm belays occurring where needed. The steeper pitches approximate 60°. When the airy arête is reached, turn right and proceed directly to the summit.

Mount Morrison (12,268)

First ascent by Norman Clyde, June 22, 1928, by Route 1. The north face of Morrison is quite impressive, and it is easily reached from the road at Convict Lake. The woods beyond the upper end of the lake provide good camping. There is an interesting hanging valley below the north face of Morrison.

Route 1. Northwest ridge. Class 2. From the upper end of Convict Lake ascend a talus slope to the base of the northwest ridge, which is followed to the summit.

Route 2. Northwest chute. Class 3 (ice axe seasonal). First ascent in 1931 by John D. Mendenhall. From the upper end of Convict Lake climb into the hanging valley below Morrison's impressive north wall. Just past the prominent buttress at the valley's entrance, turn right and ascend a steep chute. Snow may be somewhat treacherous. Follow to the crest of the ridge, joining Route 1.

Route 3. Northeast wall. Class 5. First ascent September 1946 by Charles L. Wilts and Harry Sutherland. Follow the hanging valley of Route 2 until directly beneath the summit of Morrison. Ascend the northeast face just left of the northeast buttress, working diagonally right for nearly 1,000 feet over high-angle rock, and then follow the buttress and a couloir to the top. About 18 pitons.

Route 4. East ridge. Class 2. First ascent in 1928 by John D. Mendenhall. Follow the hanging valley of Route 2, and from its head work up the east ridge to the summit. An easier but less scenic approach is from Convict Lake via the canyon that drains the east slopes of Peak 10,858.

Route 5. Direct north buttress. Grade IV; class 5.7 and A3. First ascent July 4–5, 1960, by Jim Wilson, Ron Hayes, and Allen Steck. Hike to the base of the buttress via the hanging valley as in Route 2. Make a 200 foot, right-ascending traverse to the base of the crack system on the buttress. Climb directly up the buttress for about 500 feet (class 5.7) to the base of the 60-foot headwall that marks the end of the difficult section. Ascend the wall (class 5.7; A3) and continue up the ridge for a few hundred feet. Traverse left on a wide ledge and enter a prominent reddish chimney with limestone walls (class 5.5). Proceed from top of chimney up couloirs to summit. Time for first ascent 15 hours. Hard hats are suggested because of some loose limestone rock.

Route 6. South summit (12,320+). From the east. Class 2. First ascent September 9, 1930, by James Van Patten and John D. Mendenhall. From Convict Lake follow the canyon north of Gillett to the east base of South Peak. Follow a steep, loose chute to the summit. The unsound rock demands care. A safer and more interesting climb could be made up the rocks south of the gully.

Route 7. South summit from the west. Class 2. First recorded ascent in 1928 by John D. Mendenhall. Ascend the Convict Creek trail above Convict Lake until past the west face of Morrison. Turn left and ascend a long talus slope and rocks to the summit.

Mount Baldwin (12,614)

First known ascent July 2, 1928, by Norman Clyde.

Route 1. Northwest slope. Class 2. Ascend the trail up beautiful Convict Gorge until approximately northwest of Mount Baldwin. Breaks in the cliffs east of Convict Creek allow one to easily reach the plateau below Baldwin. By skirting a few patches of steep rocks on the final peak, one may gain the summit without difficulty.

Route 2. North ridge. Class 3. Follow Route 1 onto the plateau, then ascend the north ridge (ice axe seasonal).

Peak 10,858 (0.8 NE of Morrison)

(The name Mount Gillett was used by Mr. and Mrs. Raymer, proprietors through the 1920's of Convict Camp.) From the southeast shore of Convict Lake climb talus and easy ledges to the crest of the ridge and on to the summit. Class 1. The view of the north wall of Mount Morrison is singularly impressive.

McGee Mountain (10,871)

First ascent unknown. Class one from any direction. Has been reached by jeep.

Mount Aggie (11,561)

First ascent September 1, 1952, by A. J. Reyman. From a camp on McGee Creek south of McGee Mountain, follow up the small stream (usually dry in summer) southwest of McGee Mountain and ascend to the ridge at any point west of the creek bed. Go south on the ridge to the summit, the point farthest south on the knife-edge. Class 2.

Peak 11,899 (0.8 SE of Mount Baldwin; formerly 11,846)

Mount Morgan (13,005)

First ascent July 9, 1934, by David Brower and Norman Clyde via the ridge from Mount Stanford (class 2). The southeast slope from Davis Lake is class 1.

Peak 12,268 (1.5 NW of Mount Morgan)

Red Mountain (11,472)

First recorded ascent about 1938 by John Burns. Class 1 from the south above Rock Creek watershed.

Peak 12,522 (1 E of Mount Stanford; formerly 12,506)

Peak 12,252 (1.5 SE of Mount Huntington; formerly 12,240)

This peak was climbed in 1930. It has been called Mono Mesa. It is class 1 by the southeast slope from Rock Creek Lake, and may also be climbed from the head of Mono Creek.

Mono Pass to Pine Creek Pass

HERVEY H. VOGE, JAMES W. KOONTZ, II, and
GEORGE BLOOM (1953); ARKEL ERB (1964)

THE AREA FROM Mono Pass to Pine Creek Pass, including Wheeler
Crest and Mount Morgan east of Rock Creek, lies almost entirely within
the High Sierra Wilderness Area, and is one of the finest mountain
regions to be found in California. The rock is largely granite. A few
small glaciers lie under the north or east faces of some of the peaks,
among them being Mills, Abbot, and Gabb. Map coverage is given by
the Mount Abbot and Mount Tom quadrangles. Knapsack routes and
certain other features are indicated in Sketch 10.

Trails follow the northern and southern boundaries of this area, but
the only trails that cross it are the Muir Trail in the western part, the
rough road (closed to autos) from Little Lakes Valley to Morgan Creek
and Pine Creek, and a rudimentary trail from Bear Creek past Lake
Italy to Granite Park.

Footpaths enter the Mono Recesses from Mono Creek, and also will
be found in some other canyons. To enter First and Second recesses,
proceed up the east sides of the streams that drain them. To enter Third
Recess, start up the east side, but after a short while cross to the west.
To enter Fourth Recess, leave Mono Creek east of the Fourth Recess
stream and proceed up that side to the large lake in the recess, where
the stream may be crossed to the west side; then follow a ducked trai'
that climbs high on the west wall to avoid the cliffs.

In the region east and south of Rock Creek, Wheeler Crest runs north
from massive Mount Morgan (13,748; not to be confused with the
Mount Morgan, elevation 13,005, eight miles to the northwest). The
peaks east of Rock Creek are easily accessible and can be climbed in a
single day from the roads along Rock Creek or Morgan Creek. Six summits over 13,000 feet are listed in this small region. The climbing is
not especially difficult, but the views of the main crest are excellent,
and the colorful metamorphic rocks composing this ridge add a degree
of charm.

PRINCIPAL PASSES

Mono Divide may be crossed at several places. First Recess provides a
very scenic cross-country route to Bear Creek; follow First Recess Creek

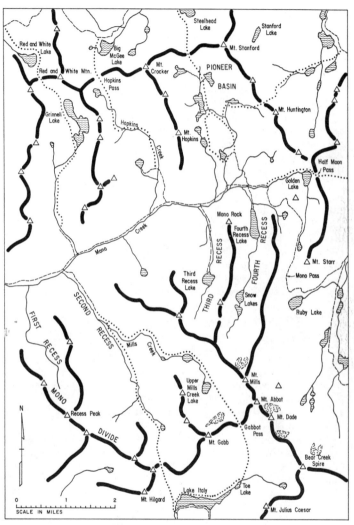

Sketch 10. The Mono Creek Area. (See legend, page 14.)

and cross a notch between Recess Peak and Peak 12,205. This class 2 pass may have snow on the northeast, but offers meadow-covered table lands on the southwest. Second Recess may be traversed on routes leading from Mono Creek to Lake Italy. The best of these leaves the meadows of Second Recess to climb the slope on the north side of the Mills Creek cascade, follows the left side of Mills Creek to its head, and crosses Gabbot Pass, between Mount Gabb and Mount Abbot. On the Lake Italy side the walking is quite easy; follow the north shore of Lake Italy to the outlet and cross to the trail on the south side. Another route from Second Recess proceeds directly up the recess, ascends a steep headwall at timberline by sloping ledges on the right (W) side, and crosses the Mono Divide at a broad pass about 0.6 mile northeast of Mount Hilgard. This route is rougher than the Gabbot Pass route. Neither is suitable for stock.

Bear Creek headwaters are splendid terrain for those who like cross-country walking, and many lovely lakes hidden away in granite bowls will be met. A shortcut from the Hilgard Branch of Bear Creek to the East Fork may be taken on either side of Peak 12,550. From the upper basin of the East Fork of Bear Creek a route proceeds south-east to a pass between Peaks 13,242 and 12,831 and follows the stream to the south down to French Canyon. Other cross-country routes may be made from the region of Sally Keyes Lake to French Canyon, cross-ing north of the Pinnacles and of Peak 12,427.

Peaks of the Main Crest

Peak 13,198 (1 SW of Mono Pass; formerly 13,202)

Route 1. West couloir. Class 3. Ascended July 25, 1946, by Fritz Gerstacher and Virginia Whitacre from the Fourth Recess by a couloir that comes down just under the highest pinnacle.

Route 2. East buttress. Ascended August 1, 1946, by Lester Lavelle and Malcolm Smith.

Route 3. West wall and north ridge. Class 5. First ascent August 17, 1953, by Jim Koontz, Ralph Perry, and Fred Peters. From between the third and fourth lakes in the Fourth Recess a large col is seen in the ridge north of Peak 13,202, with a chockstone below it, and a chimney containing chockstones at the base. Ascend the chockstone chimney and then up the face to the col. Traverse south along the ridge, mostly on the west face, to the western couloir, and climb this to the top.

Route 4. Gendarmes of crest between Mills and 13,198. A class 5 traverse of these gendarmes was made in 1963 by Mike Loughman and Jay Waller.

Mount Mills (13,468)

First ascent July 10, 1908, by J. S. Hutchinson, J. N. LeConte, and Duncan McDuffie (SCB, 1909, 9) by Route 1.

Route 1. North face. Class 3 (ice axe advisable). From the Fourth Recess ascend the glacier, cross the bergschrund, and climb the broken face on the central of three ribs of rock which comes down almost to the bergschrund, or on the west side of this central rib.

Route 2. West face. Class 4. Ascended July 23, 1953, by Jim Koontz, Marian Steineke, Louis Christian, and Jim Carl. Ascend avalanche chutes near the southern end of the face. The top 200 feet require class 4 climbing.

Route 3. East face. Class 3. There are three deep couloirs cut into the east face of the mountain. Climb over a huge chockstone into the third such couloir, counting north from the Abbot-Mills saddle. Upon reaching the ridge, cross over to the other side and continue up and southward for some 200 feet to the edge of the summit plateau.

Route 4. South notch. Class 6. In July 1960, R. Gnagy, B. Lilley, and S. Ossofsky climbed from the east to the Abbot-Mills notch and worked up the north side to the summit.

Mount Abbot (13,715)

See Sketches 11 and 12.

Route 1. Southwest chute. Class 3. First ascent July 13, 1908, by J. S. Hutchinson, J. N. LeConte, and Duncan McDuffie. From Lake Italy or the Second Recess of Mono Creek proceed to the base of Mount Abbot. A fan of talus leads just to the south (right) of the bare granite face of the summit peak. From the apex of the fan three chutes lead toward the crest. The northern one becomes a chimney with a prominent chockstone, the central one is quite broad, and the southern one leads to the crest quite a way south of the summit. Ascend the central chute, which is most easily entered from the rocks to the right (S) of the bottom. At the top of the chute the cliffs are not nearly so difficult as they appear to be from a distance, and they can be ascended by several ways to the broad summit plateau a short distance south of the summit proper.

Route 2. West ridge. Class 4. First ascent August 30, 1927, by M. Yeatman and M. L. Huggins. Follow the ridge from the Abbot-Gabb saddle (Gabbot Pass), with some minor deviations.

Route 3. Southeast buttress. Class 3. First ascent August 19, 1932, by

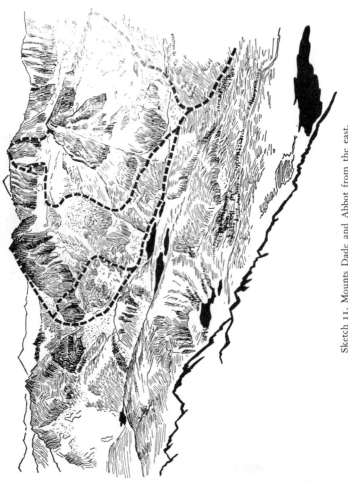

Sketch 11. Mounts Dade and Abbot from the east.

From left to right: Mount Dade, Route 1 and variation; Mount Abbot, Routes 3 and 4.

S. W. French. From Little Lakes Valley climb to the glacier between Dade and Abbot and ascend on the south side of the buttress or spur at the southern end of the east wall of Abbot, occasionally crossing to the north side of the buttress.

Route 4. Northeast buttress. Class 3. This route was descended by S. W. French on August 19, 1932. The buttress leads more or less northeast of the summit of Abbot, and is south of a prominent snow gully. The rock is fairly broken and may be ascended or descended by a variety of routes from ledge to ledge.

Route 5. West chimney. Class 4. First ascent July 22, 1953, by C. N. La Vene and Hervey Voge. Ascend the northern chute above the talus fan described under Route 1. The chockstone may be passed on the left (N) side. The chimney reaches the west ridge just southeast of a prominent, overhanging spire. From here cross the north face to the summit plateau, or go up the face.

Sketch 12. Mount Abbot from the west. From left to right: Routes 2, 5, and 1. S—Summit.

Mount Dade (*13,600+*)

First ascent August 19, 1911, by Liston and McKeen of Fresno.

Route 1. South Slope. Class 2. The south slope of Mount Dade is easily climbed and may be reached from the west or east sides of the crest.

Route 2. West chute. Class 2. From the slopes northeast of Lake Italy a chute leads almost directly to the summit of Mount Dade. The rock rib just south of the chute may also be climbed (class 3).

Route 3. On August 24, 1951, Lloyd Chorley and Don Chorley climbed by a western chute and the north ridge.

Route 4. Northeast face. Class 3–4. First ascent in September 1956 by Ray Van Aken and Kim Malville. A large gully just to the left of a steep face is climbed with the aid of an ice axe until a ledge leading to the right is reached. The ledge leads to easier slopes above a vertical section.

Route 5. East face. On August 20, 1960, Frederick Roy Suppe climbed the east face by the second chute from the northern end of the east face. The chute is followed until it ends about two-thirds of the way up. From here go left (south) a short distance and then ascend toward a depression in the crest. Follow the crest to the summit. This route is not recommended because of extremely loose and rotten rock in the chute.

Bear Creek Spire (*13,713*)

Route 1. Northwest slopes. Class 3. First ascent August 16, 1923, by H. F. Ulrichs. From Lake Italy easy benches lead around the north side of the subsidiary peak west of the Bear Creek Spire and onto the easy northwest slopes of the peak. The last few hundred feet are moderately difficult and may require use of a rope. Usually the north arête is followed on the final approach to the summit.

Route 2. Northeast face. Class 3. First ascent by Norman Clyde, October 6, 1931. A rather devious route may be worked out up this face, with good climbing most of the way.

Route 3. Northeast arête. Class 3 to 4. Ascended by Norman Clyde, May 27, 1932.

Route 4. North ridge. Class 3. From the east side the broken face may be climbed to the ridge north of the Spire. Then the north ridge can be followed to the summit or the sloping plateau can be crossed westward to join Route 1.

Route 5. From Pine Creek. Class 4. Climb to the crest about 400 yards to the southwest of the summit and traverse along the crest or on ledges on the sides to the summit (Norman Clyde).

Peak *13,120+* (*0.5 S of Bear Creek Spire*)

First ascent July 8, 1954, by Jim Koontz, Mike Loughman, Dan Popper, and Roger Popper.

Route 1. West face. Class 4. From cirque northwest of peak diagonal upward across the face of the north arête toward the summit. After passing below the low point of the north arête, reverse direction and climb northward to the summit plateau, and thence to the top.

Route 2. West ridge. Class 3. Descend by following the talus north a hundred feet from the summit. Then drop down some easy rock to a ledge that crosses the west face about two hundred feet below the summit. Follow the ledge south to the west arête. Then continue west along the arête to an easy chute that leads north to the cirque.

Mount Julius Caesar (13,196)

The name Mount Julius Caesar was proposed because of the proximity to Lake Italy. First ascent August 12, 1928, by A. H. and Myrtle Prater. The south ridge, west ridge, and southwest slopes are class 2. An ascent by the north face and east arête, from the lake in the cirque to the northeast was made August 9, 1953, by Jim Koontz, Pete Murphy, Al Wolf, and Ed Toby.

Winter ascent. March 18, 1965, by Tom Ross and Pete Lewis.

Peak 12,720+ (head of Granite Park; formerly 12,736)

First ascent July 21, 1953, by C. N. La Vene and Hervey Voge. Class 2 by west or north ridges.

Peak 12,563 (1.2 NW of Pine Creek Pass; formerly 12,542)

Ascended by Norman Clyde in 1938 via the west slope. An easy ascent except for class 3 on the summit monolith.

Peaks West of the Crest

Volcanic Knob (11,168)

The east slope was climbed August 14, 1937, by Owen Williams.

Peak 12,205 (1 NW of Recess Peak; formerly 12,135)

Ascended by members of the 1953 Sierra Club Base Camp. Class 2 by the west slope, which may be reached from First Recess by the saddle south of the peak.

Peak 12,240 (1 NE of Recess Peak; formerly 12,100+)

Ascended by members of the 1953 Sierra Club Base Camp. Class 3 by the northwest face.

Recess Peak (12,836)

First ascent prior to 1937.

Route 1. Northeast arête. Class 3. Walk up the Second Recess to timberline, climb the west wall beyond the sharp cliffs, and follow the canyon leading toward Recess Peak; this canyon holds two lakes. From the head of the canyon cross a snowfield to a large col in the arête and follow the arête to the summit.

Route 2. East arête. Class 3. Climb to the arête from the snow slope below.

Route 3. Southwest arête. Class 3. From 1.5 mi. up the Hilgard branch of Bear Creek go north crossing the ridge just northeast of point 11,338 and drop about 350 feet into a wide valley from which the southwest arête can be followed to the summit.

Peak 12,720+ (1 NW of Mount Hilgard; formerly 12,721)

First ascent August 11, 1953, by Jim Koontz, Al Schmitz, G. Wallerstein, and Fred Peters, by the east arête (class 4). The descent by the south arête into the cirque at the head of the Second Recess was class 2. The west face was climbed on July 6, 1954, by a Sierra Club Base Camp party. Class 2 from Hilgard Lake by climbing diagonally upward across the west face to the point which appears to be the highest and is the summit.

Mount Hilgard (13,361)

First ascent July 10, 1905, by Charles F. Urquhart. Class 2 from Lake Italy by the south slopes, or class 3 by the southeast face. Climbed by the northeast ridge on Sept. 8, 1963, by Arkel Erb, Ed Lane, and Barbara Lilley. Route was from Second Recess and followed the northeast ridge by crossing from one side of the ridge to the other in order to bypass several gendarmes. Class 3-4.

Mount Gabb (13,711)

First ascent June 17, 1917, by H. H. Bliss and A. L. Jordan.

Route 1. Glacier and northwest ridge. Class 2. From the head of Mills Creek ascend the glacier and the scree headwall to the northwest ridge. Follow the ridge over large blocks to the summit. This is a fine route for descent if the snow is in condition to glissade.

Route 2. East spur of the northwest ridge. Class 3. From the largest lake near the head of Mills Creek, follow talus to the notch right (W) of the prominent gendarme on the east spur of the northwest ridge. In places the talus is quite steep and loose and could be dangerous for large parties. From the notch follow the ridges over more sound rock to the summit.

Route 3. South slope or west ridge. Class 2. From Lake Italy ascend over broken rock and scree to a 100-foot cliff at about 12,000 feet. This can be climbed via several broad chutes or directly over the rock. Work to the west to avoid further cliffs, or head directly for the summit by means of broad sandy chutes and a series of chimneys.

Route 4. Northeast ridge. Class 3 to 4. Ascend directly from Gabbot Pass.

Route 5. North face. Class 4. Ascended August 13, 1953, by Jim Koontz, Ralph Perry, Fred Peters, George Wallerstein, and Al Schmitz. From upper Mills Creek climb the glacier to a point just west of the prominent split in the middle of the north face. This split diagonals upward (E to W) and ends about 300 feet directly below the summit. Climb the slabs to the split and ascend the west side of the split until a large chockstone is reached. Pass this by exposed ledges, a 25-foot crack, and a 20-foot chimney which leads to the top of the west wall of the split. Then proceed to and up the northwest ridge.

Peak 12,320+ (1.2 NW of Mount Gabb; formerly 12,367)

First known ascent September 8, 1927, by James Wright. From the largest Mills Creek lake ascend talus to a couloir, ascend the (snow-filled) couloir to the ridge, and thence go to the left to the summit. Class 3.

Peak 12,145 (2.5 NW of Mount Mills; formerly 12,124)

First ascent record illegible. Class 3 to 4 from the Second Recess by way of northwest ridge and west face. The next peaklet to the south, 12,160, was climbed for the first time by Hervey Voge, Jane Collard, and Mary Crothers on July 23, 1953. They approached over Peak 12,124 and descended the west face. Class 3 to 4.

Peak 12,691 (1.7 NW of Mount Mills; formerly 12,701)

First ascent August 3, 1864, by W. H. Brewer.

Mono Rock (11,555)

First ascent by Norman Clyde and companion, July 18, 1934.

Route 1. East slope and south ridge. Class 2. From the lowest lake of the Fourth Recess climb via the ducked trail and slopes below the buttress to the lowest point of the ridge south of Mono Rock and proceed north along the crest to the top.

Route 2. East wall. Class 4. From the top of the headwall above the lowest lake in Fourth Recess angle across the face on ledges to a small bowl from which the summit can be gained. Ascent by Bill Wallace, August 17, 1953.

Route 3. North face. Class 5. First ascent by Lester LaVelle, Paul Hunter, Joe Sharp, Willard Dean, Dan Sharp, and Homer Wellman, August 6, 1946.

Peak 12,356 (1.5 NW of Mount Mills; formerly 12,351)

Ascended July 18, 1934, by James Wright and Norman Clyde.

Peak 12,880 (0.5 NW of Mount Mills; formerly 12,934)

Climbed July 18, 1934, by James Wright and Norman Clyde.

Bear Dome (9,947)

The Tombstone (10,059)

Ascended in 1929 by Walter L. Huber.

Mount Hooper (12,349)

First known ascent in 1929 by Glen Dawson, William A. Horsfall, and John Nixon. Class 2 from Selden Pass. Head west to the small lake just to the east of Mount Hooper. Then head west up to the southeast ridge crossing it and continue up the south slopes to the summit. The summit is an impressive block and there is a 7-rung ladder and a loop of rope to assist one in reaching the top.

Peak 12,014 (1 SE of Mount Hooper; formerly 12,000)

Ascended prior to 1947. Crossing from Hooper is difficult. Class 1 from Upper Sally Keyes Lake. Ascended from Selden Pass on July 15, 1954, by Oliver Kehrlein and Jim Koontz. Class 2–3. Swing southwest from Selden Pass around the east shoulder of the mountain and climb gradually up over easy rock to the summit plateau. Cross the plateau west to a knife edge and follow this to the summit. Descent was made via the south couloirs to the pass between this mountain and Mount Hooper and then to Marie Lake.

Peak 11,615 (1.2 SW of Mount Hooper; formerly 11,583)

First ascent on July 29, 1957, by Arthur Reyman up the east slope.

Mount Senger (12,271)

First ascent 1907–9 by George R. Davis, T. G. Gerdine, C. F. Urquhart, and L. F. Biggs of the USGS. The peak is class 1 from the south or west, and class 2 from the east.

Turret Peak (*12,000+*)

Climbed prior to 1930. A south to north traverse was reported to be easy.

Peak 11,760+ (*2 SW of Mount Hilgard; formerly 11,700+*)

First ascent in July 1947 by W. J. Losh via the east ridge. Class 2.

Peak 12,287 (*1.7 S of Mount Hilgard; formerly 12,200+*)

First ascent in July 1947 by W. J. Losh, by the west ridge. Class 2 to 3.

Peak 12,550 (*1.2 S of Lake Italy; formerly 12,536*)

On July 11, 1934, James Wright found ducks on the west slope but no cairn on top.

Peak 12,756 (*1 SE of Lake Italy; formerly 12,777*)

First known ascent July 13, 1933, by George Rockwood and David Brower, who described it as one of the better sand climbs of the Sierra.

Seven Gables (*13,075*)

First ascent September 20, 1894 by Theodore S. Solomons and Leigh Bierce.

Route 1. West slope. Class 2. Ascend from the South Fork of Bear Creek, climbing up to the central valley of Seven Gables on the south side of the creek running from it. The creek is then followed through a small meadow, thence up to the saddle on the east rim. The highest point is reached by clambering southward over large broken rock and up a simple system of ledges and chimneys. If snow-filled chutes are encountered, they may be circumvented on the rock ridge above.

Route 2. East slope to saddle. Class 2. From the oblong lake northeast of Seven Gables climb slabs and snow to the chute running east from the main saddle north of the summit. Climb the north side of the chute and proceed to the summit as in Route 1.

Gemini (*12,866*)

This is a prominent twin peak. The first ascent was made July 30, 1953, by Jim Koontz and Rosemarie Lenel by the north ridge from the little lake in the saddle to the northwest. Class 2. The saddle may be reached from the east or west.

The Pinnacles (*12,240+*)

The highest point of the Pinnacles was reached, apparently for the first time, by Glen Dawson, Neil Ruge, and Alfred Weiler on July 14, 1933. There is good climbing on the east side of the ridge but not on the west. Some of the pinnacles appear very difficult. They extend for about one mile, the southern end being a little lower (12,122). Two southern pinnacles were climbed July 5, 1939, by Bruce Meyer and Jim Harkins. Another pinnacle was climbed in June 1931 by Nathan Clark.

Peak 12,421 (*2 SE of Seven Gables; formerly 12,395*)

First ascent July 12, 1933, by David Brower. Class 2.

Peak 12,427 (*1.5 NW of Hutchinson Meadow; formerly 12,363*)

Ascended July 7, 1940, by members of Sierra Club Burro Trip.

Peak 12,530 (*2 E of Seven Gables*)

First ascent was made on July 4, 1939 by Dave Brower and Jim Harkins. The route was by way of the east arête and east side, from Hutchinson Meadow. George Whitmore climbed the peak by way of the west face and south arête on July 25, 1955. Class 2.

Peak 12,831 (*1 W of Royce Peak; formerly 12,817*)

First ascent July 13, 1933, by George Rockwood. Class 2.

Peak 13,242 (*1 NW of Royce Peak; formerly 13,234*)

First ascent July 13, 1933, by David Brower. Class 3 by the southwest ridge. The name Feather Peak has been proposed.

Royce Peak (*13,253*)

First ascent June 23, 1931, by Nathan Clark and Roy Crites. A class 2 ascent over talus. From the pass between Royce and Merriam climb the southeast ridge. The southwest ridge is also easy, as is the west slope. The east face was climbed in 1936 by Ellis Porter, Herbert Welch, and Frank Richardson. The Royce-Merriam col can be approached easily either from the east over Pine Creek Pass, or from the west via Merriam Lake.

Merriam Peak (*13,077*)

Ascended July 14, 1933, by Lewis Clark, Julie Mortimer, and Ted

Waller. Class 2 by the northwest ridge. The east face was climbed July 3, 1939, by Alden Bryant and Bob Helliwell. The south and southwest sides have also been climbed (class 3).

Peaks East of the Crest

Peak 11,742 (3 SE of Red Meadow; formerly 11,757)

This peak, on the northern end of Wheeler Crest, is class 1 up the northwest slope from Rock Creek. It was climbed in 1933 by the USGS, and in 1946 there was a mining claim on the summit.

Peak 11,498 (2.2 N of Round Valley Peak; formerly 11,500)

Ascended August 7, 1945, by Chester Versteeg. Class 2 by the north ridge from Rock Creek.

Peak 10,601 (2 NW of Round Valley Peak; formerly 10,663)

First ascent by Chester Versteeg, September 29, 1944. Class 2 from the north except for a short class 3 summit pitch.

Peak 11,791 (1.1 N of Round Valley Peak; formerly 11,888)

First ascent by Chester Versteeg, September 26, 1944. Class 2 from the north, or along the south ridge from near Round Valley Peak.

Round Valley Peak (11,943)

First ascent prior to 1944. This peak may be approached from the west via a breach in Wheeler Crest just west of the peak. Class 1. Trees grow almost to the summit, and it is easy from almost any direction.

Peak 12,541 (1.5 S of Round Valley Peak; formerly 12,531)

Ascended September 24, 1944, by Chester Versteeg and Niles Werner. Class 1 to 2 by north slopes.

Peak 12,966 (2.5 S of Round Valley Peak; formerly 12,970)

The highest point of Wheeler Crest was ascended August 14, 1945, by Don McGeein and Virgil Sisson. The west slope of Wheeler Crest can be ascended in many places, although the footing is poor, consisting mostly of rubbly slate or limestone. One can walk along the top of the crest easily. Peak 12,966 is class 2 from the northeast or southwest.

Peak 13,265 (1 NE of Mount Morgan; formerly 13,200+)

First ascent by Chester Versteeg, September 25, 1944. Class 1 from the East Fork of Rock Creek by the eastern slope of the north ridge and the north ridge.

Peak 13,440+ (0.6 NE of Mount Morgan; formerly 13,450)

First ascent prior to 1942. Class 2 to 3 by the southwest ridge from Mount Morgan or from the north.

Mount Morgan (13,748)

First ascent by the Wheeler Survey, about 1870. Class 1 to 2. Mount Morgan can readily be climbed by several routes from the mines on Morgan Creek. It is probably best to go well up toward the head of the northwest fork, from which place a route can easily be picked out by inspection. In spring and early summer the mountaineer can usually avail himself of a snow-filled chute running up to the summit above. The northwest ridge from Francis Lake on the East Fork of Rock Creek is class 1. Mount Morgan is not a mountain having any very real appeal to the mountaineer, but its summit affords a spectacular view.

Peak 13,160+ (0.8 E of Mount Morgan; formerly 13,200+)

Peak 13,200+ (1.2 SE of Mount Morgan; formerly 13,206)

Peak 12,920+ (1.7 SE of Mount Morgan; formerly 13,201)

Peak 12,866 (1 NE of Bear Creek Spire; formerly 12,887)

First known ascent in 1927 by Norman Clyde. This peak is class 2 from the col immediately northeast of Bear Creek Spire.

Peak 12,640+ (1.8 NE of Bear Creek Spire; formerly 12,750)

Class 2 to 3 from saddle to west of summit. Has been called Tempest Peak.

Peak 12,808 (1 SW of Mount Morgan; formerly 12,819)

First ascent by A. J. Reyman, October 2, 1947. Class 2 by the south slope from the upper Morgan Lake.

Peak 12,571 (1.3 SE of Bear Creek Spire; formerly 12,560)

First ascent September 29, 1931, by Norman Clyde. Class 2 to 3 from Morgan Creek or Pine Creek. A number of routes are possible up chutes or intervening ribs.

Mount Humphreys Region

George Bloom, Ray Van Aken (1953);
Hervey H. Voge (1953, 1964)

THE PIUTE PASS TRAIL provides the easiest access to the Humphreys group from the east inasmuch as the North Lake roadhead is 2,000 feet higher than the Pine Creek roadhead. Off-trail approaches from the east, such as via McGee Creek, are apt to be arduous. Various knapsack routes lead to the region from the Evolution Region (which see). Golden Trout Lake is the highest comfortable campsite west of the crest for Humphreys itself; upper French Canyon timber grows at higher elevations and provides good camping for the northern peaks of the group. Map coverage is given by the Mount Tom and Mount Goddard quadrangles.

Peak 12,480+ (1.4 E of Pine Creek Pass; formerly 12,888)

Climbed prior to 1938. The name Peak of the Four Winds has been proposed.

Four Gables (12,920+)

Climbed in 1931 by Norman Clyde. Four Gables can be climbed from Horton Lake. Go to the large lake southwest of Horton Lake and follow the south side of the east ridge of the peak. Ascend the east slope and a chute between the east slope and the east ridge (Dick Jali, 1963).

Mount Humphreys (13,986)

The first ascent was made July 18, 1904, by E. C. Hutchinson and J. S. Hutchinson, who used Route 1 (*SCB*, 1905, 153). This route and others from the west side are indicated on Sketch 13. The easiest way of ascent is probably Route 2. Routes 1, 2, and 3 are easy class 4.

Route 1. South couloir and southeast face. Class 4. From Humphreys

Basin southwest of the peak proceed up a gully leading toward the very deep notch south of Humphreys. Turn left (N) and enter the deep couloir that comes down southward from the summit. This couloir leads to the southeast, secondary summit named "Married Men's Point" by those in the party of the first ascent who saw no point in going farther. Steep snow or ice may be encountered in the couloir. From the head of the couloir the steep southeastern face is climbed up a ladder-like series of small ledges.

Sketch 13. Mount Humphreys from the west. From left to right: Route 2 (variation), Route 2, Route 6, Route 1, Route 4, and Southeast Pinnacle Route.

Route 2. West slope and northwest face. Class 4. First ascent August 3, 1919, by G. R. Bunn and two others (*SCB,* 1920, 56). Follow the rocky shoulder between the two lakes nearest the west base of the mountain to the first scree-covered ledge leading upward to the left (N). Follow the ledge to the second broad gully, which ends to the north of the notch immediately north of the final pinnacle. Near the top of this gully cross over to the right (S) to the gully leading to the notch north of the pinnacle. From the notch follow a ledge to the steep trough to the right (S), and climb the trough toward the summit. When a vertical wall is encountered climb out to the right (W) and upward on an arête over good holds to the final summit ridge, which is followed eastward to the summit.

There are a number of variations of Route 2, but in all of them the final peak is climbed by the northwest face. The notch from which this final climb is made can be reached by several routes up the western slope, including one that leads up from Desolation Lake to the ridge about one mile north of the summit. The more or less flat ridge is then followed southward to the notch.

A difficult variation of Route 2, class 5.5, was climbed in July 1958 by John Dorsey, Jim Koontz, and Leif Thorne-Thomsen. They left the gully leading to the notch north of the summit some distance below the notch and worked up the west face by means of chimneys, broken ledges, and a crossing of a sharp wedge beneath an overhang. They rejoined Route 2 about halfway up from the notch toward the summit.

Route 3. East slope and northwest face. Class 4. First ascent July 18, 1920, by C. H. Rhudy, L. C. Bogue, and J. L. Findlay (*SCB*, 1921, 203). From McGee Creek go half-way around the upper McGee Lake shown on the map and then proceed westward, skirting to the south and west of a prominent ridge which projects eastward from the main range. Climb the ridge to a wide flat about one mile north of the summit, follow the north ridge to the notch north of the peak, and follow Route 2 to the top.

Route 4. Southeast buttress. Class 4. First ascent July 7, 1933, by Hervey Voge. From the west climb to the deep notch about 0.3 mile southeast of the summit. Ascend the northwest wall of the notch directly toward the peak, and then gradually work to the right (E) until the easy top of the southeast ridge is reached. Proceed along the ridge and to the summit as in Route 1.

Route 5. East arête. Class 4. First ascent June 29, 1935, by Norman Clyde. From the head of the south fork of McGee Creek enter the cirque southeast of Mount Humphreys, and climb to a notch in the crest of the cleaver-like arête to the north. This is the east arête of Humphreys; farther west it is joined by the northeast arête, and the combined ridge joins the main ridge at Married Men's Point. Follow the arête westward, passing a precipitous wall by means of a ledge at the left (S) and cracks which lead back to the top of the arête. Follow the arête to the main ridge and climb to the summit as in Route 1.

Route 6. Southwest face. Class 5. From a prominent pointed spire at the west base of the mountain, climb the face diagonally upward to the left (N) to the summit. Five pitons. Climbed July 28, 1938, by Jack Riegelhuth, Dick Cahill, George Wilkins, Bill Leovy, Bruce Meyer.

Route 7. Northeast glacier. Class 4. From the highest point of the glacier an ice-filled chute leads upward. After about 100 yards the chute branches. Follow the right (N) branch or the rocks beside it to the crest north of a small peak north of Humphreys. Climb south over the small peak and ascend to the summit by the northwest face as in Route 2.

Route 8. Southeast cirque and south couloir. Class 4. Descended June 29, 1935, by Norman Clyde. He followed Route 1 from the summit to the deep notch south of the prominent southeast buttress, then descended the headwall and a steep gully to the cirque southeast of the peak.

Southeast pinnacle. The sharp pinnacle about 0.4 mile southeast of the summit of Humphreys was climbed for the first time by Jules Eichorn and Marjory Bridge on July 20, 1933. They ascended the west face and descended the northwest ridge.

Peak 13,112 (1.2 SE of Mount Humphreys; formerly 13,116)

First ascent July 7, 1926, by Norman Clyde.

Pilot Knob (12,245)

First ascent by unknown persons. Class 2 by the east slope from Piute Creek or Humphreys Basin.

Peaks East of the Crest

Peak 12,280 (0.7 SE of Pine Lake; formerly 12,274)

Peak 12,360+ (2 SE of Pine Lake; formerly 12,388)

This peak is just east of Peak 12,575. It was ascended in 1912 by W. L. Huber and C. S. Brothers.

Mount Tom (13,652)

First ascent may have been made about 1860 by Thomas Clark. Class 2 from Gable Creek northwest of the peak. Start up Gable Creek on the west side and follow the tramway of an old mine; then cross over the creek and follow a good trail up the west slope to mines just below the summit. From there it is easy going to the summit. The climb from Horton Lake is class 1 via a jeep road to the Tungstar mine and the southwest ridge.

Basin Mountain (13,240)

Climbed by Norman Clyde September 15, 1937. Class 2 from Horton Lake by the north slope of the mountain or the north ridge.

Peak 12,228 (1.2 NE of Mount Humphreys; formerly 12,222)

Mount Emerson (13,225)

Route 1. North face. Climbed by Norman Clyde, July 1, 1926.

Route 2. Southeast face. Class 4. First ascent August 1955 by G. Ledyard Stebbins and Robert Stebbins. From North Lake hike about 1.7 miles up the Piute Pass Trail and then proceed north to the base of the face. Climb the left (SW) of two cracks that lead up the face; these cracks are to the left (SW) of the couloir separating Mount Emerson from the Piute Crags. Follow the left-hand crack or chimney, with some deviations, to a ridge that leads to the summit. The climb affords 2,500 feet of roped climbing and can be done in one day from the roadhead.

Route 3. South slope. Class 3. From the Piute Pass Trail about one-fourth mile west of the west end of Loch Leven a granite rib ascends in an easy slope toward Mount Emerson. Go up this rib, heading for the summit, which shows as two small humps on the skyline immediately to the left of the apparent highest point. Continue upward over ledges, aiming to reach the summit ridge just left (W) of a prominent overhang which is seen just below the crest. The upper part of the climb is in a couloir, from which a short scramble over broken blocks leads to the summit ridge a few hundred feet west of the summit. Still other class 3 routes are possible up the south and southwest slopes.

Piute Crags

The Piute Crags comprise the ridge that extends eastward from Mount Emerson. They may be identified on the Mount Goddard Quadrangle as the series of summits between Mount Emerson and Peak 12,089 northwest of North Lake. Since the crags are close to a road, and a trail parallels their base, they offer easy access. At the end of the North Lake road (9,400) is a public campground from which climbs of the crags may be made. There are several other campsites along the trail leading to Piute Pass.

There is much loose rock on the crags so caution must be observed. Loose rock was sent down from Crags 1 and 2 by blasting from a mine at 11,800 in 1953. Ice equipment will not be needed during the summer months, although ice may be found in the couloirs in the spring. Otherwise the couloirs to the various notches from which the climbs are made are about class 3. Sketch 14 identifies the crags.

Crag 1

Class 5. First ascent September 2, 1950, by Charles Wilts and George Harr. Ascend the couloir between Crags 1 and 2, that passes to the west of the White Tower, to the notch. Approach the crag from the northeast and traverse diagonally upwards across the 70° north face on ladder-like holds to the summit ridge. Traverse to the summit.

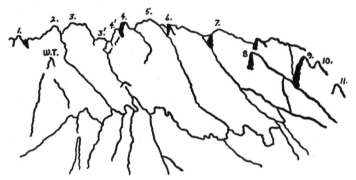

Sketch 14. The Piute Crags from the south.

Crag 2

Route 1. Class 5. First ascent August 27, 1949, by Ray Van Aken, George Harr, and Ray Osoling. From the notch between Crags 1 and 2 ascend (class 4) the west face to a belay point at the junction of the west face and the west arête. The route goes diagonally upwards and to the right on the smooth slab (class 5, 4 pitons). At the end of this pitch gain the west arête and follow it to the summit.

Route 2. Class 5. First ascent September 3, 1950, by George Harr and Charles Wilts. From slightly below the Crag 1–2 notch traverse onto the south face and ascend a series of interesting pitches to the summit.

Route 3. Class 4. First descent September 3, 1950, by George Harr and Charles Wilts. From the Crag 2–3 notch climb over loose, high angle rock up the east-northeast side.

Crag 3

Route 1. Class 4. First descent July 7, 1951, by Ray Van Aken, Wallace Hayes, and Lou Hayes. From the Crag 2–3 notch ascend the arête to the summit.

Route 2. Class 4. First ascent July 7, 1951, by Ray Van Aken, Wallace Hayes, and Lou Hayes. From the Crag 3–3' notch ascend over loose rock (class 3) to the base of the east face. Traverse around the corner to the north and ascend upwards and traverse onto the north face (class 4). Scramble to the ridge and follow it to the summit.

Crag 4

Class 5. First ascent September 1949 by Charles and Ellen Wilts, and George Harr. From the Crag 4'–4 notch traverse across the steep north face to a platform. A delicate pitch leads straight up to the east ridge from which an easy pitch-and-a-half brings one to the summit.

Crag 5

Class 3. First ascent by Norman Clyde, 1927. Traverse from the Crag 5–6 notch onto the south ridge and follow it to the summit. There is a minor but sharp summit between Crags 5 and 6; this is class 4, and was ascended June 17, 1950, by George Harr and Ray Van Aken. It may be traversed west-east or vice versa.

Crag 6

Route 1. Class 4. First ascent June 17, 1950, by George Harr and Ray Van Aken. Ascend diagonally upwards and to the right from the Crag 5–6 notch.

Route 2. Class 2. First descent June 17, 1950, by George Harr and Ray Van Aken. Ascend talus and ledges to the summit from the Crag 6–7 notch.

Crag 8

This is a prominent red pinnacle on the south face of Crag 7. Class 3. First ascent July 21, 1951, by Ray Van Aken, George Harr, and Charles and Ellen Wilts. Ascend the couloir to the east of Crag 7 and branch from this to the notch behind the crag. Climb over sound rock up the northeast face to the ridge from which the summit is easily reached. There are some excellent long climbing routes on the south face of this crag.

Crag 9

The higher of two pinnacles to the east of Crag 8.

Route 1. Class 5. First ascent July 21, 1951, by Charles and Ellen Wilts, George Harr, and Ray Van Aken. From the notch between Crags 10 and 11 climb the south ridge (2 pitons) over sound rock.

Route 2. Class 3. First descent July 21, 1951, by Charles and Ellen Wilts, George Harr, and Ray Van Aken. From the broad couloir to the east of Crag 9 gain the notch on the uphill side of the crag. Ascend the ridge to the summit.

Crag 10

The lower of two pinnacles to the east of Crag 8. Class 3. First ascent July 21, 1951, by George Harr, Charles and Ellen Wilts, and Ray Van Aken. Ascend the gully between the two crags and climb the north face over loose rock to the summit.

The White Tower

A prominent point of white rock as seen from the trail. Class 1. First ascent August 27, 1949, by Ray Osoling, George Harr, and Ray Van Aken. Scramble to the top over loose rock from the talus on the west side.

No recorded ascents have been made of Crags 7, 11, and two towers on the northeast side of Mount Emerson.

Piute Pass to Kearsarge Pass

BETWEEN PIUTE and Kearsarge passes is to be found some of the finest high country of the Sierra. Most of this high country lies within the Kings Canyon National Park. It is indeed fortunate that this magnificent wilderness area, which is not penetrated by a single road, is thus preserved for study and enjoyment by man. Climbers are probably in the minority among users of the area, and it is not likely that their little cairns, their footprints on the sandy shelves, and the evanescent tracks left upon the sparkling snowfields will cause significant changes in the landscape.

For the organization of the guide, the section from Piute Pass to Kearsarge Pass has been divided into five areas, as has been indicated in Sketch 2 in the Introduction. The areas are:

LeConte Divide and Adjacent Peaks. This includes the peaks west of the LeConte Divide to Helms Creek, and those south to Crown Mountain.

The Evolution Region and the Black Divide. This includes the main crest from Piute Pass to Bishop Pass, the Glacier Divide, the Goddard Divide, the Black Divide, and some neighboring peaks.

The Palisades Region. This includes the main crest from Bishop Pass to the Thumb, peaks south and east of Bishop Creek (south fork), the Inconsolable Range, and a few adjacent peaks.

Kings Canyon Region. Here are described Spanish Mountain, the peaks of Kettle Ridge, the White Divide, and Monarch Divide, and rock climbs of the lower canyons of the Middle Fork and South Fork of the Kings.

Palisades to Kearsarge Pass. The main crest is covered from Mount Bolton Brown, just south of the Palisades, to Kearsarge Pass, together with peaks south and east of those in the other areas. Included are the peaks around Amphitheater Lake, Cirque Crest, Goat Crest, Arrow Ridge, and the peaks around Sixty Lake Basin.

The LeConte Divide and Adjacent Peaks

FRED L. JONES (1953); HERVEY H. VOGE (1964)

THE TERRAIN of the LeConte Divide and environs is not as rugged as that of the higher peaks to the east; neither is it as austere. It has not been frequently visited by climbers.

Approach may be made from the east from Goddard Canyon, via Florence Lake and the South Fork of the San Joaquin River, or from the west by way of tributaries of the North Fork of the Kings, where a road runs from the Kings to Dinkey Creek and Shaver Lake. Hell-for-Sure Pass crosses the LeConte Divide from Fleming Creek to Goddard Canyon. This pass, at an elevation of 11,297, was crossed from east to west in 1898 by LeConte and Cory, who followed the directions of a sheep herder. They continued to Crown Valley and then to the Kings Canyon. Blackcap Mountain and Mount Goddard quadrangle maps cover this area.

Peak 11,600 (1 NW of Mount Henry; formerly 11,567)

Class 1. First ascent July 10, 1951, by Art Reyman. He ascended the west slope and the northwest ridge.

Mt. Henry (12,196)

It is not known when or by whom the first ascent of this peak was made.

Route 1. Northeast ridge. Class 2. First ascent July 7, 1939, by a Sierra Club party led by Dave Brower. They ascended the northeast side from Goddard Canyon.

Route 2. Southwest slope. Class 2. First ascent August 14, 1939, by a party of eight via the southwest slope from Fleming Creek.

Route 3. West slope. Class 2. First ascent August 29, 1940, by Bob Helliwell and Alden Bryant via the west slope from Blaney Meadows. The climb was described as long and tedious.

Route 4. North ridge. Class 3. First ascent July 10, 1951 by Art Reyman via the north arête on a traverse from Peak 11,600. Keep on the arête or to the east in order to bypass large blocks and notches. Drop to the west when the west ridge is reached and walk to the summit plateau.

Peak 12,154 (1 SE of Mount Henry)

Class 2. First ascent July 10, 1951, by Art Reyman via the northwest ridge on a traverse from Mt. Henry.

Peak 12,021 (0.5 NW of Red Mountain; formerly 12,023)

Class 1. First ascent July 11, 1951, by Art Reyman. He ascended the south slope from Red Mountain Basin.

Red Mountain (11,951)

Class 1. First ascent July 12, 1898, by J. N. LeConte and C. L. Cory via the north side. It is class 1 from any side.

Peak 11,680+ (0.3 S of Hell-for-Sure Pass; formerly 11,833)

Class 2. First ascent July 11, 1951, by Art Reyman via the northwest ridge. It is a rough knife-edge climb from Hell-for-Sure Pass.

Peak 12,034 (1.5 S of Hell-for-Sure Pass; formerly 12,028)

Class 2. First ascent July 13, 1951, by Art Reyman via the northwest arête from Red Mountain Basin.

Peak 12,011 (2.2 SE of Hell-for-Sure Pass; formerly 12,038)

Class 2. First ascent July 13, 1951, by Art Reyman via the west ridge on a traverse from Peak 12,034.

Peak 12,265 (3.2 SE of Hell-for-Sure Pass; formerly 12,254)

Class 3. First ascent July 13, 1951, by Art Reyman via the west ridge. It is a knife-edge traverse from Peak 12,011. He descended into Fall Creek Basin to the southwest.

Mount Reinstein (12,604)

Climbed prior to 1954. The southeast ridge is class 3. The south slope, from Blackcap Basin is class 2.

Mount Shinn (11,020)

First ascent August 8, 1925, by Francis A. Corey.

Fleming Mountain (10,796)

No record of ascent is available.

Peak 11,998 (1.4 S of Hell-for-Sure Pass)

Class 1. First ascent July 12, 1951, by Art Reyman up the broad southwest slope.

Peak 11,286 (0.7 SE of Devils Punchbowl; formerly 11,275)

First ascent July 1, 1936, by W. M. Wyman and eight others. It is class 1 from the west, south or east slopes.

Peak 11,398 (1.5 SE of Devils Punchbowl; formerly 11,394)

Class 2. First ascent July 12, 1951, by Art Reyman along the north ridge from the saddle.

Maxson Dome (9,547)

First ascent August 15 (year not given, but it was prior to 1933 when the second ascent was made) by Waldo Knight and M. Kaye, a survey party for the San Joaquin Light and Power Co. It is class 1 from all sides.

Blackcap Mountain (11,559)

This is a USGS benchmark so it has been climbed.

Loper Peak (10,059)

This peak is a USGS benchmark so it has been climbed.

Finger Rock (9,606)

Has been climbed. Class 3.

Castle Peak (10,677)

No information is available.

The Evolution Region and the Black Divide

ALAN M. HEDDEN and DAVID R. BROWER (1942);
ALAN M. HEDDEN (1953);
JOHN W. ROBINSON and ANDREW J. SMATKO (1964)

WELL BACK in the central High Sierra is the Evolution Region, where there are concentrated examples of almost every essential part of the High Sierra scene—cathedral-like Mount Huxley as an example of fine peak sculpture, the Enchanted Gorge for the majesty of exotic cliffs, Mount Goddard for superb views, and the Devil's Crags to provide the challenge of jagged summits. This area has remained the most remote section of the entire crest, having no one-day route into its heart for pack animals and being hardly more accessible to knapsackers.

The Evolution region lies sixty miles southeast of Yosemite Park and twenty miles southwest of the town of Bishop. Almost all of the area is within the Kings Canyon National Park. The peaks are here divided geographically into four sections: (1) peaks of the crest, (2) peaks west of the crest, from north to south through the Goddard Divide, (3) peaks west of the crest and south of the Goddard Divide, and (4) peaks east of the crest. This, the natural grouping of the peaks, is used in describing them. The Mount Goddard, Blackcap Mountain, and Mount Pinchot quadrangles of the United States Geological Survey should be referred to for cartographic detail. Sketch 15 is an outline map of the region.

HISTORICAL RÉSUMÉ

Had sheepherders spent their hours keeping notes instead of sheep, more might be known with respect to who, in this as in many other parts of the Sierra, may have been the first white—or nearly white—mountaineer. The first known record of exploration is that of the California Geological Survey party, led by William H. Brewer, who approached the region from the north in August of 1864. Four members of this party attempted to climb Mount Goddard from a camp about twenty miles distant, and of these, two, including Richard Cotter, companion of Clarence King on that same year's first ascent of Mount Tyndall, all but made it. In thirty-two hours, twenty-six without food, Cotter covered the forty-mile round trip, missing the summit by just 300 feet, according to Brewer's journal.* Next of record is John Muir, who in about 1873, according to Francis P. Farquhar *, climbed the highest mountain at the head of the San Joaquin, probably Mount Darwin.

In 1879 Lil A. Winchell's explorations took him to Mount Goddard, which he climbed with L. W. Davis; he returned to repeat the ascent in 1892. But the region remained virtually unknown and incompletely explored until July of 1895. Then, hoping to find a high mountain

* Farquhar, Francis P. (ed.). Up and Down California in 1860–1864, the Journal of William H. Brewer. New Haven, 1930.

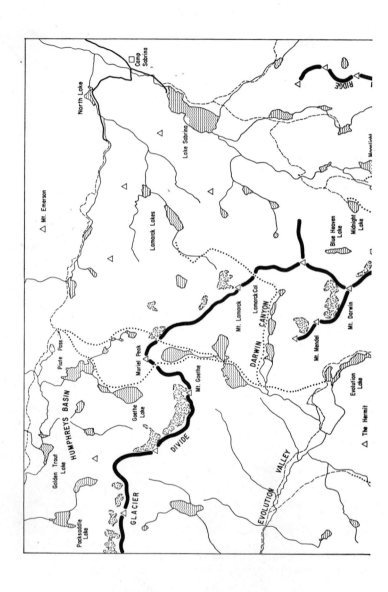

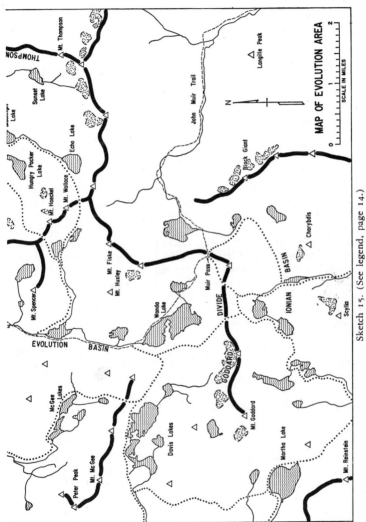

Sketch 15. (See legend, page 14.)

route between the Kings River Canyon and Yosemite Valley, Theodore S. Solomons and Ernest C. Bonner left Florence Lake on a memorable expedition into the region. Following sheep trails, they knapsacked up the south fork of the San Joaquin River and continued on into the Evolution Creek valley. At the head of what is now called Colby Meadow, a prominent mountain shaped like a sugarloaf suggested to Solomons a name, The Hermit, which he promptly bestowed. From here, also, he named the flat-topped Mount Darwin, Evolution Creek, Evolution Lake, and, to complete the homogeneity of the place names and to honor the respective philosophers, Mounts Huxley, Fiske, Spencer, Haeckel, and Wallace. Retracing their steps to the junction of Evolution Creek and the Goddard Canyon, the two men turned south and followed the canyon to its source, southwest of Mount Goddard, and made the third ascent of this peak. Dropping down the southeast side of Goddard Divide, Solomons and Bonner entered the deep Enchanted Gorge, passing through a gateway formed by two black metamorphic peaks, which became Scylla and Charybdis, and descended Disappearing Creek, then Goddard Creek, and finally the Middle Fork of the Kings to Tehipite Valley. Thus they succeeded in finding a route from Yosemite to the Kings. The complete route has seldom been used since, but the place names Solomons left behind—and almost all in the region are his—are some of the most pleasing in the Sierra.

The rest of the story follows a familiar pattern. Explorers had done their work. Then came the decades of scrambling, with the last of the important summits going down before the onslaught of members of high-mountain outings. As yet, relatively little roped climbing has been done in the region. A glance at the rugged terrain, however, is enough to convince a rock climber that there are still many excellent and difficult routes to be pioneered.

Topography and Its Relation to Climbing

In the Evolution Region, as in nearly all parts of the High Sierra, there is an easy way to climb almost every peak. In general, the peaks on the crest are most easily climbed from the southwest, while the northeast sides present higher, more vertical faces for the rock climber. The small glaciers of the region provide interesting routes for climbs of several peaks, such as Darwin, Goddard, and Mendel.

For the most part, the peaks of the crest are of granite. A substantial part of the region is composed of dark metamorphic rock, resembling the highly metamorphosed ancient lava of the Ritter Range. The Black

Divide, Scylla, Charybdis, the Enchanted Gorge, Mounts McGee, Goddard, and the Black Giant are all, as many of the names imply, of dark rock, much of it beautifully sculptured. The beauty is not so apparent, however, to the rock climber, who will find much of the metamorphic rock unsound and easily fractured. Chutes in the Devil's Crags are particularly unsound and should be avoided during storms.

APPROACHES AND CAMPSITES

From the east, Bishop Pass, 11,972. At an elevation of 9,755 feet, leave the end of the road which follows the South Fork of Bishop Creek. From here a horse trail continues from South Lake over Bishop Pass into Dusy Basin, then down into LeConte Canyon. Excellent campsites are found in Dusy Basin and at Grouse and Little Pete meadows in LeConte Canyon.

From the east. Piute Pass 11,423. From the roadhead at North Lake the Piute Pass trail leads past Mount Humphreys and descends through Humphreys Basin and Hutchinson Meadow, following Piute Creek to its junction with the South Fork of the San Joaquin River. Here the Muir Trail may be followed southward into the Evolution Region. Campsites are both good and plentiful anywhere along Piute Creek or the upper reaches of the South Fork, particularly on Evolution Creek.

From the east. Lamarck Col, 12,920+. Lying ¼ mile southeast of Mount Lamarck on the main Sierra crest, this high pass provides the most direct route for knapsackers into the Evolution Region. Because of the difficulties encountered by many climbers who did not follow the exact route, it will be described in detail. At the end of the road above North Lake leave the Piute trail and follow a fork to the south (left) toward Grass Lake. Shortly after reaching the level of the first bench, on the northwest side of Grass Lake, the trail again divides. Here, follow the west(right) branch to Lower Lamarck Lake, skirting its southeastern end and continuing on westward toward Upper Lamarck Lake. Shortly before arriving at this latter lake, the trail forks into a western branch, which continues on to the lake, and a southern branch, which leads toward the spur forming the southern boundary of this upper lake basin. Follow the southern branch and climb the spur in a southerly direction to the first of several sand flats. (When crossing from west to east it is highly advisable to follow the side of the spur rather than to drop directly down to Upper Lamarck Lake.) Proceed in a southwesterly direction to the second sand flat, at which point the crest comes into view. Continue toward what appears to be a low gap to the southwest. On the north (right) side of this and somewhat beyond the low wall in which the gap is situated is a prominent butte with a large monolith. Continue up and through the gap, beyond which is a third sand flat which leads into the final cirque basin, after curving around the southern side of the butte with the monolith. At the head of this cirque valley is a tiny lake, to the south of which can be seen a jagged spire somewhat higher than its neighbors. To the east (left) of this spire is a low notch, which leads to Bottleneck Lake. To the northwest (right) is a series of three or four notches in the arête leading up to Mount Lamarck. The first notch to the northwest (right) of the jagged spire is Lamarck Col, and it is best reached by passing to the south (left) of the lake, climbing between it and the tall spire, and then ascending directly to the col itself.

When the summit has been reached, the "trail," now no more than a route, drops down toward the upper lakes of Darwin Canyon. After a descent of several hundred feet, it ends altogether save for an occasional duck. It is not imperative to follow the ducks, for any route may be followed over the talus and down the north side of Darwin Canyon. From the lower end of the canyon a ducked trail contours south to the Muir Trail at Evolution Lake. Fair campsites for small groups may be found around the lowest lake in Darwin Canyon. Excellent campsites are available on Darwin Bench halfway between the mouth of Darwin Canyon and Evolution Lake.

From the west. At Florence Lake, where the road from Fresno ends, a pack trail follows the South Fork of the San Joaquin River, joining the Muir Trail in Blaney Meadows; the Muir Trail ascends the South Fork into Goddard Canyon, and leads up Goddard Canyon to the Evolution Creek junction. The Muir Trail, following Evolution Creek, winds up a steep canyon, passes Evolution, McClure, and Colby meadows and continues on past Evolution Lake and over Muir Pass. With its vast supply of pasturage, wood, water, and scenery, Colby Meadow is one of the finest camping spots in the Sierra.

On the south shore of the large peninsula which enters Evolution Lake from the east and about one hundred yards from the trail there is a fairly well sheltered campsite for a small group, with feed for a few animals, firewood, and an excellent view of the southern half of the lake.

From the west. Hell-for-Sure Pass, 11,297. One of the first routes of access to the Evolution country, but now seldom used, is the trail from Dinkey, on the North Fork of the Kings, over Hell-for-Sure Pass, and down to Goddard Canyon. Knapsackers may easily travel directly up Goddard Canyon, taking the east branch for the Evolution Peaks or Muir Pass, or taking the main branch on south to Mount Goddard. Martha Lake, at the head of Goddard Canyon, is above timberline.

From Blackcap Basin it is readily possible to cross the saddle (11,800+) just north of Mount Reinstein. There is good camping at Lake 10,212, near the head of Goddard Creek.

From the south. Mather Pass (12,080+). The John Muir Trail descends Palisade Creek to its junction with the Middle Fork of the Kings River. Just north of this junction is Grouse Meadow, a perfect little alpine valley. For climbs among the nearby Devil's Crags there is an excellent site high up on the south fork of Rambaud Creek at about 10,200 feet.

PASSES

The Goddard Divide. Muir Pass. The only trail that crosses the Goddard Divide is that over Muir Pass, 11,955. At the summit of the pass is the John Muir Memorial Shelter. Through the generosity of George Frederick Schwarz, the Sierra Club was able to build this stone hut in 1930. Since it is high above timberline, its fuel supply is strictly limited. Signs along the trail at the bottom of the pass advise the traveler of the last place to get wood before beginning to climb to the hut. Every extra branch that he can carry to the pass is just so much added insurance that the weary hiker, caught in a sudden summer storm, will find warmth in the hut.

Knapsackers may cross the Goddard Divide at the gap southwest of Wanda Lake. It is also practicable to go from Davis Lake to Martha Lake by a route west of Mount Goddard. A pass north of Davis Lake may be crossed to upper McGee Lake. To get into the Ionian Basin, knapsackers may cross the Goddard Divide by going over the saddle just west of Peak 13,016 (about ½ mile southwest of Muir Pass).

The Black Divide. Black Giant Pass, 12,200+. Black Giant Pass offers the best approach to the Enchanted Gorge from Muir Pass. It is an easy, broad, knapsack pass, located about ½ mile due west of the Black Giant and about ¼ mile north of a large lake at the headwaters of Disappearing Creek.

The Black Divide. Rambaud Pass, 11,553. There is an old trail which ascends Rambaud Creek and crosses the Black Divide, dropping down its western slopes to Goddard Creek.

Glacier Divide. At the eastern end of Glacier Divide are two very rocky (class 2) knapsack passes connecting Piute Pass with Evolution Lake. From Piute Pass go southwest to Muriel Lake. Above the head of the southeastern tributary to this lake is a low notch, The Keyhole, 12,560+, so named because the climber may pass through it rather than over it. There is a short class 3 pitch on the west side immediately below The Keyhole. On this western side the slope drops sharply to a small lake basin, which is descended to its junction with Darwin Canyon. (See Sketch 15.)

Another tributary to Muriel Lake, which enters from the southwest, leads to a large basin filled by Goethe Lake, 11,528. Above the southeastern end of this lake a small tributary stream comes down the ridge wall from a small notch, Alpine Col, 12,320+, which leads to Darwin Canyon, and thence to Evolution Lake.

Peaks of the Crest

Peak 13,160+ (1.5 S of Piute Pass; formerly 13,162)

Class 2. First recorded ascent July 3, 1939, by James R. Harkins, Fred L. Toby, and Herbert L. Malcolm on a traverse of the crest from north to south; class 3 by this route, but estimated as class 2 from the head of the north fork of Lamarck Creek.

Mount Lamarck (13,417)

Class 1. First ascent in the summer of 1925 by Norman Clyde, who found it an easy scramble from the south. The high point is on the northwest side of the broad summit plateau.

Peak 13,248 (1 NE of Mount Darwin; formerly 13,252)

Class 2. First recorded ascent by Norman Clyde in the summer of 1925; however, he found a cairn. Class 3 by the north ridge.

Mount Darwin (13,830)

The broad, sandy, nivated summit table of Mount Darwin is a fascinating indication of what the ancient Sierra was like, before the great uplifts and the extensive glaciation. It is particularly odd that an unsteady-looking pinnacle, well detached from this summit plateau and southeast of it, is actually the highest point.

The first ascent on record was made by E. C. Andrews, Geological Survey of New South Wales, and Willard D. Johnson, of the United States Geological Survey.

Route 1. West wall. Class 3. First ascent by Andrews and Johnson, August 12, 1908. Although their exact route is not known, it seems to parallel closely the following. Near the south end of Evolution Lake ascend a small tributary east of the lake, through meadows leading to the base of the west face. Here, cross to the left (N) to the base of the third of three talus fans, counting from south to north, and ascend the chute from which the fan emanates. Midway to the crest this chute branches, and the right-hand (S) branch is followed to the saddle just above the first pinnacle on the right (S) side of the chute. By a series of easy ledges drop down into the middle chute and continue up its right-hand (S) side to an indented trough, which leads to the crest of the main shoulder. The only difficulty yet to remain in traversing to the nearly flat plateau is a knife-edge which must be straddled.

Variations are possible for most of this route. The chutes forming the first and second talus fans may also be climbed, thus avoiding the knife-edge. The climber must be prepared, however, to cross from one chute to another frequently. No one has yet determined which combination of chutes and traverses is best.

Route 2. Via glacier and west ridge. Class 3. First ascent by Robert M. Price and Peter Frandsen, August 21, 1921. Between Mounts Mendel and Darwin there is on the ridge a large notch with a smaller one about one hundred yards farther to the east. In an approach from the north via Darwin Canyon the glacier presents a problem. If weather is favorable and adequate equipment is available, the quickest route is directly up the glacier to the bergschrund, over it if possible, and on up to the smaller, eastern notch. The easier but longer route is to skirt the right (west) side of the glacier and then traverse above it from west to east to any of several routes to the small notch. The route then proceeds along the ridge to the summit plateau and thence to the higher, southeastern end.

Route 3. North face. Class 3 to 4. First ascent by David R. Brower and Hervey Voge, July 5, 1934. Two ribs or arêtes run down the north face, partly dividing the glacier. The east (left) side of the east rib, which lies one-quarter of a mile west of the northeast ridge, is ascended a short distance over talus and snow. The route then goes up onto the rib itself and ascends, via easy ledges, up to the point where the rib merges with the face. Here a moderate pitch is passed by a crack to the left, and the final climb to the summit may be made via a small chimney (see Sketch 16). A variation is to follow the snow slope east of the rock rib as far as possible.

Route 4. Northeast ridge. Class 4. First ascent in 1945 by Austin, Pabst and Wilts who climbed some 800 feet of difficult class 4 terrain to the summit.

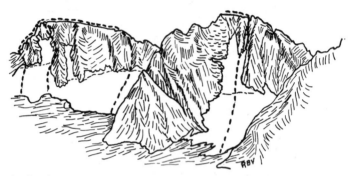

Sketch 16. Mounts Darwin and Mendel from the north. From left to right: Mount Darwin, Routes 4, 3, and 2; Mount Mendel, Route 4.

Route 5. East face, left side. Class 4. First recorded ascent by Morrough O'Brien and Dick Leigh on September 9, 1955. George Wallerstein (second ascent, 1958) reports route as follows: From Blue Heaven Lake (above Midnight Lake) proceed west toward east face. The central and deepest chute in the face leads to the top, but is inaccessible from the bottom due to cliffs. From a point below the rib just to the left of this chute climb up and to the left for about four pitches to get into the leftmost (southernmost) of the chutes in the face. After this the angle eases off. Ascend this chute to its end and traverse right (N) on a broad ledge of darker rock to the deep central chute which is followed to the notch between the Plateau and the Summit Pinnacle. The climbing is class 4 near the bottom, then becomes class 3 and is again class 4 near the top due to the loose nature of the rock.

Route 6. East face, right side. Class 4. Climbed in July, 1960, by a Sierra Club Base Camp party. Many routes are possible and have been worked out on this side of the peak. The primary difficulty is passing the band of cliffs that undercut the avalanche sculptured upper portion of the face. The following route is probably the easiest: From the highest lake under the east face proceed north up a deep scree chute to the Sierra crest. Follow the crest to the northeast ridge of Mount

Darwin. Move left and climb a moderate 60-foot chimney. Follow easy ledges out onto the face, crossing two sharp ribs and working gradually up into the main avalanche chute in the upper portion of the face. Once this chute is gained, the summit plateau is most easily reached by keeping right (N) and coming onto it near the top of the northeast ridge.

Route 7. Southeast ridge. Class 5. Climbed September 6, 1964, by Fred Martin, George Wallerstein, Herbert Weidner, Donald Wilson, and Robert Wyman. From above the south end of Blue Heaven Lake climb class 4 rocks to a notch in the ridge by a band of yellow rock. Follow the ridge to the base of the steep section. Ascend a seventy-foot crack to a ledge on the face of the last gendarme; climb around the corner and up an exposed diagonal crack on the west face of the gendarme. Then it is class 3 to the summit.

Summit Pinnacle. Class 4. The detached summit pinnacle was first climbed by E. C. Andrews on August 12, 1908; he descended into the chimney east of the arête between the summit and the pinnacle, thence reaching the top by means of a "monstrous icicle," referring doubtlessly to the snow tongue which lies in the chimney well into the summer. Ascent of this chimney fortunately does not depend upon the existence of the icicle. It is a rock scramble permitting several variations, exposed just enough to warrant a belay for the unsteady.

Peak 13,280+ (¾ SE of Mt. Darwin; formerly 13,332)

Class 3. Climbed on July 19, 1933, by Glen Dawson, Neil Ruge, and Bala Ballantine. There was no evidence of previous ascent. The southeast face, from the basin west of Hungry Packer Lake is class 2 (Tom Ross).

Mount Haeckel (13,435)

Route 1. West shoulder. Class 3. On July 14, 1920, a party of nine climbers, led by Walter L. Huber, left Evolution Lake, going around the west shoulder of Mount Spencer, and climbed into a small basin between Mounts Spencer and Huxley. From this point they crossed along the left of the basin and then ascended a chute to the top of a ridge which joined the crest just south of the summit. The only serious obstacle remaining, a vertical face of 30–40 feet, was surmounted with the help of a number of excellent hand-holds.

Route 2. South ridge. Class 3. First ascent by Edward O. Allen, Francis E. Crofts, and Olcott Haskell, also on July 14, 1920. From the small basin between Mounts Spencer and Huxley, proceed directly across this amphitheater, climb to the saddle between Mounts Haeckel and Wallace, and traverse the many sawteeth to the summit. Allen, Crofts, and Haskell were quite surprised to find that they had been beaten to the summit by a matter of minutes. Yet, still greater was their surprise on learning that they had not, as they had intended, climbed Mount Darwin.

Route 3. Northwest arête. Class 4. Climbed in 1933 by Jack Riegelhuth. From the notch northwest of the peak follow the crest. It is somewhat easier to stay in the chute left (E) of the arête.

Route 4. East ridge and southeast face. Class 3. Climbed by O. H. Taylor, Angus Taylor, and Merton Brown in 1935. From the saddle east of the peak, traverse southeast slopes upward to the summit.

Route 5. North face. Class 4. Climbed by Mike Loughman and Jay Holliday in 1958. From the lake to the north, climb directly up steep snow and slabs. Traverse right (W) through a notch in a sharp rib and finish in the northwest chute.

Mount Wallace (13,377)

Class 2. First ascent by Theodore S. Solomons, July 16, 1895. From the amphitheater west of the summit, climb up a rock-filled chute that leads to a splintered wall whose highest point is the summit. From Moonlight Lake northwest of the peak, ascend to the Haeckel-Wallace saddle, then south over easy blocks to the summit.

Clyde Spires (13,267)

Between Mounts Wallace and Powell on the main crest are two small granite spires. The north spire (13,267) was first climbed on July 22, 1933, by Norman Clyde, Jules Eichorn, Theodore Waller, Helen LeConte, Julie Mortimer, Dorothy Baird, and John D. Forbes. The south spire was ascended the same day by Clyde, Eichorn and Waller and proved to be a difficult slab climb. The spires were named after the party's leader. The ascents are best made from the southwest (Muir Trail) side. The northeast (Bishop Creek) approach is not advisable due to loose, rotten rock on the approaches.

Mount Powell (13,360+)

There is some confusion as to the true summit of this peak. The high point, containing the official register, is just southeast of the Powell Glacier, and equidistant from Mounts Wallace and Gilbert. An earlier map error was corrected in the 1957 printing. (The lower peak. 0.3 NW of Powell, is class 3 by the west ridge.)

Route 1. South plateau. Class 2. First ascent August 1, 1925, by Walter L. Huber and James Rennie. From Helen Lake climb an intervening ridge of about 12,200 feet, and drop down several hundred feet into a small cirque. Then climb the ridge just south of the summit and follow the long, barren plateau to the top. The final peak is a huge summit block where "a careless step might result in a drop to the glacial ice far below, under the north face."

Route 2. Northwest chute. Class 3. First ascent by Norman Clyde on June 29, 1931, who described it as "an interesting climb from the northwest." Members of the 1950 Sierra Club Base Camp proceeded past Moonlight Lake and ascended snow patches between the Powell ridge and the eastern lateral moraine. They crossed the snow below that flat turret which marks the northeast end of Mount Powell and climbed up the southernmost of two large, parallel cracks in the west wall for twenty feet, after which they climbed the face of the wall itself toward the south.

Route 3. Northeast Ridge. Class 3. First ascent by Norman Clyde (date unknown) who ascended to the col between Mounts Powell and Thompson, then southwest along the broken ridge to the summit.

Route 4. North face. Class 2. First ascent unknown; a large Sierra Club party took this route in June 1961. From Sunset Lake (1 mile SE of Baboon Lake) ascend south up the rock rib that forms the west border of the Thompson Glacier moraine. From the glacier ascend a prominent, steep, scree-filled chute on the left (east) side of the north face. Above the chute, a broad slope leads northwest to the summit.

"Mount Powell—West." Class 3. Northwest Chute. From the outlet of Echo Lake, traverse high into the steep cirque and glacier between the north and west ridges. Climb the glacier and talus to the obvious notch in the west ridge near the summit. Note: The route along the west ridge is broken by a 20-foot jam crack down a slab on the knife-edge, west side of the notch.

Mount Thompson (13,480+)

The first ascent of this peak, which marks the junction of Thompson Ridge with the main crest, was made by Clarence H. Rhudy and H. F. Katzenbach in 1909. Their route is unrecorded. Several routes have since been used.

Route 1. Northwest face. Class 3. First ascent, June 30, 1931, by Norman Clyde. From Sunset Lake ascend the Thompson Glacier to a steep chute near the junction of the northwest face and the Thompson Ridge. Ascend the chute, avoiding an obstruction by traversing left, up and around it, to a notch between the Thompson Ridge and the peak. From the notch, ascend upwards just left (west) of the ridge to the summit. Care should be taken on this route to avoid loosening rocks. Variations are possible using chutes further west on the northwest face; most of these involve class 4.

Route 2. Southwest face. Class 2. First ascent by Jack Sturgeon on August 14, 1939. Ascend via steep slopes and a narrow chute on the face itself. This route can be reached from the north (Sunset Lake) by a class 3 route from the Thompson Glacier to the lowest point on the crest between Mounts Thompson and Powell, then traversing along the steep south side of the crest to the easy south face of the peak.

Route 3. Thompson Ridge. Class 3. In September 1959 Henry Mandolf, Charles Bell, and Stuart Ferguson followed the creek, which leads west southwest from the small lakes east of the peak. At the end of the creek, turn right (WNW) and ascend a long scree slope to the top of the Thompson Ridge. Follow the ridge, a jumbled mass of rocks, south to where it is separated from the main Sierra crest by a deep gap. Descend into the gap (some 100 feet), then ascend via broken benches onto the east face of the peak and up to the summit plateau.

Mount Gilbert (*13,103*)

Route 1. Southeast ridge. Class 2. From Treasure Lakes ascend into the large basin east of the peak. At the head of the basin, ascend a prominent, loose chute to the southeast ridge, then over easy slopes to the summit. First ascent by Norman Clyde on September 15, 1928, who described it as an easy ascent except for a chute which may at times be icy.

Route 2. Southeast slopes. Class 1. From Big Pete Meadow ascend easy southeast slopes to the summit. On August 14, 1939, Jack Sturgeon followed the crest and climbed it by these slopes.

Mount Johnson (*12,868*)

Route 1. North ridge. Class 3. Ascend to the saddle immediately north of Mount Johnson and then up the north ridge to summit.

Route 2. Southeast face. Class 2. From Treasure Lakes ascend south to Lake 11,586, then southwest along the boulder-strewn creek bed and up the southeast slope to the summit.

Route 3. West arête. Class 2. Jack Sturgeon ascended the peak via this route on August 14, 1939, and noted that it had previously been climbed twice by Norman Clyde.

Peak 12,960+ (0.4 W of Mount Goode)

This peak on the Sierra crest appears to be a moderately difficult climb from any side. The northeast side is a sheer, smooth, trapezoidal wall 400 feet high, and the name Trapezoidal Peak is proposed.

The northwest face and the west ridge are class 3, as is a chute that descends to the right of the northeast face.

North buttress. Class 4. Climbed by a Sierra Club Base Camp party in July 1962. They found a cairn, but no records. The ridge that extends to the north of the peak terminates in a prominent, pyramidal peak. Climb the east ridge of this peak and follow the ridge south to the main peak. This route affords more than half a mile of splendid climbing along an airy arête, class 3 with a few class 4 pitches.

Mount Goode (13,092)

Class 1. The first recorded ascent, via the easy southeast face from Bishop Lake, was made by Chester Versteeg, July 16, 1939; a cairn was found but no record. An ascent of the south ridge was made by Jack Sturgeon on August 12, 1939, while traversing the crest from Bishop Pass to Mount Thompson. The sheer north face appears to offer possibilities for rock climbing.

Peak 12,916 (0.5 S of Mount Goode; formerly 12,903)

Class 1. This peak was mistakenly climbed by a Sierra Club party led by Charles Miller in August 1957. Thinking they were climbing Mount Goode, the party upon reaching the summit facetiously named the peak "Mount No Goode." On July 12, 1939, Chester Versteeg made the first recorded ascent of the higher summit. Norman Clyde, in 1936, climbed the lower but more difficult summit, which Versteeg considered to be class 3.

Peaks West of the Crest: The Goddard Divide and North

Peak 12,045 (0.3 SW of Ramona Lake; formerly 12,026)

Class 2. The first ascent of this northernmost peak of the Glacier Divide was made on July 4, 1939, by Marion Abbott and Scott Smith.

Peak 12,591 (1 SE of Ramona Lake; formerly 12,592)

Class 2. First ascent on July 14, 1933, by Hans Helmut Leschke, Dr. Hans Leschke, and Helen LeConte, from the north.

Pavilion Dome (11,846)

Class 2. Appears to be an easy ascent via the southeast slopes. North-west face offers rock climbing possibilities.

Peak 12,241 (1.5 NE of Evolution Meadow; formerly 12,251)

Class 2. Weldon Heald and Alden Smith made the first ascent on July 5, 1939.

Peak 12,498 (1 S of Golden Trout Lake; formerly 12,486)

Class 3. First ascent by Glen Dawson and Neil Ruge on July 11, 1933.

Peak 12,873 (1 S of Packsaddle Lake)

The north arête (class 4) was climbed in 1959.

Peak 12,971 (1.8 S of Golden Trout Lake; formerly 12,961)

Class 2. Northwest of the Goethe Glacier and lying on the crest of the Glacier Divide, this peak was first climbed by R. S. Fink on July 25, 1942. The second ascent was on August 29, 1942, by August Frugé, Neal Harlow, and William A. Sherrill, who climbed from McClure Meadow to the saddle between Peak 12,971 and Peak 13,240+ to the southeast and thence directly to the summit.

Muriel Peak (12,942)

Class 2. First ascent on July 8, 1933, by Hervey Voge, who described it as an easy rock climb from the west. In May 1963 a Sierra Club party ascended the southeast ridge from The Keyhole. Andrew Smatko describes it as high class 2 to low class 3 in a few spots along big blocks until the sloping summit plateau east of the peak is reached.

Mount Goethe (13,240+)

Class 1. First recorded ascent by David R. Brower and George Rock-wood on July 6, 1933. This, the highest point on the Glacier Divide, is an easy ascent from the east. The northeast ridge from Alpine Col is class 3. The north face above the central lobe of the glacier was climbed by Jay Holiday and party in 1959 (class 5).

Peak 12,720+ (1 W of Mount Lamarck; formerly 12,741)

Class 2. First ascent July 5, 1934, by David R. Brower, who climbed the south side and descended the west ridge. There is some scrambling among the large blocks of the summit ridge. Brower could not determine which end of the ridge was higher.

Ridge 12,355 (1.5 NE of Colby Meadow; formerly 11,922)

First ascent July 29, 1941, by members of the Sierra Club knapsack trip.

Peak 13,385 (0.5 NW of Mount Mendel)

No record is available of an ascent of this precipitous peak at the northern end of the Darwin-Mendel Ridge. It appears to offer rock climbing possibilities.

Mount Mendel (13,691)

For many years this peak was erroneously labeled Mount Wallace on the topographic map. On the 1937 edition it bore only the elevation and soon acquired among climbers the rather inelegant title of "Ex-Wallace." On the 1951 edition it has at last been named correctly and thus assumes its rightful place among the great Sierra summits.

The first recorded ascent was by Jules Eichorn, Glen Dawson, and John Olmstead on July 18, 1930; they found a cairn. The chimney by which they ascended was considered more difficult than the climbing on Darwin. It is quite possible that the first ascent was made in error by climbers, seeking the summit of Darwin, who started climbing, as has so often been done, too far north along the shore of Evolution Lake.

Route 1. Southwest face. Class 3. This route is readily apparent from The Hermit. About 400 yards along the Muir Trail south of the peninsula jutting into the lower end of Evolution Lake, a massive buttress of glaciated granite descends from the peak, in contrast to the extensive accumulation of talus bordering the lower half of the east shore. Ascend this buttress for 1,500 feet, diagonally up and southward, until the glaciated granite gives way to the broken rock of the summit mass. Then continue upward by crossing right (SE) to a talus fan, the first fan southeast of the buttress, and ascend this fan into the chute from which it emanates, keeping in the north branch of the chute, to the notch at its head. Thence, traverse north along the broken and serrated ridge to the summit.

Route 2. East slope. Class 3. From upper end of Darwin Canyon, ascend across the north part of the Darwin Glacier to the east face of Mount Mendel. Follow obvious ledges and chutes up to the summit plateau. Near the top keep to the right. This route has much loose rock.

Route 3. Northeast ridge. Class 3. First recorded ascent by Bud Bingham and Don Clarke in 1956. At the base of the northeast buttress, start up a sloping slab leading from the left into a shallow chute on the nose of the buttress. Ascend the chute to about 50 feet short of the crest, then traverse left and gain the ridge. Follow the ridge to the summit.

Route 4. North couloir. Class 5. Two of the most spectacular snow couloirs in the Sierra descend the north face of Mount Mendel. A first ascent of these very steep couloirs was made by Felix Knauth and John Whitmer on June 21, 1958. This route should be attempted only by those well trained in advanced snow and ice techniques. From the base of the north face, ascend steep snow to the bottom of a buttress which splits the couloir. Traverse into the right-hand (western) branch of the couloir, crossing just under the first large ice patch to gain the rocks. About 300 feet of class 4 rock climbing brings the climber to the crux of the route: a 60° ice slope that spans the couloir and stretches upward out of sight. Ascend the ice, using the rock walls for handholds and belay points whenever possible. Ice pitons should be used at several points for safety. The final pitch is a 15-foot vertical wall of crusty snow (possibly ice in late summer) that leads into a notch. From the notch several class 3 pitches are ascended to the summit.

The Hermit (*12,360*)

The cleanly sculptured granite of The Hermit culminates in an inviting summit that dominates the view from Colby Meadow. It was first ascended by L. Keeler, R. Brandt, and party, July 2, 1924, and again by G. R. Bunn, July 28, 1924, by unstated routes.

The final summit monolith was ascended by Keeler and Brandt, and in 1925 by James Rennie and Norman Clyde. Bunn had declared that the "20-foot summit slab" was unclimbable. However, it was climbed by sixty-five persons in three days in July, 1939. Because of the exposure, a rope is recommended for the final pitch. A shoulder stand is usually used and dexterity is required.

Route 1. From Evolution Lake. Class 2. The easiest and most often used route is to cross just below Evolution Lake, contour to the base of the peak, and climb the eastern talus chute to the notch just south of the summit, traversing from there to the summit. From the base of the peak on the east side it is also fairly simple to work out on the more exposed face and thence directly to the summit.

Another variation is to ascend the eastern talus chute about a third of the way up. Just before the chute divides, ascend an obvious slanted ledge on the right (north) that leads out of the chute and onto the east face. Ascend directly up the east face (class 3) over numerous ledges to the summit block.

Route 2. From McGee Canyon. Class 2. Ascend McGee Canyon to about 10,400 feet and proceed east up the first tributary to the small lake that feeds it; thence, ascend over talus and scree to the top of the chute heading in the notch south of the summit, from which point proceed as in Route 1. Special care must be taken to avoid loosening the rocks in the chute.

Route 3. North ridge. Class 3. First ascent on July 9, 1936, by Richard G. Johnson and Peter Grubb. From Colby Meadow ascend through forest and over easy, open granite to a shelf on the north shoulder, usually sheltering a snow bank, just beneath the high-angle granite slabs of the final 1,000 feet of the summit. From here traverse to the left (E) under the cliffs and proceed diagonally up and westward over granite slabs, now more broken and at a lower angle, to the final summit pitch which must be reached by traversing to the south of the peak, 25 feet below the summit.

Route 4. Northwest face. Class 3. First ascent July 9, 1939, by Harriet Parsons, Madi Bacon, and Maxine Cushing. Follow Route 3 to the snow-bearing shelf. Here a broad ledge extends up and around the west face to a chute leading back to the shoulder, but above the cliffs that shelter the snow. Continue over the steep but broken ridge to the summit, as in Route 3.

Peak 12,350 (½ SE of The Hermit; formerly 12,341)

This peak erroneously bore the name of The Hermit on an earlier edition of the map. It was first climbed by Dr. Grove Karl Gilbert and Mr. Kanawyer, the packer, in July, 1904. It is a class 1 climb by either the southeast ridge or from the saddle on the northwest ridge.

Mount Spencer (12,440+)

Class 1. First climbed by Robert M. Price, George J. Young, H. W. Hill, and Peter Frandsen on August 20, 1921. About one-half mile above Evolution Lake ascend one and a half miles east along a tributary creek, reaching lake 11,592. Climb over broken granite and talus to the east saddle of the peak, thence westward and up to the summit. The saddle is just as easily reached from the lake basin east of Sapphire Lake.

Mount Fiske (13,524)

Named in 1895 by Theodore S. Solomons for John Fiske, historian and philosopher, this peak was first climbed by Charles Norman Fiske, John N. Fiske, Stephen B. Fiske, and Frederick Kellet on August 10, 1922.

Route 1. Southeast ridge. Class 1. First ascent by the above party on August 10, 1922. From Muir Pass contour at about 12,000 feet around the southeast side of Peak 13,231, and then drop down about 200 feet to the small lake to the northwest of Helen Lake. A steady climb then leads to the southeast peak, whence the ridge may be followed to the summit.

Route 2. Southwest ridge. Class 2. First ascent on August 18, 1939, by Jack Sturgeon, who traversed from Peak 13,231 and the basin to the south, ascending by way of the southwest arête. The southwest saddle is easily accessible from the group of lakes, nestled between Mounts Fiske and Huxley, which drain into Sapphire Lake. The nivated slope east of this ridge provides a class 1 route.

Route 3. Northeast ridge. Class 2. First recorded ascent by Andrew Smatko, Peter Hunt, and John Robinson on August 20, 1958. From the basin west of Mount Wallace, ascend the steep northeast ridge to the east peak of Mount Fiske, then across easy slopes to the main summit.

Mount Huxley (13,117)

Class 3. First ascent by Norman Clyde on July 15, 1920. From the trail on the first bench above Sapphire Lake, ascend the southern side of the western shoulder until the angle steepens appreciably; then continue up the shallow chute, which empties almost on the shoulder itself, to the slabs and large blocks of the sharp summit arête. Descent of the southwest chute and face may require the use of rope.

Peak 13,231 (1 N of Muir Pass; formerly 13,223)

Class 1. First ascent in 1926 by Nathaniel Goodrich and Marjory Hurd. This is an easy traverse from either Muir Pass or Mount Huxley. The best opportunities for rock climbing are found on the east face and in the small cirque to the north of the summit, between Mounts Huxley and Fiske, but no climbing has yet been reported there.

Peak 12,800+ (0.7 W of Muir Pass)

Class 2 from east ridge. First ascent by Jack W. Sturgeon in 1939.

Peak 13,016 (0.5 SW of Muir Pass; formerly 13,012)

Class 2. The first ascent was made by M. H. Pramme and T. F. Harms on August 12, 1929. It is an easy climb directly from Muir Pass via the northeast shoulder or by the snow chute which heads in very loose rock just under the flat summit. By way of the southwest ridge it is a class 1 climb, but the ridge itself is remote. The summit affords a striking view of Scylla, Charybdis, and the Ionian Basin.

Peak 13,081 (1 S of Wanda Lake; formerly 13,070)

Class 1. First ascent by Jack Sturgeon on August 16, 1939. Held to be an easy climb by the northeast ridge or almost anywhere on the southern or western slopes.

Mount Goddard (13,568)

The early history of the Evolution Region is, in many respects, the early history of Mount Goddard. Many were the explorers who were enamoured of its summit, and for good reason: it was not only one of the highest summits in the range, but also it was well isolated, distinctly set off to the west of the crest, and could promise a unique view and admirable triangulation station for topographic mapping. Members of the Whitney Survey viewed the peak from far to the south in 1864, named it in honor of civil-engineer George Henry Goddard, attempted to climb it twice, and estimated the height to be 14,000 feet. It was not climbed, however, until fifteen years later, when, on September 23, 1879, Lil A. Winchell and Louis W. Davis made the first ascent. A winter ascent was made February 4, 1964.

Mount Goddard has twin summits about 200 yards apart, and there is some dispute as to which one is higher. The register has been moved back and forth between the summits for the last 35 years, and presently (1963) rests on the southern one. Sighting back and forth with a hand level, the north peak appears to be several feet higher.

Route 1. Northeast couloir and ridge. Class 2–3. Walter Starr, Jr., has given a detailed description of this approach from the Muir Trail, which is essentially as follows:

At the lower end of Wanda Lake, ford the outlet, cross the saddle to the southwest at its lowest point, and descend into the rocky basin beyond. Continue almost due south across the basin, fording several small streams some distance above Davis Lake, and proceed toward the very steep spur which ascends from the floor of the basin southward to the crest of the Goddard Divide. Rock climbers may proceed straight up the very steep top of the ridge from the floor of the basin. Those who prefer snow climbing may work their way onto the buttress higher up from the snow on the right. A short distance below the crest, where the buttress becomes almost perpendicular, a ledge leads around the left side, above the long snowfield, and comes out on the crest to the left of the point at the top of the buttress. From here a long talus slope leads up the crest to the summit.

Route 2. Goddard Divide and east slope. Class 2. Russ and Paul Mohn report this route is easier and faster than the traditional Starr route. Take the relatively low angle gully south from Wanda Lake to the Goddard Divide, then traverse along the south side of the divide and up the long east talus slope to the summit. The Mohns' time from Wanda Lake to the summit was 3¼ hours, faster than any register entries for the Starr route.

Route 3. Southwest ridge. Class 2. Ascend east from Martha Lake and then northeast up the talus slopes to the summit.

Peak 12,410 (1.2 SW of Mount Goddard)

Climbed August 25, 1963, by Karl and Paul Leavitt and Ed James, via the southwest ridge. Class 2.

Peak 12,913 (1 N of Mount Goddard; formerly 12,908)

First ascent by R. S. Fink on July 27, 1941, by an unrecorded route. Second ascent on September 2, 1942, by August Frugé, William A. Sherrill, and Neal Harlow whose route was as follows:

Class 3 to 4. After leaving the Muir Trail at the outlet of Wanda Lake, proceed over the low saddle to the southwest and thence across the large basin toward the narrow ridge connecting Peak 12,913 with the crest of the Goddard Divide. Ascend this ridge via the steep, blunt buttress to the southeast of the summit. Then follow the ridge, passing to the right (E) of a large pinnacle and then out onto the left (W) side of the ridge, traversing onto the steep south face of the summit mass itself. A narrow chimney then leads up to several chutes which may be followed to the summit.

Peak 12,290 (1 NW of Wanda Lake; formerly 12,279)

Class 1. First ascent by Kenneth Adam, 1933. This peak may be easily climbed from the north or east.

Mount McGee (12,969)

Mount McGee dominates the westerly panorama from Muir Pass.

Sharply sculptured, dark with metamorphic rock, it is situated just far enough from the Muir Trail to have discouraged most climbers who might have liked to reach the summit. It may be approached from Goddard Canyon, Colby Meadow, or from Wanda and Davis lakes. It was first climbed July 11, 1923, by Roger N. Burnham, Robert E. Brownlee, Ralph H. Brandt, and Leonard Keeler; their route is unrecorded.

Route 1. North chute. Class 4. First ascent by Glen Dawson, Charles Dodge, Jules M. Eichorn, and John Olmstead on July 16, 1930. From Colby Meadow proceed up McGee Canyon directly toward the summit, turning southwest when past timberline to climb over moraine and talus toward a spur at the base of the west peak, which resembles a massive inverted shield. Ascend the ridge that circles west of the residual glacier and which deflects westward the drainage from the mouth of the steep snow-chute cleft in the north face of the peak, but well to the west of its center. It is usually possible to ascend this chute along the edge, where the snow has melted back from the rock wall. The last 800 feet of the chute is exposed enough to merit use of a rope for safety. From the notch at the top of the chute, proceed east along the well-broken ridge to the summit.

Route 2. West face. Class 2. First ascent by Glen Dawson, Neil Ruge, and Bala Ballantine on July 17, 1933. From Goddard Canyon ascend the east fork of North Goddard Creek to about 11,000 feet. Proceed northwest to the base of the west face and ascend the talus to the summit of the west peak, traversing from there into the notch at the head of Route 1.

Route 3. South chute. Class 2. (Probably the route of the first ascent.) From the lower end of Davis Lake ascend the broad fan of scree and talus to the prominent chute ending in the notch between the west and east summits. Ascend the scree in this chute to the notch and proceed east to the summit. The sliding nature of the scree makes this route a bit disagreeable as a means of ascent.

Peter Peak (*12,543*)

Class 2. First ascent on July 11, 1936, by Peter Grubb and Richard G. Johnson. Ascend to the northeast notch from the head of McGee Canyon, and climb the ridge to the summit. Grubb and Johnson also climbed the eastern buttress of the peak when making the first ascent. The metamorphic rock of the peak, and particularly of the chute leading to the notch, is quite unsound. One must "hold the mountain together with one hand while he climbs it with the other."

Peak 12,400+ (¾ SE of Emerald Peak; formerly 12,407)

First ascent July 9, 1939, by Alden Smith and Grace Nelson.

Emerald Peak (12,543)

Class 2. First ascent made by Norman Clyde, Julie Mortimer, and Eleanor Bartlett, August 8, 1925. From Evolution Meadow ascend the steep south wall of the canyon and continue over the gradual slope above to the north base of Peak 11,778. It is perfectly feasible to climb this peak first, traversing the northwest ridge of Emerald Peak to its summit. It is much easier, however, to contour a mile at 11,000 feet (timberline) until almost due west of the peak, thence climbing over talus and nivated slope to the top.

South of Goddard Divide

South of the Goddard Divide, between LeConte Canyon and the White Divide, is the wildest part of the High Sierra. Place names are rather far between. From the old map it is apparent that the Geological Survey parties were not too familiar with the topography. Lack of trails, rugged terrain, high altitude and low timberline, remoteness, and the lack of any great number of mountaineers who would prefer to cope with these conditions—all this has contributed to the final result: a knapsacker's wilderness, black, rugged, and enchanting.

Peak 12,760+ (0.7 SE of Muir Pass; formerly 12,700+)

First ascent by Jack W. Sturgeon in 1939; route unknown. This peak was climbed in July 1952 by Oliver Kehrlein, Toni Gamero, Peter Raven, George Wallerstein, and John Williams via the col northwest of it; class 2.

Scylla (12,939)

Class 2. First ascent by David R. Brower and Hervey Voge on July 3, 1934. From Muir Pass ascend southwest to the col immediately west of Peak 13,016 and drop into the Ionian Basin. Contour southwest around the west side of Lake 11,560+ and along the east shore of Lake 11,824 to the lake just north of Scylla. From here the route up the northwest slope to the summit is an easy scramble. The three pinnacles east of Scylla have been called The Three Sirens. The central and western ones were climbed (class 4) in August 1963 by George Wallerstein, Don Wilson, and Mike Raudenbush.

Peak 12,855 (0.5 SW of Scylla)

Class 1. First ascent by Robin McKeown and Frank Orme on August 17, 1954. Easy talus climb from north or west.

Peak 12,960+ (0.5 S of Peak 12,855)

Class 1. This high point of the Ragged Spur south of Scylla was climbed by Robin McKeown and Frank Orme, August 17, 1954.

Peak 11,833 (1 SW of Scylla)

Class 1. First ascent by Paul J. Sullivan on August 31, 1954. Easy climb from Goddard Creek.

Peak 12,841 (1.5 S of Scylla)

Class 1. First ascent by Robin McKeown and Frank Orme.

Peak 11,587 (1.2 SE of Peak 12,841)

No record is available.

Peak 10,927 (1 SE of Peak 11,587)

No recorded ascent of this peak at the southeast end of the Ragged Spur is available.

Charybdis (13,091)

Class 3. First ascent on July 7, 1931, by Anna and John R. Dempster. Cross Black Giant Pass to the large lake at the head of the east fork of Disappearing Creek and follow up the northeast ridge, going somewhat to the south of the ridge at times. There are several chutes on the north face, any of which may be used.

Peak 12,800+ (1 E of Muir Pass; formerly 12,818)

Class 1. First ascent by Kenneth Davis and John U. White on August 3, 1938, from Muir Pass via the west slope.

Black Giant (13,330)

Class 1. First ascent by George R. Davis in 1905. Along the western side the climb is little more than a rock scramble. On the eastern approaches, however, the whole ridge is sharply broken off. Any ascent from this side would be considerably more difficult.

Peak 12,804 (1 SE of Black Giant)

Class 2. First recorded ascent by Andrew Smatko, Tom Ross, Phil Clayton, Gordon MacLeod, Jess Logan, Ellen Siegal, and Neko Colevins in August 1963. Easy ascent from northwest, west, or southwest. The east ridge appears to be class 3.

Peak 13,046 (1.5 E of Charybdis)

Class 2 up northwest slopes. First known ascent by Carl Miller in October 1952. Frank Orme and Robin McKeown ascended the peak on August 13, 1954, by means of a steep chute on the southwest side, and reported it class 2 with some class 3 the last 200 feet.

Mount Duncan McDuffie (13,271)

This peak was named after a former Sierra Club president.

Route 1. North ridge. Class 3. First ascent by Charles Bays Locker, Karl Hufbauer, and Alfred Elkin on July 23, 1951. From the northwest, climb to the saddle between Mount McDuffie and Peak 13,046, and thence south along the ridge, keeping 100–150 feet below the crest on the west side. Upon nearing the peak, ascend the rocks to the left (E) of the wide snow chute on the north-northwest side of the summit mass. A slightly more difficult variation is to take the narrower and shorter snow chute on the west face. Proceed up the left (N) side of the chute about two-thirds of the way up, then cross to the right (S) side of the chute and climb over exposed class 3 to the summit.

Route 2. Southeast ridge. Class 2. First ascent by Charles Bays Locker, Don Albright, Gary Hufbauer, and Karl Hufbauer on July 15, 1952. From Ladder Lake proceed west southwest up the broad ridge to the small lake at about 12,000 feet. From here it is a short climb to gain the southeast ridge. Follow the ridge mostly on the west side to the summit.

Route 3. Southwest ridge. Looking from Wheel Mountain, Andrew Smatko reports that there appears to be an easy class 2 route up the southwest ridge from Enchanted Gorge. From the small lake southeast of the summit, head northwest, contouring to gain the southwest ridge. Then ascend easy class 2 slopes to the summit. Although this is possibly the easiest route up the peak, it is also the most inaccessible.

Peak 12,125 (1 W of Langille Peak; formerly 12,114)

Class 2. First ascent by George R. Davis and George W. Hoop on

August 19, 1907. This is a class 2 climb by either the southwest ridge or on a traverse from Langille Peak.

Langille Peak (11,991)

Class 3. The first ascent of this magnificent example of finely sculptured, gleaming granite was accomplished in August 1926 by Nathaniel L. Goodrich, Marjory Hurd, and Dean Peabody, Jr. The route of their ascent is unrecorded, possibly via the west ridge. They descended by way of the south face, a vast glaciated granite apron of polished smoothness (class 3). The first ascent by this latter route was made by Glen Warner and Suzanne Burgess on August 5, 1941. From LeConte Canyon ascend the tributary opposite the Dusy Branch and climb the cirque wall just north of the prominent waterfall above 11,000 feet. Traverse to the north onto the west ridge, and follow this to the summit.

Peak 12,652 (1.3 S of Mount Goode; formerly 12,699)

Class 1. First recorded ascent by Chester Versteeg on July 14, 1939. An easy climb either by the southeast ridge or from Dusy Basin on the south.

Peak 12,520+ (2.2 E of Charybdis; formerly 12,566)

First ascent August 5, 1941, by Glen Warner and Suzanne Burgess. From LeConte Canyon ascend the tributary opposite Dusy Branch to 10,500 feet. A narrow snow chute provides a class 3 route up the north face.

Peak 12,483 (1.5 N of Ladder Lake; formerly 12,400+)

First ascent July 13, 1952, by Charles Bays Locker, Karl Hufbauer, and Don Albright. A difficult class 3 climb from Ladder Lake via the south arête.

Peak 12,920+ (1 SE of Charybdis; formerly 12,935)

Class 2 from the west. First ascent by Frank Orme and Robin McKeown on August 14, 1954.

The Citadel (11,744)

Route 1. West ridge. Class 2. First ascent on June 24, 1951, by Richard Searle and William Wirt. Proceed from Ladder Lake directly up the west ridge to the summit.

Route 2. Northeast face. Class 4. First ascent by Donald Goodrich and Robert Means on June 24, 1951, arriving on top several hours after the party of the first route. Ascend the northeast face via several gullies and chutes to the summit ridge, climbing southwest along this ridge over the subsidiary East Peak and traversing along the ridge to the higher West Peak.

Route 3. North wall. Class 4. First ascent by Charles Bays Locker, R. J. McKenna, S. Hall, D. E. Albright, and Karl G. Hufbauer. Ascend to the base of the northwest buttress from the eastern end of Ladder Lake. Climb up the first chute on the northwest side of the peak. From the top of the chute proceed along the ridge to the left (E) directly to the summit.

Peak 12,009 (1.5 W of Grouse Meadow; formerly 12,015)

Route 1. Southeast arête. Class 2. First ascent on August 9, 1934, by H. B. Blanks and B. S. Kaiser who climbed from the Rambaud Lake Basin via the southeast arête. This party made a complete traverse of the ridge from east to west.

Route 2. North ridge. Class 2. First ascent by this route by Charles Bays Locker, Donald Albright, Gary Hufbauer, and Karl Hufbauer. Climb from Ladder Lake in a southeasterly direction to the north ridge and follow it to the summit; no particular obstacles are encountered.

The western summit of this peak (approx. 12,000) was also climbed by both parties and is a class 1 traverse from the eastern summit.

Peak 12,425 (1 SW of Ladder Lake; formerly 12,400+)

Class 3. First ascent on August 9, 1934, by H. B. Blanks and B. S. Kaiser who traversed the ridge from the east.

Peak 12,760+ (1 NW of Wheel Mtn.; formerly 12,767)

First ascent by Charles Bays Locker, Donald Albright, and Gary and Karl Hufbauer, July 15, 1952. Class 3 from the crest of the Black Divide.

Wheel Mountain (12,781)

Route 1. Northwest slopes. Class 3. First ascent on July 26, 1933, by Marjory Bridge, John Cahill, Lewis F. Clark, and John Poindexter. Ascend from the lakes at the head of Rambaud Creek to the saddle in the southeast ridge (11,553), then drop 300–400 feet to the plateau southwest, west, and northwest of the mountain. Ascend the northwest slopes either on shallow ridges or up steep snow to the main ridge east of the summit. Proceed about 100 feet on class 3 rocks to the summit.

Descent is possible by means of two steep, loose gullies on the south face.

Route 2. Southeast ridge. Class 3. First recorded ascent by Phil Clayton, Jess Logan, Tom Ross, and Andrew Smatko in August 1963. Ascend the southeast ridge from the saddle (11,553). Upon approaching jagged rocks above and to the right, contour below them on the west. A 30-foot wide chute heads up east between sheer walls for about 60–75 feet. Ascend this easy chute and gain the rocks on the left (north) at the head of the chute. Ascend 30–40 feet of easy class 3 to the summit. Note: A landmark for the chute described above is a small lake that lies immediately below and to the west.

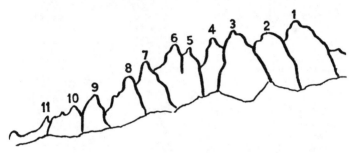

Sketch 17. The Devil's Crags from Rambaud Peak.

Rambaud Peak (11,040+)

Class 2. First ascent in 1925 by Albert Tachet and Ruth Prager. This is a scramble from Rambaud Creek campsites to the north, and is an excellent point from which to study the Devil's Crags.

Devil's Crags (12,600–11,240+)

The Devil's Crags are about two miles southwest of Grouse Meadow and form the southern end of the Black Divide. They are slightly over a mile in length, have a northwest-southeast trend, and the highest crag is at the northern end. Although several systems of numbering have been employed, the system here used numbers only those crags which rise 150 feet or more above their notches (see Sketches 17 and 18). Since this nomenclatorial system is rather recent, the numbers in the crag registers will not always be in agreement. There are eleven crags, and the routes of ascent lie, generally, in their neighboring chutes. From the southwest the chutes which are fairly easy to climb (class 4 mostly) are those between Crags 2–3–4, 6–7–8–9–10. From the northeast, they are 2–3, 4–5, 8–9.

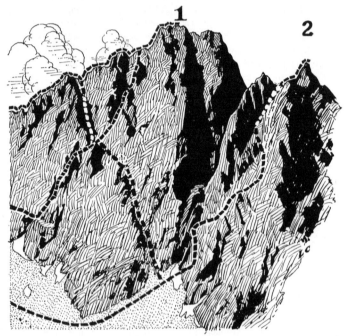

Sketch 18. Devil's Crags 1 and 2 from the west.

Crag 1 (12,600+)

Route 1. Southwest face. Class 4. First ascent made by Charles Michael on July 21, 1913. Andrew Smatko reports the best route as follows: From Rambaud Creek ascend to the prominent saddle (11,553) one-half mile southeast of Wheel Mountain. Proceed southeast to an easy high point, then descend to the saddle immediately below. Descend about 500 feet down a fast scree slope that heads south into the gradually sloping basin west of the crags. Then ascend any one of several obvious routes into a long diagonal chute that crosses the southwest face of Crag 1 from the lower right (south) to the upper left (north). Ascend this chute all the way to the arête, and proceed southeast along the arête to the summit. A more difficult variation is to ascend the chute about halfway up, then take a steep chute directly up to the arête just northwest of the summit.

Route 2. Northwest arête. Class 4. First ascent by Jules Eichorn, Helen LeConte, and Alfred Weiler on July 25, 1933. Follow the crest of the northwest arête to the summit.

Route 3. Northeast face. Class 4. First ascent by Raffi Bedayan, Kenneth Davis, and Jack Riegelhuth on August 5, 1938. From the upper end of the lake at 10,450 feet on Rambaud Creek, proceed southeast half a mile to the notch just under and northeast of the face; this is the roping-up point. Traverse to the right (northwest) and up over somewhat loose rocks of a delicate pitch to the chute marking the middle of the face, planning the traverse so as to end well above the overhanging lower portion of the chute. Ascend this chute toward the summit over rock that is fairly sound. Belay positions are good for the most part. When 35 feet below the summit, cross to the north wall of the chute, ascend a high-angle pitch to the summit ridge, and scramble to the top.

Crag 2 (12,350)

Class 4. First ascent by Jules Eichorn, Glen Dawson, and Ted Waller on July 26, 1933. Climb the first chimney south of the summit on the northeast side. It is most difficult in the lower portion. From the notch the ridge is easily climbed to the summit. From the southwest it is possible to climb the chute that heads between Crag 2 and the subsidiary crag to the north. From the notch follow the arête.

Crag 3 (12,350)

First ascent by David R. Brower, Hervey Voge, and Norman Clyde on June 24, 1934.

Route 1. From the northeast. Class 4. Climb the northeast chute between Crags 2 and 3, remaining on the floor of the chute and passing under the huge chockstone. From the notch climb the first pitch by the left side of the broken face. Contour out and up on the broad, sloping ledge on the north face to the north arête. Climb the left side of this to the northwest arête, and thence to the summit. With little more difficulty the northwest arête may be followed from the notch.

Route 2. Traverse. Class 4. The southeast arête may be descended 250 feet without too much difficulty. Descend a sloping, broken ledge heading on the east side of the peak. Follow this down and to the south, traversing easterly to a very broad shelf when the angle becomes too severe. Climb down an additional 60 feet just west of the southeast arête. Ensuing overhangs will suggest roping down into the notch between Crags 3 and 4. Descend via the southwest chute. If this route is used for an ascent, pitons are necessary for safety while climbing the largest overhang, 100 feet above the notch.

Route 3. From the southwest. Class 3. Climb the southwest chute between Crags 2 and 3 to the 2–3 notch, following Route 1 from the notch.

Crag 4 (*12,250*)

Class 3. First ascent by David R. Brower, Hervey Voge, and Norman Clyde on June 24, 1934. From the southwest reach the 3–4 notch and follow the much-broken westerly side of the northwest arête to the summit. Descend the same route. A traverse would involve an 800-foot descent on a steep, ledgeless face.

Crag 5 (*12,250*)

Class 3. First ascent by David R. Brower, Hervey Voge, and Norman Clyde on June 25, 1934. From the northeast climb the floor of the northeast chute between Crags 4 and 5, keeping to the left branch at the extreme top. From the notch contour into the shallow western chute, up which there are several variations in route to the arête above. Follow the arête to within about 25 feet of the summit monolith, contour around the western side, and walk up the south debris to the summit. There are several routes of descent on the southeast arête.

Crag 6 (*12,250*)

Class 3. First ascent by David R. Brower, Hervey Voge, and Norman Clyde on June 25, 1934. From the northeast follow the arête from Crag 5 to the 5–6 notch, and ascend the west side of the northwest arête.

Crag 7 (*12,250*)

Class 3. First ascent by David R. Brower, Hervey Voge, and Norman Clyde on June 25, 1934. From the northeast walk up the northwest arête from the 6–7 notch, which has been reached by the traverse of Crags 5 and 6. Descend the southwest chute, roping down in the lower portion.

Crag 8 (*12,250*)

Class 2. First ascent by David R. Brower, Hervey Voge, and Norman Clyde on June 25, 1934. From the southwest climb the southwest chute between Crags 7 and 8, and follow the northwest slope to the summit.

Crag 9 (*11,950*)

First ascent by Glen Dawson and Jules Eichorn on August 1, 1933.

Route 1. From the northeast or the southwest. Class 4. Climb to the notch between Crags 8 and 9 by either the northeast or southwest chutes. From the notch climb up and slightly to the west onto the arête, which is followed just below and to the north of its crest to the summit.

Route 2. Traverse. Class 4. A traverse involves a little climbing and two rope-downs into the 9–10 notch, from which one may descend by traversing Crag 10.

Crag 10 (*11,950*)

First ascent by David R. Brower, Hervey Voge, and Norman Clyde on June 23, 1934.

Route 1. From the northwest. Class 4. Traverse Crag 9 to the 9–10 notch and follow the west side of the northwest arête to the summit.

Route 2. From the southeast. Class 2. Climb the northeast chute between Crags 10 and 11 to the 10–11 notch. Traverse to the northwest, over a subsidiary crag and along the arête to the summit.

Crag 11 (*11,950*)

Class 4. First ascent by David R. Brower, Hervey Voge, and Norman Clyde on June 23, 1934. Climb the northeast chute between Crags 10 and 11 to the 10–11 notch. From the notch climb up toward the summit over rather exposed pitches on somewhat broken rock.

Mount Woodworth (*12,219*)

Class 2. First ascent by Professor Bolton Coit Brown on August 1, 1895, who climbed straight up the southwest spur, and above this followed along the base of the jagged spires bounding the southern face. Descent was along the easterly edge of the south face.

The north ridge is also class 2, and can be readily reached from the basin northwest of the peak.

Peaks East of the Crest

Peak 12,320+ (*0.7 SE of Piute Pass; formerly 12,317*)

First ascent on July 3, 1939, by Jim Harkins, Fred Toby, and Bert

Malcolm. Contour from Piute Pass to the north shoulder and then follow this to the summit.

Peak 12,707 (1.5 SE of Piute Pass; formerly 12,702)

Class 2. First ascent by John Cahill and Neil Ruge on July 9, 1933, from the north fork of Lamarck Creek. Arkel Erb and Andrew Smatko climbed this peak via the west ridge in May 1963. Their route was as follows: Proceed south from Piute Lake over the spur west of Emerson Lake, drop into the basin, and then gain the west ridge one mile west of the summit. Proceed along the class 2–3 ridge to the top. Their descent was via the northwest slopes directly to Emerson Lake (class 2).

Peak 11,215 (1 SE of Lake Sabrina; formerly 11,257)

Class 3. First ascent by Chester Versteeg on July 21, 1939, who suggested it be named "The Axe Blade." An easy climb from Lake Sabrina southeast and up to the summit monolith, which is a rock climb.

Table Mountain (11,696)

Class 1. First ascent October 24, 1931, by Norman Clyde. The easiest route is along the trail between George and Tyee lakes until beneath the summit rock pile.

Peak 13,198 (1 SE of Mount Lamarck; formerly 13,202)

First recorded ascent of this peak was made by Norman Clyde in 1925. Class 2 up north or northwest slopes.

Peak 11,760+ (2 S of Lake Sabrina; formerly 11,827)

Class 2. First ascent by Angus E. Taylor on July 29, 1936. This peak is an easy climb from the west and south except near the summit.

Peak 12,993 (1.5 N of Mount Thompson)

First ascent by Norman Clyde on November 7, 1931. A class 1 climb along the east arête and a class 2 climb from the southeast face.

Peak 13,120+ (0.7 E of Mount Haeckel)

First ascent by Norman Clyde in 1931.

Route 1. Southwest side. Class 3. The chutes that descend this side are generally easy, but terminate in short cliffs.

Route 2. North face. Class 4. Climbed by Sierra Club Base Camp party in 1960. From the cirque north of the peak, ascend scree about two-thirds of the way to the deep notch between the main peak and the spectacular northeast buttress. Climb diagonally across a broken face toward the summit, and ascend a chute to the top. Tho rock is unsound on this route.

Route 3. East side. Class 5. Dick Grunebaum, Mike Loughman, Bob Orser, and Rick Polsdorfer reached the northeast notch and the top of the northeast buttress from the east in several hundred feet of rock climbing in 1958.

Peak 12,400+ (0.5 W of Sunset Lake)

Class 2. First ascent by Kenneth Taylor and party on July 15, 1961.

Peak 13,000+ (1 NE of Mount Thompson; formerly 13,029)

Class 2. First ascent by Chester Versteeg on July 24, 1939, who suggested the name "Mount Fusilade." Class 2 from the northwest. Third class along south wall of a divide about 600 yards from the top; summit rock mass class 5.

Peak 13,323 (0.4 NE of Mount Thompson; formerly 13,350)

Norman Clyde made the first ascent of this peak on September 6, 1931.

Peak 13,300+ (0.5 N of Mount Powell; formerly 13,000+)

First ascent of this peak was accomplished by Walter L. Huber and James Rennie on August 1, 1925.

Hurd Peak (12,219)

First ascent by H. C. Hurd in 1906, route unknown. It is a class 3 climb from Treasure Lakes via the west face. The south ridge is class 4.

The Palisades Region

HERVEY H. VOGE and DAVID R. BROWER (1939); LARRY WILLIAMS (1964)

ALTHOUGH there are higher peaks in the Sierra Nevada than those found in the Palisade Group, there are none of bolder or more rugged relief, or more beautifully alpine in character. The Palisades divide the watersheds of the Middle Fork of the Kings and the branches of Big Pine Creek; they rise 6,000 feet above LeConte Canyon to the west and nearly two vertical miles above the desert environs of the little town of Big Pine to the east. The Palisades form the second highest group in the Sierra. They are about 40 miles northwest of the higher Muir Crest peaks which culminate in Mount Whitney, and about 70 miles southeast of Yosemite. North Palisade (14,242) is the third highest peak in the Sierra. Five other points of the Palisade range exceed 14,000 feet in elevation: the northwest peak of North Palisade (about 14,200), Mount Sill (14,162), Middle Palisade (14,040), Thunderbolt Peak (about 14,040), and Polomonium Peak (about 14,040). Split Mountain (14,058), formerly known as South Palisade, is actually apart from the Palisades, and is not included in this area of the Guide. Maps for this region are the Mount Goddard and Big Pine quadrangles. Sketch 19 is an outline map.

Historical Résumé

THE PALISADES were named by the California State Geological Survey in 1864; the heights of North Palisade and Split Mountain were determined at over 14,000 feet in 1875 by the Wheeler Survey. Four years later Lil A. Winchell was in the region and named Mount Winchell, after his father's cousin, geologist Alexander Winchell, and Agassiz Needle, after naturalist Louis Agassiz. It is hardly possible that "Agassiz Needle" could have been intended for the gradual peak which bears the name on the topographic map, and, in order to correct a false impression, the name "Mount Agassiz" has been substituted. Winchell also gave the name "Dusy Peak" to North Palisade, but the name did not become established. In 1895 Professor Bolton Coit Brown renamed it "Mount Jordan"; but finally the original "North Palisade," an admirably descriptive name, was restored, and David Starr Jordan was commemorated by a peak on the Kings-Kern Divide.

Approaching the Palisades from Cartridge Creek in 1903, Joseph N. LeConte, with James S. Hutchinson, James K. Moffitt, and Robert Pike attempted to climb North Palisade. Stopped in their first attempt, they turned to Mount Sill, and met with success on its easier slopes. The following day, however, July 25, 1903, they discovered a route, and LeConte, Hutchinson, and Moffitt made the first ascent of North Palisade.

Middle Palisade did not fall so soon or so easily. An unsuccessful attempt was made July 20, 1919, when H. H. Bliss, A. L. Jordan and J. M. Davies climbed a peak just south of the true summit, which they named "Peak Disappointment" upon discovering their error. A storm stopped a subsequent attempt upon the correct peak. Two years later, Francis

P. Farquhar and Ansel F. Hall, unaware of the earlier attempt, repeated the mistake, but upon discovering their error descended 2,000 feet and then climbed the true summit, thus accomplishing the first ascent, on August 26, 1921.

For the pioneering of new and more difficult routes in the region principal credit must go to Norman Clyde, veteran of at least a thousand Sierran ascents. Because of his residence in Owens Valley, it was natural that his interest in the Palisades should center upon routes from the glaciers. Clyde, a remarkable man, has written numerous articles about the Sierra, and has long remained active in climbing, exploration, and rescue work. As recently as the summer of 1963, when in his late seventies, Norman offered to help in the difficult removal of the body of a climber from the Middle Palisade.

Several fourth class routes were established in 1931, when a party of nine, led by Robert L. M. Underhill, of the Appalachian Mountain Club, and Farquhar and Clyde, of the Sierra Club, introduced the proper use of the rope to the Sierra. Routes of still greater difficulty have evolved from the application of pitoncraft. One should not conclude that all the climbs of moderate difficulty have already been made, although it is likely that quite a few not reported below have been done.

TOPOGRAPHY AND ITS RELATION TO CLIMBING

Unlike most peaks in the Sierra, the Palisades have few easy approaches. The southwest walls, where one usually expects gradual slopes, are high; while the northeast sides are severely glaciated, with steep-walled amphitheaters and residual glaciers to complicate the climbing routes. The main Palisade Glacier is the largest in the Sierra. The peaks above it are shown in Sketch 20. For details of the topography reference is made to the maps of the United States Geological Survey, Mount Goddard and Big Pine quadrangles.

In 1864, members of the California State Geological Survey, seeing the Palisades at a distance, spoke of them as of volcanic origin. This was wrong, however, for the area is largely of granite, very much disintegrated along lines of cleavage, but very sound and excellent for climbing. Nevertheless, the ceaseless testing and care inevitably associated with climbing above timberline are essential. The glaciers, although contributing much to the scenic magnificence of the Palisades, do not figure largely in mountaineering except as convenient avenues of approach. Crevasses are small and do not often impede progress; however, late in the season of a dry year, the crevasses in Palisade Glacier

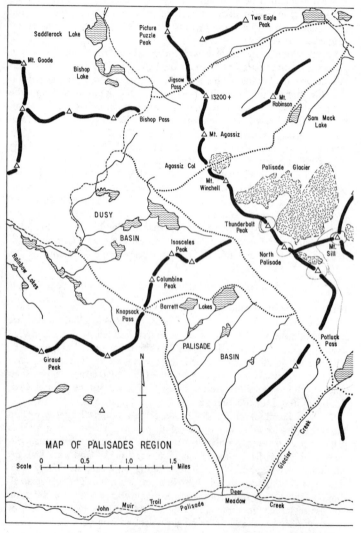

MAP OF PALISADES REGION

Scale 0   0.5   1.0   1.5 Miles

Sketch 19.

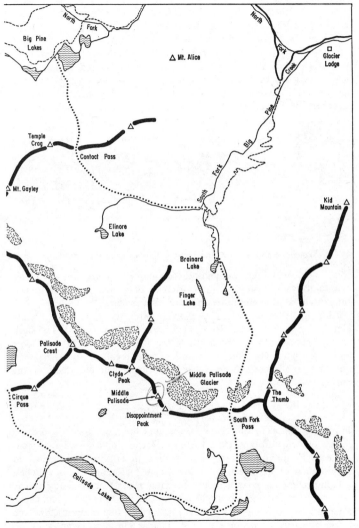

(See legend, page 14.)

may open to a width of fifteen feet and will measure a rope-length in depth. California climbers, who frequently are good on rock but lack ice experience, have been tricked by these little glaciers when descending the warm soft snow in late afternoon. Some of the bergschrunds can be difficult to negotiate and often stop or slow down parties of otherwise competent climbers. In chutes and couloirs steep ice is frequently encountered, and though it may sometimes be avoided, an ice axe is necessary if peaks are approached from the northeast. Climbers who approach the Palisades from this side should use lug

Sketch 20. Peaks above the Palisade Glacier from the northeast.

soles. They will find crampons useful in the couloirs. Snow and ice conditions vary greatly, and the exercise of sound judgment backed by experience is prerequisite to many of the climbs.

Although climbers who are familiar with the routes can usually climb on good solid rock, loose rocks are a frequent hazard. The steep chutes and couloirs on the north of the Palisades contain much loose rock, especially when the snow is low, and rockfalls caused by man and nature are perhaps more common here than elsewhere in the Sierra.

APPROACHES AND CAMPSITES

From Big Pine. The quickest approach and the most dramatic, because of the sudden transition from barren desert to alpine splendor, is from the east. From Highway 395 in Big Pine an 11-mile road extends to an elevation of 7,800 feet at Glacier Lodge (accommodations, supplies, packing, climbing guides, mountaineering school) and slightly above. A horse trail continues up the North Fork of Big Pine Creek and above Fourth Lake with short laterals to many lakes, fine campsites, and the Palisade glaciers. One of the most popular climbers' campsites is at Sam Mack Meadow, located below the lake of the same name, at

11,000 feet elevation. A higher campsite is on the south shore of Sam Mack Lake. From Glacier Lodge there is also a trail into the South Fork basin, and knapsackers will find many campsites beyond the end of the trail, up to 11,400 feet under Temple Crag, and to 11,000 feet beneath Middle Palisade. There are good campsites just south of Contact Pass, by a little meadow.

From Bishop. A road follows Bishop Creek 20 miles to an elevation of 9,750 feet at Parcher's Camp (accommodations, supplies, packing), from which a horse trail continues over Bishop Pass to popular campsites in Dusy Basin.

From the Muir Trail. The Bishop Pass lateral approaches Dusy Basin campsites. The Muir Trail passes within two miles of Middle Palisade on the way to Mather Pass on the South Fork of the Kings River. Fine campsites are to be found in Little Pete, Grouse, and Deer meadows. Palisade Basin is quite desolate, but knapsackers can camp at its lower border (11,200) and also along Glacier Creek or at 10,500 feet on Palisade Creek.

Principal Passes

There are no passes over the Palisades for stock. The following passes are suitable for highly competent knapsackers or for climbers. The passes over the crest are listed from north to south, followed by passes over the eastern and western spurs.

Jigsaw Pass (12,622). Class 2. This pass offers an interesting route from Fifth Lake to Bishop Pass. *East to west:* Follow the south shore of Fifth Lake, and ascend talus and slabs south of the creek flowing from Mount Agassiz. It is well to stay about 300 feet above the stream to avoid the bluffs over which it cascades. Follow the north branch of the creek for about one mile and then angle to the left over easy ground that may be covered with snow to the pass. Jigsaw Pass is not the lowest point on the divide, but lies a few hundred yards south, beyond a minor rise. It is marked with a cairn. Peak 13,200+ separates the pass from Mount Agassiz. Descend on the west by a steep but easy chute and cross large talus blocks to the nearest point of the Bishop Pass trail, just north of Bishop Pass. *West to east:* As with many climbs in the Sierra, the west approach to Jigsaw Pass is a problem in choosing the correct chute. From the trail at Bishop Pass one sees that the ridge north of Mount Agassiz extends one mile to the first important peak of the Inconsolable Range (Peak 13,278). Jigsaw Pass is just south of the low point of this ridge, and is separated from the low point by an angular but low peak. Proceed up the southern of two chutes. The climb, over scree, grass, and well-fractured granite, will be found much easier than it had appeared. On the two-mile descent to Fifth Lake all one need remember is to keep south of the inlet stream and stay well above it for the last 400 yards. The large boulder fields make backpacking very tedious over this pass.

Agassiz shoulder. Class 2 to 3. As a rugged route from Palisade Glacier to Bishop Pass, Alfred Wilkes has suggested a 13,000 foot pass just north of Mount Agassiz. From the foot of the Palisade Glacier cross the east ridge of Mount Agassiz and follow the contours around to the pass. Descend a small ridge just south of the pass to the top of Bishop Pass.

Agassiz Col (13,200+). Class 2 to 3. This pass is higher and more difficult than Jigsaw Pass, but provides climbers the opportunity for sidetrips to Mount Agassiz or Mount Winchell. *East to west:* Follow the Palisade Glacier trail south to Sam Mack Lake, turn west from the upper end of the lake, and proceed north of the east spur of Mount Winchell, which cannot be seen until the lake is passed. The route leads past a small lakelet, up through a series of moraines, and across the small glacier north of Winchell. The col is the low point at the head of the cirque, and is best reached by climbing to the top of the right (N) side of the glacier and then continuing diagonally up to the left over broken rock. The descent over scree and talus to Dusy Basin is not nearly as tedious as the climb back. *West to east:* The correct chute is the largest between Mounts Agassiz and Winchell. Ascend the chute to the col and descend the stream from the Winchell Glacier.

The U Notch (13,900+). Class 3 to 4. This spectacular alpine notch separates North Palisade from the Mount Sill massif, and from it both peaks are accessible. It is a climber's route and is not suitable for knapsackers. For details, see North Palisade, Routes 2 and 3.

Southfork Pass (12,560+). Class 2 to 3. The summit of the pass is located just above the *S* in "Southfork Pass," not above the "ou," in that place name on the Mount Goddard quadrangle map (1:62,500). This route is a severe knapsack route between the South Fork of Big Pine Creek and the Muir Trail near Palisade Lakes. *North to south:* From the end of the trail at Brainard Lake, follow the stream course up the canyon past a small lake. Work up between the open granite slopes on the right and the moraine on the left to a small glacier west of the Thumb. There is a cairn with a pole in it at the pass which is visible from here. Early in the year the glacier may appear to be a smooth snowfield, but later a small bergschrund opens beneath a funnel-shaped chute. Work up the glacier into the chute. Loose rock on the ice is the primary hazard if there is not sufficient snow cover. Once through the narrow chute, the angle of climb lessens. The scree and talus slope down the southern side leads to Lake 11,767. It is easy to keep to the right of Lake 11,632 and follow the stream course to the Muir Trail. *South to north:* Follow the stream course to Lakes 11,632 and 11,767. From the benches above the upper lake you may see the cairn and pole in the first notch east of the broad slopes of Disappointment Peak. North of the summit of the pass the slope gradually steepens. Depending on conditions, an ice axe and/or rope may be needed before you reach the glacier. Follow the stream course to Brainard Lake. From Brainard Lake the southfork trail cuts left and winds down through the forest to the right of Willow Lake. The trail improves from here down.

Contact Pass (11,760+). Class 1–2. This rounded notch just east of Temple Crag affords a good route between the two forks of Big Pine Creek. It receives its name from the contact zone between two different granites, to which it also owes its origin. *North to south:* From the upper end of Second Lake follow the contact zone to the notch. A few hundred feet below the pass is a small lake that drains into Willow Lake, with the connecting stream about one and a half miles long. Follow the north side of the stream, crossing shortly above Willow Lake, and climb about 200 feet to the trail on the bench south of the lake. *South to north:* Follow the north inlet of Willow Lake and the north branches of this inlet stream to the little amphitheater and lake at timberline just under Temple Crag, which may be identified by its beautifully castellated summit. From the lake Contact Pass is unmistakable, and the route of descent to Second Lake is likewise obvious. If there is heavy snow this north slope will require a little care in glissading or step-kicking. A fisherman's trail leads from Second Lake to Third and Fourth lakes.

Glacier Notch (13,120+). Class 2–3. The saddle between Mounts Sill and Gayley, called Glacier Notch, is not difficult on either side, and forms a part of a route from the Palisade Glacier to the Sill Glacier. A small bergschrund may have to be negotiated on Palisade Glacier just below a loose rock chute to the pass. Keep close to Sill Glacier on the southeast side of the pass.

Knapsack Pass (11,673), Potluck Pass, and *Cirque Pass.* Class 1–2. Although stock has been taken from Dusy Basin to Palisade Basin over the pass south of Columbine Peak (Knapsack Pass), it is recommended only for knapsackers or hikers. The divide between the two basins may also be crossed just northeast of Columbine Peak (12,000+), or where the divide joins the Palisade wall (12,360+). The route across Knapsack Pass is an interesting way for knapsackers to proceed from Bishop Pass to Mather Pass, and it will therefore be described in a little more detail. Leave the Bishop Pass trail in Dusy Basin where the trail swings close to the lower lakes, and head southeast across easy open country to Knapsack Pass, which is the obvious gap just south of Columbine Peak. The route from the top of the pass goes to the left, where a well-defined trail leads below the cliffs of Columbine Peak, eventually dropping into Palisade Basin. A fairly well ducked route can then be followed to the dike west of the largest and highest lake in Palisade Basin (Barrett Lakes). Travelers should be warned that there is no wood at this lake, or, in fact, anywhere in the basin above 11,200 feet. It is probably best to skirt the lake around its north and east banks, staying right at the edge of the lake. A stream flows into the southeastern corner of the lake. A ducked route can be followed, starting up the south bank of the stream, and leading up the ridge and across gentle country to Potluck Pass (12,120), which marks the division between Palisade Basin and Glacier Creek Basin. The east side of Potluck Pass is quite steep; bear to the right while descending and work off the sloping ledges to a slope of scree, and then descend to the north shore of the large lake, from which Mount Sill can readily be climbed (see Mount Sill, Route 1). One can camp a little ways down the steep canyon of Glacier Creek below the lake. To continue on the route, cross Glacier Creek at the outlet of the lake and ascend the cliff. A ducked route starts at the base of the cliff somewhat to the right of the pass (Cirque Pass, 12,040+), and zigzags up a series of ledges to the top. From this pass a route is picked down to the west side of a small tarn (11,400+) in the mouth of the cirque. Continue southeast and work down a cliff to a small stream which may be followed to the Muir Trail just below the Palisade Lakes.

Other Passes. There are doubtless many routes, not described here, which can be traversed by climbers or knapsackers. One, known as Chimney Pass, crosses the southwest spur of Palisade Crest from Glacier Creek Basin to Palisade Lakes at (12,600+). The gap on the main divide between Palisade Crest and Peak 13,390 is easily approached from Glacier Creek, but has a cliff on the northeast. The col southeast of Mount Winchell involves a 100-foot rappel when going from east to west, and therefore should be considered a climbing route.

Peaks of the Crest (North to South)

Mount Agassiz (*13,891*)

Ascended August 30, 1925, by Norman Clyde.

Route 1. West slope. Class 1. This is the easiest of the major peaks of the Palisades. A good view of the North Palisade and the basin of the Big Pine Lakes is obtained from the summit. The ascent is made via the spur of the peak that extends to Bishop Pass.

Route 2. Southeast face and south ridge. Class 2. See Agassiz Col, under Passes, for approach. From the terminal moraine of the Winchell Glacier work up the debris-filled chute that empties just north of the moraine, follow the chute to the ridge north of Agassiz Col, and follow the ridge to the summit. It is also possible to follow the east side of the south ridge all the way from the Col, and this route may be preferred since it avoids the scree of the chute.

Route 3. Northeast face. Class 4. First ascent by Norman Clyde. Approach by the canyon leading directly from Fifth Lake to Mount Agassiz. From the glacier (which is northeast of the mountain and is not indicated on the quadrangle map) proceed to the foot of the Y-shaped couloir that heads on the north arête, ascend half-way up to the "Y," then climb left (S) to the rocks. Continue diagonally upward and halfway to the summit over the moderately difficult face, and then it will be possible to traverse right (N) to the little arête dividing the lower portion of the route from the south branch of the "Y." Follow this arête a short distance, and then either continue along the east face to the top or cross the ridge to the less exposed northwest face and climb it to the top.

Mount Winchell (*13,768*)

The ascent of Mount Winchell is not difficult, but it is quite satisfying as the peak is rugged and the view down the sculptured western face is impressive. The first ascent was made June 10, 1923, by H. C. Mansfield, J. N. Newell, and W. B. Putnam by Route 1.

Route 1. East arête. Class 3. From near Sam Mack Lake walk up south of the east arête to within about 500 yards of the col southeast of Winchell. Climb the south face to the east arête and follow the arête westward until it becomes a knife-edge. From here an exposed route leads a short distance to the left into a steep chute which leads to the spectacular summit. A variation of this route, ascended in September,

1953, by George and Kay Bloom and Glenn Cushman, is also class 3. Go to the north of the large buttress at the end of the east arête and climb up a broken face to the top of the arête. Then follow the arête to join the usual Route 1.

Route 2. West face. Class 4. First ascent July 29, 1930, by Jules Eichorn, Glen Dawson, and John Olmstead. Jim Eder and Tom Matthes describe the route from a 1961 climb: At the foot of the west face, enter a prominent chute from which a fan-shaped talus slope emerges. Follow this diagonally up and to the left about halfway to the top. After climbing over a large boulder which obstructs the narrowing chute, traverse right and follow a broad sloping chute diagonally up and to the right. This leads to a notch on an arête leading down from the summit. From here the summit is visible and four class-4 pitches lead to the top.

Route 3. Southwest chute. Class 4. First ascent August 11, 1938, by W. K. Davis and Jack Riegelhuth. Start in the largest chute on the west face of Winchell that has a large buttress on the north side. From the top of the chute traverse left into a notch east of the buttress. Then climb to the top. There are many possible routes on the west face, most of them class 4. The most northerly chutes lead to the north arête, which may involve class 5 or class A climbing.

Route 4. Southeast face. Class 5. Don Harmon and Bob Dohrmann describe their ascent of June 21, 1959: Climb a half-dozen pitches of class 3 scrambling from the Winchell-Thunderbolt Col to a rather prominent chute. From this point three easy class 4 pitches over loose rock bring you to a broad ledge. A long pitch of moderate class 5 leads over a small overhang and up a rather delicate crack to a secure alcove below a second overhang. This overhang is turned on the right through a cleft leading onto the east face. From here a class 4 scramble brings you to the top of the south arête a short distance from the summit.

Route 5. North face. Class 4. The north face was climbed on August 14, 1955, by Robert Stebbins, Bill Rogers, and G. Ledyard Stebbins. The route went from the top of Winchell Glacier between the northeast buttress and the north couloir. At one point in the route there is a long diagonal traverse (one rope length) where one may wish to use a piton for protection. The route comes out just east of the summit cone on top of the east arête.

Winter ascent. January 10, 1938, by Norman Clyde, Morgan Harris, and David R. Brower by Route 1.

Thunderbolt Peak (*14,000+*)

The name of this peak was inspired by a thunderstorm which harried the first ascent party and hurried them off the ridge after a bolt had struck very close to one of the climbers. First ascent by Route 1 on August 13, 1931, by Norman Clyde, R. L. M. Underhill, Bestor Robinson, F. P. Farquhar, Glen Dawson, Lewis Clark, and Jules Eichorn.

Route 1. East couloirs. Class 4. From Palisade Glacier twin couloirs lead to the notch between Thunderbolt Peak and the northwest peak of North Palisade. The right (NW) one is the so-called Underhill Couloir. Climbing in these couloirs depends greatly on snow conditions, and sometimes one may be preferred over the other (see *SCB,* 1950, 127). Ice may be met in either. To reach the notch the left (SE) couloir may be climbed about halfway and then the arête between the two may be followed the rest of the way. However this left couloir contains much dangerous loose rock if the snow is low, and then the right one is better. During the summer of 1963 there were many severe rock falls in the left couloir.

About two-thirds of the way up, the floor of the right couloir is blocked by a large chockstone, which may be passed on the right up a rock wall with good holds. From the notch climb slabs leading to the north, and then work upward along the southwest side of the ridge, finally climbing to the crest and following it to the summit block. The smooth summit block may be climbed with the aid of a shoulder stand or with protection from a rope thrown over the top.

Route 2. Southwest chute number 1. Class 4. From the Palisade Basin side of the Palisade-Dusy Basin divide, take the first chute east of the divide. This chute heads between the twin summits of Thunderbolt. First descent September 3, 1949, by the party of Route 6. This is probably the easiest route of ascent of Thunderbolt yet found. About one-third of the way up the chute there is a narrow chimney choked with stones. The chimney can be passed on the right side (looking up) by traversing out on a three-foot, scree-covered ledge. Above the chockstones the chute divides several times. Wherever it divides, always take the right-hand chute, looking up. Ascend the chute to the notch between the twin summits. At the notch the highest peak is to the right (SW). There is one class 4 pitch directly up from the notch which leads around to the left of the peak to the flat ridge on the east side, and then a large crack leads to the south side of the summit block.

Route 3. Southwest chute number 2. Class 4. First ascent August 3, 1933, by Norman Clyde, John Poindexter, Philip Von Lubkin. Climb the largest chute southeast of the divide between Palisade and Dusy basins to the deep notch southeast of Thunderbolt, and proceed to the summit as in Route 1.

Route 4. Northwest ridge. Class 5. First ascent August 11, 1938, by W. K. Davis and Jack Riegelhuth. They followed the ridge from the col southeast of Mount Winchell. The first third of the route was class 3, while the rest was class 4 and 5. The first ascent was made as part of a climb from Dusy Basin to the summit of Winchell and then along the ridge to North Palisade; the total time was 13 hours.

Route 5. Northeast buttress. Class 4. First ascent by Norman Clyde on an unknown date. There is a large, ice-filled couloir west of the great northeast buttress of Thunderbolt. Cross the bergschrund about 20 feet to the right of the eastern margin of the lower end of the couloir, and cut steps up to accessible ledges, all the while being protected from falling rocks by an outward bulge in the wall of the couloir above. After a short distance on the ledges, climb upward and eastward to the crest of the buttress, and follow this to the main ridge, where an upward traverse to the right leads to a notch of the main ridge. From this traverse to the left around a shoulder and into a couloir which leads to the summit block.

Route 6. West face. Class 4. First ascent September 3, 1949, by Oscar Cook, Sylvia Kershaw, Mildred Jentsch, and Hunter and Isabella Morrison. They ascended the first feasible chute on the Dusy Basin (N) side of the Palisade-Dusy Basin divide. They followed the right (SE) branch of the chute until it ended in an ice-filled chimney, and then worked to the right to an arête which was left higher up by a vein of rotten quartz that led to next chute to the southeast. A chockstone in this chute was passed on the left by a class 4 pitch. The chute led to a spur which was followed to the main ridge west of Thunderbolt, and from there they followed the ridge southeast to the small notch between the twin summits of Thunderbolt. The highest is the southwest peak, and a class 4 pitch from the notch takes one to the east side of this.

Route 7. East buttress, right side. Class 5. First ascent July 1959 by Richard Gnagy and Ellen Wilts. Start in the couloir between the east and northeast buttresses (the furthest right couloir shown in Sketch 20). Climb on the north wall of the east buttress, working up and to the right and eventually onto the top of the buttress.

North Palisade (14,242)

First ascended July 25, 1903, by J. N. LeConte, J. K. Moffitt, and J. S. Hutchinson, by Route 1.

Route 1. Southwest chute (LeConte route). Class 3. See Sketch 21. Enter the chute which leads to the U Notch (this is the deep notch southeast of North Palisade) from the southwest. This chute may be identified from the upper end of the highest and largest of the lakes in Palisade Basin, where one sees at the base of the southwest wall of North Palisade three white cliffs, resembling inverted shields, and marking the entrances to two chutes. The right (SE) chute is ascended, and would lead to the U Notch if followed to the crest. About half-way up, at the upper end of a bare granite bottom area in the chute, where

Sketch 21. North Palisade from the west, and Route 1.

it widens out somewhat, is a narrow ledge running to the left (NW). Follow the ledge, which is only a few feet wide at one point, around to the next chute. Climb this second chute until progress is stopped, and then cross to the right to a third chute, which usually has snow in it and which is not visible from below, and ascend to the crest of the ridge. Then proceed northward over large blocks to the summit.

Although this is a third class route on an otherwise fourth class mountain, it can be a tricky route. It should not be attempted without ropes and reasonably experienced persons. The summit blocks are exposed.

Route 2. Southwest chute to U Notch. Class 4 or 5. First ascent July 19, 1921, by Hermann Ulrichs. Enter the first chute described under Route 1 and climb to the U Notch. If there is no snow cover, loose rock near the top of the U Notch may be quite a hazard. At the top of the notch, a steep, open chimney leads up the west wall. About halfway (100 feet) up, you will notice pitons with rappel slings on the right wall. Since the climbing is exposed and at an elevation of 14,000 feet, most climbers will use a piton or two for safety. From the top of the chimney proceed along the serrated ridge first on the right and then left toward the summit. *Clyde's variation:* From a point 120 feet down the southwest side from the top of the U Notch, there is a body-wedge crack leading to the top of a small buttress. Climb on the wall slightly to the right to a ledge where one can walk to the left (SW) past a cairn and around the corner of the arête. Climb up the chute about two long rope lengths and come out at the top of the U Notch wall, where you will see rappel slings of the chimney route, and go around the end of the southeastern serrated ridge and proceed toward the summit. Route 3 with Clyde's variation is the most frequently climbed way up the mountain.

Route 3. Via U Notch from the glacier. Class 4. First ascent in June, 1928, by Norman Clyde. Follow the trail to the main Palisade Glacier and cross the glacier to the broad, steep couloir leading to the U Notch. Neither the couloir nor the notch can be mistaken; the notch is the most prominent one between North Palisade and Mount Sill. Late in the season the bergschrund may be a serious obstacle; it is usually best crossed at the northwest side of the couloir. Ice is always present in the couloir, and any snow surface should be carefully probed before it is trusted. Late in the season bare ice will be met. It is well to work up along the northwest edge of the couloir, out of range of rock or snow sliding down the couloir. About halfway up a peninsula of rotten granite is reached, and this can be followed without difficulty to the notch. From there proceed as in Route 2. An ice axe is a must for this climb. There is a real danger of rockfalls in this, as in other, couloirs on the northeast side of the Palisades, especially in late afternoon, during storms, or late in the season of a low snow year. Some remarks by Norman Clyde on this subject are of interest (*SCB,* 1950, 127). Clyde says: "More ricocheting rocks and rockslides come down the Palisade than was the case when there was more snow. These [rockfalls] are rather numerous in the latter half of July and are still numerous in August. They are most common also in the afternoon, but may occur at any time—even early morning."

Route 4. North face. Class 4. First ascent in July, 1929, by Norman Clyde. This climb starts up the steep and rather narrow couloir west of the couloir leading to the U Notch. This couloir splits the north face of North Palisade, and heads at a high notch between the summit and the northwest peak. Sometimes the bergschrund below this couloir is nearly impassable. Climb the west wall of the couloir between the snow and the rock for about 200 feet above the bergschrund. Here the couloir narrows and falling rocks are a hazard. The route proceeds diagonally up rock to the right to the ridgetop of a narrow arête. Follow this arête and the slopes above it keeping to the right of the couloir until you are a few hundred feet below the summit. Here you should cross the couloir and proceed directly toward the summit blocks (watch for loose boulders) or proceed diagonally left (SE) across North Palisade's large distinctive snow band to the summit ridge where you turn right to get to the summit. This is said by many climbers to be one of the finest alpine routes in the Sierra. John Mendenhall and Dick Franklin followed the icy couloir nearly all the way up in 1955, but considered the route quite hazardous.

Route 5. West chute. Class 4. First ascent July 13, 1933, by James Wright. The exact route is uncertain, but approximates a combination of Thunderbolt Route 3 and North Palisade Route 6.

Route 6. Northwest ridge. Class 4. First ascent June 29, 1934, by Norman Clyde, David R. Brower, and Hervey Voge. From the notch between Thunderbolt Peak and North Palisade (see Thunderbolt Peak, Route 1) work upward along ledges on the southwest side of the ridge. When progress becomes difficult, climb by an intricate route behind some large blocks to the crest and follow it to the northwest peak of North Palisade. From there the best route follows the crest rather closely, crossing from side to side several times, and, in particular, crossing to the north at a prominent gendarme in order to pass a difficult gap. *Variation:* Cross to the northeast (glacier) side of the ridge when progress on the southwest side becomes difficult, and proceed along ledges and snow until directly beneath the main summit; then climb to the top.

Route 7. West face. Class 5. First ascent in August, 1936, by Richard M. Jones and Mary Jane Edwards. Start to the left of a black streak on the base of the mountain, cross to the right above this mark by going under a large, fallen slab on the slanting shelf, continue up a fairly wide chute to a point where it becomes very narrow, cross to the right into the next chute on a horizontal white vein, passing slightly above a large block. Then proceed more or less directly to the summit.

Route 8. Northeast Buttress. Class 5. First ascent in July 1961 by Larry Williams, John Sharsmith, Burton Turney, and Genevieve Turney. From just above the right (W) side of the bergschrund below the U Notch Couloir (Route 3) proceed up a great open chimney of light gray rock for about 300 feet. Here the wall becomes vertical. Traverse right on a slightly overhanging portion of the wall toward some solid but weathered brown granite. Although holds are good it is a strenuous climb. You are then at the top of the buttress which slopes gently up toward the summit.

Winter ascent. North Palisade was climbed March 17, 1940, by David R. Brower and Fred Kelley, by Route 3.

Northwest peak of North Palisade (14,080+). This peak may be reached by the northeast face, by a variation of Route 4 for North Palisade, either directly up the face or by returning from the notch separating it from North Palisade. It can also be climbed by North Palisade Route 6, either from the summit of North Palisade, or from the notch southeast of Thunderbolt. The first ascent was made July 9, 1930, by Norman Clyde. The summit is a large block somewhat resembling a milk bottle; this block can be climbed without artificial aid.

Polemonium Peak (14,000+)

This peak, which lies directly southeast of the top of the U Notch, is the source of the highest glacier in the Sierra.

Route 1. Class 2. From the glacier described in the Route 1 climb of Mount Sill, proceed directly up.

Route 2. Class 4. From the top of the U Notch climb the southeast wall and thence to the summit. (see Mount Sill, Route 3)

Route 3. Class 4. Looking south from Palisade Glacier the V Notch Couloir, about 200 yards east of the U Notch Couloir, presents a fine bergschrund and a steep snow slope that extends up to 13,800 feet at the crest. Climb to the V Notch and proceed west along the ridge to the summit. Ice axe and crampons are needed.

Mount Sill (14,162)

Route 1. Southwest slope. Class 2–3. First ascent July 24, 1903, by Joseph N. LeConte, James K. Moffitt, James S. Hutchinson and Robert D. Pike. Go up Glacier Creek to a cirque, then up a steep talus slope to the left to the foot of the small glacier southeast of North Palisade. The summit of Sill is not visible from here. There are two alternatives. One can ascend the steep cliff on the northeast side of the glacier directly to the summit, or follow up the glacier and the snow field at its head and then work to the east over the slopes to the top.

Route 2. Northwest face. Class 3. Ice axe necessary. First ascent, June 10, 1927, by Norman Clyde. A number of routes are possible up the wall to the ridge west of the summit. However, in recent years, some loose rock has been coming down this west ridge which is part of the headwall of Palisade Glacier, and Route 4 is usually preferred. For Route 2 the bergschrund of the main Palisade Glacier may cause difficulty, but it can almost always be crossed along the left margin of the lower edge of the large couloir running up toward Mount Sill.

Route 3. Traverse from the U Notch. Class 4. First ascent, July 27, 1930, by Jules M. Eichorn, Glen Dawson, John Olmstead and Charles Dodge. From the U Notch (see North Palisade, Routes 2 and 3) climb about 20 feet up the southeast wall and traverse right to the southwest arête. Then follow the ridge to the summit.

Route 4. North couloir. Class 4. First ascent, September 25, 1931, by Walter A. Starr, Jr. From Glacier Notch go up the chute between the face of Sill and a small pyramid under the face. Pass through the gap and traverse on ledges across the face to an arête which leads to the crest on the north side of the summit. Then ascend the ridge to the summit. This is the most frequently climbed route from the northeast. A variation of this route is suggested by George Wallerstein. Climb five short pitches directly up from the traverse. On the third pitch you will probably want to use pitons for safety.

Route 5. East couloir and southeast ridge. Class 3. Descended June 16, 1934, by Norman Clyde, Hervey Voge, and David R. Brower. For an ascent proceed from the east to the Sill Glacier and up to the first deep notch southeast of the summit of Mount Sill. A couloir just south of the precipitous east face leads up to this notch; this couloir is best entered by the left (SE) branch. From the notch follow the easy ridge to the summit. An ice axe is necessary.

Route 6. North buttress. Class 5. First ascent July 3, 1938, by Spencer Austin, Ruth Dyar, Ray Ingwersen, Richard M. Jones, and Joe Momyer. From Glacier Notch cross the north couloir diagonally upward to the buttress. Climb to the ridge of the buttress and follow it about halfway to the summit. Then traverse around an awkward corner to the right (W) on a series of ledges formed by a prominent band of light colored rock. One can climb back on the ridge from several places on these ledges. On the ridge proceed up over huge blocks to the summit. This route has more exposure than Route 2, but is almost free of loose rock.

A class 4 variation may be made by traversing to the right (W) earlier and farther.

Route 7. East face. Class 5 or A. From Sill Glacier Tom Condon and Fred Kepfelsberger climbed the east face. No details are available. Later, in September 1963, a parallel route further south (class 5.7) was ascended by Burt and Gen Turney, Rick Gnagy, and John Mendenhall. Start at the highest reach of the glacier in a chimney with a huge overhanging chockstone and go almost directly up, ending 200 feet south of the summit.

Winter ascent. John Mendenhall and Henry Mandolf made the first winter ascent of Mount Sill in 1960.

Peak 13,840+ (0.2 miles SSE of the summit of Sill)

This peak was climbed via several class 2 and 3 chutes from the headwall of Glacier Creek by a group that included Tom Kendall.

Peak 13,390 (0.5 miles SE of Mount Sill)

Class 2 from the south. Records of ascents by Don McGeein, Chet Errett, and Evelyn Errett on July 3, 1939, and by Ted Sanford and Tom Jukes on July 4, 1940, are known.

Palisade Crest (13,520+)

This impressive wall, capped with pinnacles, rises above small glaciers feeding the South Fork of Big Pine Creek. John and Ruth Mendenhall climbed the three easternmost pinnacles on July 4, 1954. The couloir east of the crest terminated in a difficult rock pitch. The east pinnacle had some interesting fourth and fifth class pitches. The other two were easier ascents.

Clyde Peak (13,920+; 0.4 NW of Middle Palisade; formerly 13,956)

This peak stands sharply against the sky as the most prominent peak from the vicinity of Glacier Lodge. Norman Clyde's Route 1, and the later climbed Route 3 can be clearly seen from the canyon.

Route 1. North face. Class 3 to 4. First climbed by Clyde on June 9, 1930. Go up the glacier north of the peak and climb the left hand couloir and the north face to the summit ridge. Then traverse southeast, over the ridge, around an arête and onto the ridge just west of the summit, and thence to the summit.

Route 2. South face. Class 3 to 4. First ascent June 19, 1930, by Norman Clyde from Palisade Lakes.

Route 3. North face and northeast ridge. Class 4. A. Erb and M.

McNicholas, July 22, 1961. From the glacier on the north side go up the left side of the peak to the northeast ridge and follow the ridge to the top.

Route 4. Northeast face. Class 4 to 5. First climbed in August 1961 by Allen Steck, Larry Williams, and John Sharsmith. From the northern end of the north icefield of Middle Palisade Glacier climb almost straight up, bearing to the left of a distinctive circular snow patch at 13,000 feet, and working directly toward the summit. It is an exposed route and does not offer good cracks for pitons.

Middle Palisade (*14,040*)

The thin ridge with its finely serrated summit, seemingly held up by fragile arêtes, makes Middle Palisade easily identifiable from the switchback on the road above the campgrounds on Big Pine Creek. This peak was first climbed on August 26, 1921, by F. P. Farquhar and A. F. Hall, who climbed Route 1.

Route 1. Southwest chute and south face. Class 4. The history of this route reveals much disappointment that has resulted from the choice of the wrong chute. Those wishing to climb Middle Palisade instead of Disappointment Peak should take the third chute north of the angle between the Middle Palisade wall and its southwest spur, counting the chute that marks the angle as the first. The first and second chutes lead to Disappointment Peak, while the third leads to Middle Palisade, and heads just north of the little sawtooth peak between the two peaks. The route is intricate at the top, and there are a number of possible variations. Three-fourths of the way up, work to the left out of the chute and ascend the face south of the summit to the top.

Route 2. Northeast face. Class 4. First ascent by Norman Clyde, June 7, 1930. The northeast face may be climbed by means of several routes up chutes and arêtes leading up from the glacier. This face is west of the prominent buttress that projects eastward from the peak.

Route 3. Northwest ridge. Class 4 or 5. Traverse along the ridge from Peak 13,920+ (Clyde), with a few deviations to pass gendarmes. First done July 30, 1933, by Jules Eichorn and Glen Dawson.

Route 4. Southeast ridge. Class 4. Traverse from Disappointment Peak, mostly on the northeast side of the ridge. First done July 20, 1939, by David Brower, Bruce Meyer, and Keith Taylor.

Route 5. East face. Class 3. This route is probably the easiest way to the top of Middle Palisade; it follows a prominent chute or couloir directly below the summit and directly above the moraine that divides the glacier to the northeast of the peak (see Sketch 22). First ascent uncertain. From the top of the moraine that divides the glacier proceed onto the left hand (S) glacier. About half way up the glacier a ledge is seen leading up the buttress to the right. Follow this ledge to the broad couloir and follow this couloir until it ends; then cross over to the next couloir to the north. After a short distance this couloir divides and the left branch may be climbed to a notch on the ridge just northeast of the main peak.

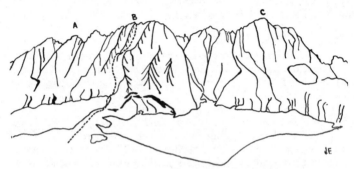

Sketch 22. Middle Palisade from the northeast, and Route 5.
A—Disappointment Peak. B—Middle Palisade.
C—Clyde Peak.

Winter ascent. Tom Condon and John Mendenhall climbed Route 5 on January 5, 1960.

Disappointment Peak *(13,917)*

This is the highest peak just southeast of Middle Palisade, and the central one of three on that ridge. From some places it appears to be higher than Middle Palisade. First ascent July 20, 1919, by J. M. Davies, A. L. Jordan, and H. H. Bliss, by Route 1.

Route 1. Southwest chute. Class 3. Climb up the large chute just north of the prominent buttress or spur that extends to the southwest from the main ridge. The chute leads to a point just south of the summit.

Route 2. Northeast couloir. Class 4. First ascent June 20, 1930, by Norman Clyde. It was stated to be a good climb, with some difficulty at the foot of the couloir in a chimney. The couloir used is the right (N) of two, and does not run all the way to the ridge. The left-hand couloir leads to the notch southeast of the peak.

Route 3. East ridge. Class 3. From the north climb to the main ridge about midway between Southfork Pass and Disappointment Peak and follow the ridge to the summit, sometimes deviating to the north side. William Dunmire and Allen Steck climbed Middle Palisade by this route in September, 1953, but they bypassed the summit of Disappointment.

The Thumb (*13,388*)

This peak has sometimes been called East Palisade. The first ascent was made December 12, 1921, by W. B. Putnam.

Route 1. Southeast slope. Class 2. The peak was first climbed by this slope after an approach from Birch Creek. From Birch Lake (little or no wood for camping) proceed southwest to the cirque southeast of The Thumb. The wall of the cirque can be climbed near the southwest end on ledges (class 3). Then proceed up the easy southeast slope of the peak. To climb The Thumb from the Muir Trail, follow the stream that comes from the east into the upper Palisade Lake. Cross the Sierra Crest by ascending the more easterly of the two talus-filled chimneys in the wall to the right of a small peak to the right (E) of Southfork Pass. The Thumb lies north of the main crest. Proceed up the easy southeast slope.

Route 2. Northwest face. Class 4. First ascent June 5, 1930, by Norman Clyde. Climb up a couloir of the northwest face, then circle around the final peak to the south or southeast slope.

Route 3. North northeast ridge. The west wall of this ridge, just north of the summit was climbed on September 12, 1957, by Leigh and Irene Ortenburger. They climbed in a deep couloir with three large chockstones toward the headwall and then went up the steep right-hand wall to a knife-edged subridge that joined the summit ridge. The route requires some fifth class pitons near the top of the ridge.

Peaks East of the Crest

Chocolate Peak (*11,658*)

Class 1 by the southeast ridge. First recorded ascent by Don McGeein on July 4, 1932.

Inconsolable Range, Cloudripper (*13,501*)

First know ascent June 15, 1926, by Norman Clyde. Class 1 from Seventh Lake via the east ridge, or class 2 from Green Lake via the north ridge. The western slopes are class 3 from Chocolate or Ruwau lakes (Ted Waller, 1962).

Inconsolable Range, Picture Puzzle (13,278)

First recorded ascent in 1937 by Norman Clyde. The north slopes are class 3 from Ruwau Lake. The southwest face is class 4 from the Bishop Pass Trail (Mike Loughman, 1962).

Sky Haven (12,834; 1 N of Fifth Lake)

Climbed prior to 1940 by Morgan Leonard.

Peak 13,200+ (0.5 N of Mount Agassiz)

Climbed in 1934 by David R. Brower and Hervey Voge. A class 3 ascent from Jigsaw Pass or the glacier northeast of Mount Agassiz.

Two Eagle Peak (12,880+; 0.7 W of Fifth Lake; formerly 12,986)

First ascent July 6, 1929, by Norman Clyde. The ascent from Fifth Lake by the east ridge and the north side of the east ridge is class 3. The summit is a large, smooth block.

Mt. Robinson (12,800+; 0.8 NE of Mount Agassiz; formerly 12,981)

Route 1. Northeast face. Class 3. First ascent July 4, 1930, by Norman Clyde, who described it as a good rock climb, involving the passing of numerous pinnacles.

Route 2. West ridge. Class 3. First ascent June 14, 1934, by David R. Brower and Hervey Voge. Follow the ridge from the little glacier northeast of Mount Agassiz.

Route 3. Southeast face. Class 3. Descended June 14, 1934, by the party of Route 2. The face is cut by rough, broken chutes, which are readily climbed or descended.

Mount Gayley (13,510)

This is the peak just northeast of Mount Sill. The first ascent was made June 10, 1927, by Norman Clyde, by Route 1. It offers the finest view of the glaciated peaks of the north and south forks of the Big Pine Creek basin.

Route 1. Southwest ridge. Class 3. Follow the ridge from Glacier Notch. An alternative (Norman Clyde, 1949) is to climb from the Palisade Glacier to the ridge north of the buttress north of Glacier Notch, rather than first climbing to the notch.

Route 2. South face. Class 3. Descended September 28, 1931, by W. A. Starr, Jr. A number of routes are possible.

Route 3. West face. Class 3. First ascent June, 1950, by Robert Cogburn and Ed Robbins. A fairly large gully comes down the west wall south of Gayley. Ascend on the northeast side of this gully for a short distance in a rotten chimney, and then traverse left (N) on a series of ledges underneath a prominent gendarme to a couloir that leads up to the summit ridge.

Route 4. North face. Class 4 to 5. Various routes have been made by Smokey Blanchard and others. One interesting route is to climb diagonally across the face to the left to a notch on the northeast ridge. From here you can ascend the east face to the summit.

Temple Crag (*12,999*)

From the north Temple Crag is one of the most beautiful mountains of the Sierra, chiefly because of the splendid sculpture of the precipices on that side, which are of dark, massive granite and rise 3,000 feet above the lower Big Pine Lakes. The north face is cut by two deep and narrow snow chimneys; the northwest face by a broader couloir. These have carved the intervening buttresses into tremendous, fantastic towers. The first ascent was made by the USGS in 1909, probably by Route 1.

Route 1. Southeast face. Class 3. Climb the deepest chute in the broken southeast face to the gradual nivated slope above it. A shallow chute connects the top of this slope with a spectacular knife-edge leading to the summit. As a variation, the nivated slope of Route 1 may be reached by a steep crack or chimney up the west wall of Contact Pass, just south of the highest point of the pass. Fourth class climbing up the crack, or up the wall outside, leads to the slope above.

Route 2. Northwest face. Class 3. First ascent by Norman Clyde in 1930. Go up the chute to the right (SW) of the broad northwest couloir until it joins the latter, then follow the right wall of the main couloir to the broken face at its head. Here cross to the left of the left branch of the chute for a way and work up to the west arête of the Crag, which is followed to the summit.

Route 3. North face. Class 4. First ascent August 11, 1931, by Norman Clyde, R. L. M. Underhill, Glen Dawson, and Jules Eichorn. Climb the narrow crack just east of the western snow-chimney of the north face. The crack goes more or less up the center of the north buttress. Then climb the east wall of the snow-chimney to a point below the notch between Temple Crag and its north peak. Proceed diagonally upward and east to the summit knife-edge.

Route 4. North peak from the northeast. Class 4. First ascent July 7, 1940, by John and Ruth Mendenhall. From Third Lake ascend scree and snow slopes and enter the first deep chimney or couloir southeast of the north buttress. Well up in the chimney the angle diminishes and climbing becomes class 3 until the notch looking down the northwest face is reached. To reach the north peak, first ascended by the Mendenhalls, climb north along the ridge, winding in and out of, and over, rocky teeth.

The summit of Temple Crag was reached from the notch between it and the north peak by the Mendenhalls in 1957, after a climb to the notch from the northeast, up a chimney just southeast of that used in Route 4.

Route 5. North peak from the northwest. Class 5.4. First ascent August 1963 by John and Vivian Mendenhall, Roy Coates, and Ed Lane. From Third Lake ascend talus to the base of the couloir just west of Temple Crag. Climb up the face toward the north peak, reaching the north ridge a little north of the summit.

Peaks West of the Crest

Columbine Peak (12,652)

First ascent prior to 1925, by persons unknown. Class 2 by the northeast or south ridge.

Peak 12,359 (1 E of Giraud Peak)

First ascent by John White in August 1938. A class 2 traverse from Knapsack Pass.

Isosceles Peak (12,240+)

This is the most striking feature of the south wall of Dusy Basin, and is a good class 3 climb by the northwest face. The first ascent was made in July 1938 by Wear and Morse.

Giraud Peak (12,585)

First ascent in September 1925 by Norman Clyde. Class 2 by the east arête.

Peak 12,692 (1.3 S of North Palisade)

First ascent in 1925 by Ralph A. Chase.

Kings Canyon Region

ROBERT L. SMITH (1953, 1964)

FOR WILD and rugged grandeur the Kings River Canyon Region of the Sierra Nevada has no peer. A mighty panorama, beginning at the thundering snow-fed streams, sweeping up the terrifying gorges past jagged spires, and culminating in towering granite peaks and domes presents itself to the adventurer. In this vast, largely unknown area the opportunities for exploration are limitless. With the imposing array of peaks and rock towers, and with many unclimbed summits still awaiting an ascent, the climber can fare very well. Maps for this area are the Tehipite Dome and Marion Peak quadrangles.

Deepest of all Sierra canyons are those of the Kings River and its two main forks. The great canyon of the Middle Fork of the Kings River is one of the most spectacular parts of the entire Sierra. It is indeed an awe-inspiring sight to break out of the pine forest onto the rim of the Tehipite Valley and gaze across at the opposite mountain wall, fantastically cut up into multiple flying turrets soaring in the blue haze. The thin ribbons of streams, sweeping down the myriads of steep gorges from the high country, line the mountain sides with bands of silver. The great river, four thousand feet below, sends its dull roar echoing about the valley. Here also is the graceful and symmetrical Tehipite Dome, the sentinel of this seldom-visited domain.

To the southwest stands an even greater mountain wall. Spanish Mountain, on the edge of an immense plateau, towers 8,200 feet above the Kings River. The expanse between, dropping off in dizzy contours, is a vast jumble of deep gorges, madly cascading and falling streams, and steeply-tilted spurs, all more vertical than horizontal.

HISTORICAL RÉSUMÉ

In this section of the Sierra, as well as many of the others, the sheepherders played an important part in early exploration. Perhaps the best known and certainly the most ambitious of this group was Frank Dusy. In 1869, Dusy and Bill Helm set up partnership in sheep raising at Dinkey on Dinkey Creek. On a hunting trip the same year, Dusy shot a grizzly bear near Crown Creek, and followed the wounded bear all the way down to the Middle Kings Canyon. He hiked up to the

Tehipite Valley and can presumably be given credit for its discovery. Dusy also built the Dinkey Trail to Crown Creek and its extension, the Tunemah Trail, to the upper Middle Fork Canyon, both of which were needed to get his sheep to Simpson Meadow.

Around 1876 there was a Hydrographic Reconnaissance of the area. Among other things, the height of Tehipite Dome was estimated.

Known primarily for his early mountaineering in the Kings Canyon area was Professor Bolton C. Brown. Among his many achievements were first ascents, in 1895, of Mount Woodworth and Avalanche Peak and his extensive work in exploration and route finding.

Until recent years, very little climbing has been done here. Some of the peaks above the canyon walls were climbed in past years by hikers or members of the USGS, but the more difficult peaks and the rock climbs remained untouched. In 1935 an attempt was made on the Sphinx, but it was not until 1940 that it was finally conquered. In the years that followed many of the difficult rock towers fell to Sierra Club climbing parties. First was the Obelisk in 1947, and then the towers of the Grand Dike, Gorge of Despair, and Silver Spur in 1951 and 1952.

Many towers and faces above the South Fork Canyon have been climbed since 1954, but unclimbed spires and pinnacles can probably be found in the maze of gorges yet unexplored.

TOPOGRAPHY AND ITS RELATION TO CLIMBING

The canyons of the Kings River owe their astounding depth mainly to streamwork, although they have been remodeled and enlarged by intense glaciation. Often compared with Yosemite, the Kings Canyon is actually different in most respects. While Yosemite has its hanging valleys and great water falls, nearly all the tributary streams in Kings Canyon have cut their valleys down to so great a depth that they now descend in broken cascades engulfed in slot-like gorges, dark and narrow. The walls are further scored by great avalanche chutes. In the canyon of the Middle Fork of the Kings River, particularly on the southern wall above Tehipite Valley, the actions of streams, glaciers and the elements through countless centuries have left in their wake many fantastic spires and towers. It may be safely said that these are the finest rock climbs in the entire Sierra, outside of Yosemite Valley. The fact that they lie in lonely, barely accessible country only adds to their enchantment.

The great canyon of the South Fork also has attractions for the mountaineer. The best climbing is undoubtedly on the Grand Dike, an immense steep and broken ridge comprised of eight large towers and a number of minor summits.

Many interesting climbs can be found on the canyon walls above State Highway 180 from Windy Cliff east to Cedar Grove. Farther up this canyon may be found the Grand Sentinel and the Sphinx, also fine climbs, which are easily reached from the road end.

In general, the rock in this region is fairly sound granite, but that of a crumbling nature is occasionally encountered. Many of the rocks have peculiar knobs protruding from their surface shells, a remarkable characteristic seldom found elsewhere. These knobs can be found on the towers above the Gorge of Despair, where they enable one to climb high-angle walls, and on the Obelisk, where they are sound enough to safely hold a rappel rope.

Approaches

From the north. A trail leaves the John Muir Trail at the mouth of Palisade Creek (8,125) and follows down the Middle Fork of the Kings River to Simpson Meadow. Here the trail divides, one branch continuing to Dougherty Meadow, and still upward to cross the Monarch Divide at Granite Pass (10,673), then dropping down to meet the Kings River Canyon at the old Kanawyers campsite.

From the south. Starting from Giant Forest in Sequoia National Park, the most direct route is over J. O. Pass (9,410) to Rowell Meadow, where two branching trails lead to the same route. One joins at Horse Corral Meadow and the other goes over Marvin Pass (9,100) to join between Horse Corral Meadow and Summit Meadow. The trail descends by switchbacks to the floor of Kings River Canyon at Cedar Grove (4,635).

From the east. Leaving the John Muir Trail at the forks of Woods Creek, a trail goes down the creek to its intersection with the South Fork of the Kings River. After fording the river, the trail follows down the west bank through Paradise Valley to a junction with the Kings River Canyon trail. Farther south on the Muir Trail, the Bubbs Creek trail leads westward to the Kings River Canyon.

From the west. Highway 180 from Fresno leads first to General Grant Grove, then continues to Cedar Grove. From here all points of the Kings Canyon area are accessible with the exception of the Tehipite Valley and peaks on the north wall of the Middle Fork. A long trail from Cliff Camp on the North Fork of the Kings River passes through Three Springs, Collins Meadow, and finally drops into the Tehipite

Valley, from which Simpson Meadow may be reached. At Collins Meadow an obsolete trail branches eastward over Tunemah Pass (10,879), and descends a steep and unsafe route to Simpson Meadow.

The Tehipite Valley may be reached from Cedar Grove by crossing the Monarch Divide at Happy Gap and following down the east bank of Silver Creek. This is a dangerous route, unfit for pack animals, and is further complicated by the fact that it is often impossible to cross the Middle Fork of the Kings in the valley. In the spring, at high water, this river may present an impassable barrier at many points, as the only bridge is at Simpson Meadow.

The rock climbs on the great spurs above Tehipite Valley are not easily approached from any direction. The only feasible route is to start from the South Fork of the Kings River, following up either the Lewis Creek or Deer Cove trails to Wildman Meadow. Just west of this meadow is Grizzly Creek, which can be followed along its west bank to the top of the Monarch Divide. The divide is crossed at a saddle just west of Hogback Peak. Care must be taken at this point to descend into the correct canyon. A route due north would continue past Swamp Lakes and then down into Lost Canyon, which is virtually unexplored. A one-half mile traverse to the west must be made from the saddle to enter the upper end of the Gorge of Despair. This gorge can be followed down, keeping on the north side of the creek, until a suitable campsite can be found at about 8,000 feet elevation. Many fine rock climbs are available from this point.

A packer's trail now follows the west bank of Grizzly Creek from near Wildman Meadow going several miles upstream, and then climbing out of the west fork of Grizzly Creek at Grizzly Lakes. This canyon can be followed up under Mount Harrington to the top of the Monarch Divide. It is advisable to stay on the right (east) side of this canyon to avoid cliffs.

Because of the three thousand foot precipice at the lower end, it is impossible to enter the Gorge of Despair from the Tehipite Valley. Those exploring the other great spurs and canyons in this area will find that the obstacles to cross-country traveling are often great, and sometimes insurmountable. Because of this fact, there are many rock towers that have never been closely approached, some of which may well prove to be more than worth the arduous trip to their base.

CAMPSITES

Most of the meadows in this region provide excellent campsites, having water available all year. Especially to be recommended because of their beautiful setting are Collins Meadow in the Crown Valley, Simpson Meadow on the Middle Fork of the Kings River, and Zumwalt Meadows in the Kings River Canyon. Pasturage is good in general, but is very meager on portions of the Granite Pass Trail, especially between the pass and Granite Basin. The floor of Tehipite Valley is also quite barren, except in early spring. Not shown on the USGS quadrangle map are several meadows about one-third mile northwest of the Obelisk, which are the best campsites in that vicinity.

A good base camp can be established alongside the creek in the Gorge of Despair at an elevation of approximately 8,000 feet, which is near the base of Cobra Turret, and close to the best climbs in the region.

ROUTES AND RECORDS FOR THE PEAKS

The peaks covered in this section of the guide lie in an area partially within the borders of Kings Canyon National Park and partially in the Sierra and Sequoia National Forests. This region extends from Mount Woodworth on the north to Sentinel Dome on the south. The western boundary follows from Finger Peak south along Kettle Ridge to the Obelisk, and jogs over to include Spanish Mountain. The eastern boundary, starting at the intersection of Goddard Creek with the Middle Fork of the Kings River, follows down the Middle Fork to the Granite Pass trail near Simpson Meadow. This trail serves as the easterly limits of the arbitrary region from here on south. Avalanche Peak and The Sphinx are also included in this section.

Because they are widely scattered, the peaks and rock climbs in the Kings Canyon area cannot be grouped in any strict order. Therefore, they are arranged in order from west to east as follows:

Middle Fork of the Kings River region
  Spanish Mountain and Tombstone Ridge
  Kettle Ridge and vicinity
  White Divide and vicinity
  Gorge of Despair and Silver Spur
Monarch Divide
South Fork of the Kings River region
  Peaks on the North Wall
  Peaks on the South Wall

There is, however, an exception to the west-to-east rule. On spurs having a number of rock towers on them, the towers are grouped according to elevation, from the lowest to the highest. The spurs themselves will follow the original west to east classification.

Middle Fork of the Kings River Region

SPANISH MOUNTAIN AND TOMBSTONE RIDGE

Spanish Mountain (B.M. 10,051)

Climbed in 1921 by Hermann F. Ulrichs. May be climbed from the northwest by a number of routes, but the most interesting route lies along the southeast ridge, where the best view of the 8,000 foot deep canyon can be had. Class 2.

Obelisk (9,700)

Route 1. Class 5. First ascent in 1948 by Jim Wilson and Allen Steck. The route starts up a long, well broken chimney on the south face. The chimney ends at the foot of a steep wall about 100 feet high. This pitch is the crux of the climb, for it is quite exposed and the holds are unreliable. Several pitons are used here for safety. The lead is about 100 feet with no intermediate belay spots. The route to the summit is easy from the top of the wall. Six rappels are required to reach the ground. Length of climb: 500 to 600 feet.

Route 2. Extreme class 4. First ascent June 1951 by Anton Nelson, David Hammack, John Salathé, and Alice Ann Dayton. The climb starts on the short 45° ridge near the center of the north face. The slabs are ascended for about 100 feet, at which point the ridge ends. A traverse to the right (west) is made around the face on very small, exposed ledges to the west arête. The arête is followed to the summit on excellent holds. Time required: 1½ hours.

The rope-down, if made from the northeast shoulder over the great overhang, involves a 130-foot rappel. Some of the large knobs that protrude from the surface of this rock make excellent anchor points. Care should be taken to see that the rope will run around the knob used.

KETTLE RIDGE AND VICINITY

Kettle Dome (9,446)

First ascent July 20, 1920, by Hermann Ulrichs. Climbing data is meager on this dome as ascents are rare. In the notes of Ulrichs, we find this description: "Only one or two narrow cracks in the smooth rounded granite afford finger holds sufficient to make an ascent possible." The climb is class 3 via the northeast slope.

Tehipite Dome (7,708)

First known ascent by Allan L. Chickering and Walter A. Starr on July 31, 1896. The summit can be gained by climbing out along a sloping ledge on the west face or by going out the backbone, which involves nothing more than a rock scramble. The easiest way to reach the north base of the dome is to leave the Tunemah trail at the 7,500 foot level and contour around, as severe brush is encountered at higher elevations.

Southwest face, main buttress. First ascent by Fred Beckey and Herb Swedlund on June 1, 1963, and on the following day by John C. Ahern and Ken Weeks. The length of this climb is 3,600 feet, and the first ascent took five days. About ten bolts were used, as well as a wide selection of pitons. Part way up the face there is a ledge system which makes it possible to traverse off the climb to pick up more supplies. Class 5.8.

WHITE DIVIDE AND VICINITY

Peak 12,479 (0.8 S of Mount Reinstein)

The left (westerly) of several chutes on the southwest face leads almost to the summit. About 20 feet from the top of the chute climb out to the left onto the south ridge. First ascent August 9, 1958, by Gordon Oates and George Wallerstein. Class 2–3.

Peak 12,209 (1.5 S of Mount Reinstein)

First ascent August 8, 1958 by Gordon Oates and George Wallerstein. Ascent was by the east ridge. The easiest way to get past the steep lower portion of this broad ridge is to go behind a huge boulder and then up. Descent can be made by the southwest ridge. Class 2–3.

Peak 12,309 (1.7 S of Mount Reinstein)

First ascent August 8, 1958, by Gordon Oates and George Wallerstein. The east peak is class 2 from the basin to the east or from Peak 12,209. To get to the higher west peak go down the south ridge to a chute on the west side. Descend the chute and then traverse north toward the notch. Cross a sandy chute and climb rocks onto the ridge leading to the west peak. Class 3.

Finger Peak (12,404)

First ascent by government survey party. Records of the climb are not available. It is class 3 by the northwest ridge from Cathedral Lake. The southwest and southeast slopes are class 2.

Blue Canyon Peak (11,849)

First ascent by Robin J. McKeown and Frank Orme on August 27, 1959, by a class 2 route from the east.

Peak 11,920 (0.5 S of Blue Canyon Peak)

Climbed on August 4, 1960, by Martial Thiebaux and George Wallerstein on a traverse from Peak 12,081. Class 2. Descent was by the west face, class 2–3.

Peak 11,969 (1.2 SE of Blue Canyon Peak)

First ascent on August 3, 1960, by Martial Thiebaux and George Wallerstein. The climb is Class 3 via the west ridge, which can be reached either from the col south of Blue Canyon Peak by crossing a rocky basin and a low ridge, or from Tunemah Lake. It is reported to be the best climb in the area.

Peak 12,081 (1 S of Blue Canyon Peak)

Climbed by Martial Thiebaux and George Wallerstein on August 4, 1960. They found a cairn. The route was the northwest ridge, class 3. Descent was by the northeast ridge to Peak 11,920. Class 2.

Peak 11,872 (1.2 S of Blue Canyon Peak)

Climbed by Martial Thiebaux and George Wallerstein on August 3, 1960, from Tunemah Lake via the northeast ridge. Class 2. Descent was down the south ridge to a notch, and then down into Blue Canyon. Class 2–3.

Burnt Mountain (10,608)

Probably climbed by early exploring parties. There appear to be no climbing difficulties to surmount this peak, and it is easily approached from the Tunemah trail.

Tunemah Peak (11,894)

The west, southwest, and southeast slopes are class 2, as is the south ridge.

Gorge of Despair and Silver Spur

Sketch 23 shows the location of the turrets and towers of this area.

Fascination Turret (7,000)

First ascent June 16, 1955, by Kim Malville, Fred Martin, and Robert Tambling. This is the lowest rock tower on this immense spur, being almost out of sight of the large towers above. It is located on the extreme end of the spur, immediately above the tremendous drop-off into Tehipite Valley. It may be reached from the notch below the east face of Frustration Turret by descending the steep flood channel to the north. Turn up into the second gully on the left (W) and climb over loose rock to the base of the turret. The climb is class 3 via the east face.

Gendarme near Frustration Turret

This is the needle-shaped gendarme on the ridge between Frustration and Fascination turrets, first climbed in June 1955 by Kim Malville, Fred Martin, and Robert Tambling. It may be reached by descending the flood channel to the north from the Frustration Turret notch and turning up the first gully on the left (W). It is a short class A climb.

Frustration Turret (7,500+)

First ascent June 18, 1952, by David Hammack, Jules Eichorn, Clinton Kelley, and Bob Smith. The climb starts from just below the notch at the base of the east face, and goes straight up this face for about 100 feet to a small tree ledge, which serves as the first belay point. The holds up to this ledge are very small at the start, but improve farther up. From this ledge continue upward on good holds for another 15 feet to a smaller ledge. Traverse around the face to the right, passing under the huge overhanging slab to a broken shoulder. This is ascended to the large friction ledge above. Cross this outward slanting ledge to the other end and up a semi-chimney. By going upward and to the right, a large steep slab on the northwest corner of the tower is ascended. The route follows up the vertical jam crack from the slab, and then up to the right to a small platform. Several variations of the route can be made here. By going up to the left, a class 5 route on small holds can be followed. The other choice is to work slightly to the right (W) and up a highly-polished trough at the limit of friction. At the upper end of the trough a traverse is made to the left. Either route brings one to a narrow ledge under a vertical face about 100 feet below the summit, which

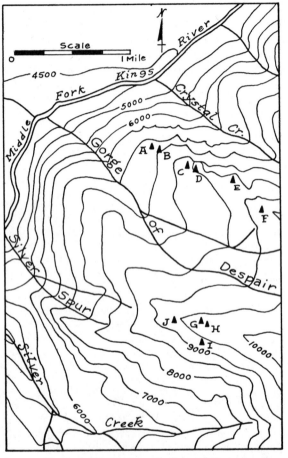

Sketch 23. Turrets above the Gorge of Despair.

A—Fascination Turret   F—Crystal Turret
B—Frustration Turret   G—Silver Turret
C—El Corporale   H—Fang Turret
D—El Commandante   I—Silver Maiden
E—Cobra Turret   J—Friday's Folly

can be climbed with one or two pitons for direct aid, and with the aid of a small crack. Continuing slightly to the left, the route goes up a short, steep pitch requiring long arm pulls on hidden holds, and finally brings one out on the northeast shoulder at the summit block. A traverse around the block to the south side of the tower leads to an easy route to the summit. The rope-down is made on the north face down to the large friction ledge in two rappels. The first ascent party climbed down from here to the tree ledge on the east face, and then rappelled from there. Length of climb: 400 feet. Class A.

El Corporale Turret

First ascent July 25, 1951, by David Hammack and Anton Nelson. The climb is made up the prominent gully, making use of the large solution knobs, and is just difficult enough to justify a rope. Class 4.

El Commandante Turret (8,530)

Route 1. First ascent on July 25, 1951, by David Hammack and Anton Nelson. Class of climb: 5.5. The only apparent route on this tower is the obvious chimney that starts from the south (lower) corner and leads to a large platform about halfway up. The climb is started by ascending the chimney for about 30 feet until it begins to steepen, and then out on to the southwest face, where use is made of the large solution knobs. The chimney is intersected again at the platform. From the platform, which is at the northwest corner, a class 5 route zig-zags up the 70° face to a point just below the summit block. Here a delicate friction pitch, either up a steep arête or across the face to the southwest corner leads to a point from which the summit may be attained. Length of climb: 300 feet.

Route 2. First ascent on July 19, 1952, by a Sierra Club party of nine. Class 5.2. The climb starts in the same chimney as Route 1, but instead of going out on to the face, the chimney is followed up until it ends. Here a short traverse is made to the right (NE) which leads to the platform. From this point the deep chimney is climbed until it also ends. The route traverses slightly to the right, and then up a high angle class 5 crack involving a lieback, to the platform just below the summit. From here a narrow, steeply-inclined ledge leads to the summit block. Then it is an easy scramble to the summit.

Cobra Turret (9,050+)

First ascent July 26, 1951, by David Hammack and Anton Nelson. The highest point on the northwest side is reached by skirting the cliffs.

This point, from which the climb is started, is just to the southwest of the ridge above Crystal Creek. A large tree may be seen about 75 feet above the ground on the face of the turret, and may be reached by a 3rd class scramble. From the tree, the route leads to the southwest for about 50 feet, and then up and back into a semi-chimney, passing the overhang to the right (SW), and continuing to a suitable belay spot. This lead is a full 120 feet, and requires the use of several class 5 pitons. From here, the climbing continues directly up by a number of possible routes. Solution knobs allow one to ascend the vertical face in several spots. It would seem best, however, to remain just above the prominent semi-chimney. Length of climb: 500 feet. Class 5.8.

Crystal Turret (9,600)

This is the highest rock tower in this group. First ascent July 25, 1951, by David Hammack and Anton Nelson. This climb is started from the southeast corner, up a short steep rib. A long class 5 traverse is then made to the right (W) on small, polished holds to a difficult jam crack. Above the jam crack is a platform and a "window" through which the route passes. Once through the window turn right (N), and climb the steep arête to the large platform, and then traverse around the south side of the summit block to the southeast corner. From here an easy pitch leads directly up to the summit. Length of climb 200 feet. Class 5.4.

Tenderfoot Peak (10,621)

This peak is the highest point on the north ridge of the Gorge of Despair, located above a large lake, and can be identified by its prominent red and white bands. First ascent in June 1955 by Fred Martin, Kim Malville, and Robert Tambling. This is a class 2 climb from the lake at the base.

Friday's Folly (9,388)

First ascent July 8, 1955, by Felix Knauth, Harold Sipperly, and John Whitmer. This is the large wedge shaped mass below and to the southwest of Silver Turret. The route follows an overlapping flake formation midway down the east side. It provides about 250 feet of high angle climbing. Class 5.3.

Silver Turret (9,913)

This is the most prominent feature on Silver Spur when viewed from the 8,000-foot contour in the Gorge of Despair, and is shown on the USGS quadrangle map (elevation). The approach should be made to the left (E) from the Gorge of Despair. The summit is reached by a class 3-4 scramble from the south. First ascent by David Hammack and Anton Nelson on July 27, 1951.

Fang Turret.

A very difficult 100-foot rock spire immediately to the south of Silver Turret. From the southeast notch, the route is easily seen. Pitons for direct aid and safety are required on the almost vertical route. First climbed on July 27, 1951, by David Hammack and Anton Nelson. Class A.

Silver Maiden (9,300)

This is a large tower located in Silver Creek Canyon about 500 feet below the notch between Fang and Silver Turret, and southeast of it. First ascent August 3, 1962, by Bruce Edwards, Howard Lewis, Bob Smith, James Smith, and Ed Sutton. The route starts on a broken wall on the northeast side, and goes up on large holds for about 30 feet to a sharp arête. A traverse on the exposed north side of the arête leads to a platform, the first belay position. From here descend to the south for about 50 horizontal feet to the base of a prominent rib. The route follows up this polished rib using lieback to an alcove under a large block. This position must be used as a belay point although it is precarious. From here the route goes directly up the wall, first in a chimney, which disappears into an almost vertical classic lieback crack. This pitch continues for about 70 feet, ending on the shoulder just below the summit. One bolt, three pitons for direct aid, and two pitons for protection were used in the crack. From here an easy class 4 pitch leads to the summit on large solution knobs. Length of climb: 250 feet. Class A.

The Python

This is the next high point up the ridge from Fang Turret on Silver Spur. First ascent in June 1955 by Fred Martin, Kim Malville, and Robert Tambling. Class 4.

Monarch Divide

Wren Peak (9,450)

No recorded ascents. This is the large dome-shaped peak at the upper end of Junction Ridge. It appears to be a class 2 climb from any direction. The best approach would be from Happy Gap. There is a group

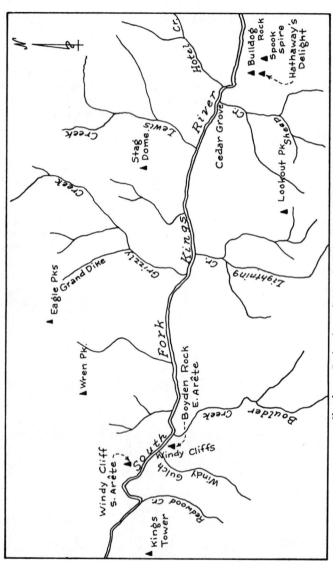

Sketch 24. Peaks above the South Fork of the Kings River.

of formidable-looking crags below and to the south of Wren Peak, some of which may prove to be difficult climbs.

Eagle Peaks (9,750)

While there are no records of ascents in this group of peaks, some of them may have been climbed by exploring parties. All of them appear to be rock scrambles from their bases.

Mount Harrington (11,005)

First recorded ascent July 27, 1951, by David Hammack and Anton Nelson. The best approach to the base is from the north. The lower part of the mountain presents no serious climbing difficulties. The jagged summit spire is a climb of extreme class 3 difficulty, with large holds all the way up.

Hogback Peak (11,077)

This peak can be climbed from the saddle just to the west over huge talus blocks. First ascent by James M. Carl and John Ohrenschall, September 10, 1955.

Slide Peak (10,915)

No recorded ascents. The north and west faces of this peak are very steep and would no doubt provide some interesting class 4 routes. There appears to be an easy route from the south, however.

Kennedy Mountain (B.M. 11,433)

First ascent by government surveying party. This peak appears to be a class 2 ascent from any direction except the north, where the face drops a sheer 600 feet. An easy climb from Kennedy Pass.

South Fork of the Kings River Region

Sketch 24 indicates the location of some of the South Fork climbs.

PEAKS OF THE NORTH WALL

Windy Cliff—South Arête

First recorded ascent July 20, 1954, by Merle Alley and George Sessions. This is the prominent arête just north of the bridge crossing the

Kings River at Boyden's Cave. Follow the gully to the east until an easy traverse is possible left to the very edge of the arête. The climb consists of 350 feet of fourth and fifth class rock work along the left side of the arête. Several pitches up, a variation to the right is possible but requires the use of direct aid to reach the summit. Descend via the back third class to the east gully. This route, as well as the arête on Boyden Rock, is on limestone and extra care must be taken to test for loose rock. Class 5.

The Grand Dike (7,500–8,500)

A traverse of seven of the nine towers was made on July 28, 1951, by David Hammack and Anton Nelson, which constituted first ascents of all but Towers No. ½ and 4. The towers are numbered starting from the lower (SE) end.

The Towers

Tower No. ½. First ascent Nov. 26, 1954, by Kim Malville, John Ohrenschall, and Richard Smyth. The route begins in the notch between Tower No. 1 and this pinnacle. Descend a few feet down the other side of the notch in a southwest direction. Go through a little key-hole formed by a chockstone that rests between the walls of Tower No. 1 and the pinnacle. Ascend a little ledge diagonally along the wall of Tower No. 1 to a point directly above the notch, from which the tops of chockstones can be crossed. Cross over to the northeast corner of the summit tower. Traverse a ledge on the northwest face to the base of a short chimney. Up to the base of the chimney the climbing is class 3. Roping up, ascend the chimney to a small platform at the base of a chockstone. Gain the top of the chockstone by ascending to its right (SW). Several pitons should be used on this pitch. The top of the summit block can be reached by a short class 4 pitch. After climbing down from the summit block, descent can be made by a short rappel from its southeast corner. Class 5.3.

Tower No. 1. The route leads up the eastern face of Tower No. 2 for about 70 feet to a broad, horizontal ledge. (A diagonal upward ledge from low down on Tower No. 2 is not the route.) The broad ledge leads to the notch between No. 1 and No. 2. From the notch, Tower No. 1 is easily climbed by circling around to the west face. Class 4.

Tower No. 2. This is the truncated, small tower between the larger towers No. 1 and No. 3. From the broad ledge mentioned above, a short chimney continues up the east face to the summit. Class 4.

Tower No. 3. Route 1. From the notch between Nos. 2 and 3 a traverse is made around the southeast face. After it becomes impossible to traverse easily any further, the route goes up and back to the right (SE) on a high angle face with good holds, to a large ledge. The next lead bears to the left (NW) and follows, in general, the northwest corner. This brings one to the base of the main pitch of the climb, a 70 degree face with few prominent holds. This pitch should be done by working slightly to the right (S) and up until a cornice is reached that supplies a few underholds. From the top of this pitch the summit is easily reached. Length of climb: 300 feet. Class 5.5.

Route 2. First ascent November 27, 1954, by Kim Malville, John Ohrenschall, and Richard Smyth. In beginning the climb make the traverse from the notch between Towers 2 and 3 as in Route 1, but continue around the southeast face to a platform with a tree on the northwest face. From the platform ascend directly up, using the tree to get started. Reach some bushes and traverse right (S) around a corner to a large ledge to join Route 1. Class 5.3–5.4.

Tower No. 4. First ascent June 15, 1952, by David Hammack, Bob Smith, George Larimore, and Bob Purington. The route starts in a large chimney on the northeast side. The chimney is ascended about 30 feet, or until it is possible to work out to the right on small holds onto the face. The route follows up a short distance to a suitable belay point on one of the small ledges, where a piton anchor should be placed. Continue straight upward and then traverse slightly to the left (S) to reach a large, partially detached flake. The broken edges of the flake make a ladder, enabling one to ascend the vertical face quite easily. From here the ascent continues up the northeast face at a high angle on good holds, and up a tight chimney to a small but conspicuous tree ledge, a good belay point. The face is climbed until the great north shoulder is reached. From here a short class 3 pitch leads to the summit. The best method of descent is to climb down to the shoulder and rappel down the northwest side into the notch between Towers 4 and 5. This is a 110-foot rappel. Length of climb: 350 feet. Class 5.3.

Tower No. 5. From the notch between Nos. 4 and 5, the summit may be attained by climbing up the broken southeast face. There is only one spot that offers any difficulty, and that is a short, slightly overhanging wall that must be climbed to get out of an alcove about halfway up. From there the main arête is more or less followed to the summit. The rope-down is to the notch between Nos. 5 and 6. Class 3 to 4.

A class 3 route on the north face was ascended on November 27, 1954, by Kim Malville, John Ohrenschall, and Richard Smyth.

Tower No. 6. From the notch between Nos. 5 and 6, there is only one obstacle on the entire climb and that is the 10-foot overhanging wall that extends along the base immediately beside the notch. This is overcome by climbing a small tree about 30 feet below the notch (W side) and traversing across to the wall. The rest of the climb is 2nd and 3rd class. There is apparently an easy class 3 climb on the north side of this tower.

Towers No. 7 and No. 8. May be climbed by any number of routes, none of which offer any serious difficulties. Each of these summits may be attained by second and third class routes.

Stag Dome (7,710)

Records of first ascent are not available, but there is now a USFS lookout station on the summit.

Comb Spur (11,618)

A traverse was made of this spur from July 11 to 25, 1931, by Robert A. Owen.

North Mountain (8,632)

No recorded ascents.

Mount Hutchings (10,785)

First ascent on April 1, 1933, by Norman Clyde and an unnamed companion. It is a class 2 climb from the Granite Pass Trail by following the ridge.

North Dome (8,717)

First ascent June 30, 1940, by Neil Ruge and Florence Rata via Granite Creek and Copper Canyon.

PEAKS ON THE SOUTH WALL

Kings Tower

First ascent May 16, 1954, by Wayne Kincheloe, Richard Sessions, George Sessions, Larry Hawley, and Chris Jessen. This short spire, mushrooming from a thin base when viewed from the east, is located above the road about three miles up-river from the Ten-Mile Creek bridge. It is most easily approached from the west up a brush-filled gully to the south notch. From an alcove above the belayer, a difficult lieback leads to a secure platform. The route then goes up the left side of the south face to a thin ledge which traverses the face to the right edge where the climb finishes on the east face. A 60-foot rappel is required to regain the notch. Piton protection is poor on the hard move below the thin ledge; a very-short, thick wedge is needed. Class 5.2–5.4.

Boyden Rock—east arête

First recorded ascent June 30, 1954, by Mark Powell, Merle Alley, and George Sessions. This route lies on the large peak above Boyden Cave. Follow the Cave Trail on around the buttress and bushwhack high up the arête until difficult rock is encountered. From here, the climbing involves several hundred feet of fifth class rock on the arête, passing above and left of Cliff Cave, to the summit. A rappel to the southeast leads to the third class pinnacles on the southeast and/or the watercourse leading down northwest of the Rock to the road. Class 5.0–5.5.

Lookout Peak (8,501)

First ascent by Elisha Cotton Winchell on September 27, 1868. The climb is described as an easy scramble from Summit Meadow. It is probably no more difficult than class 2.

Hathaway's Delight and Bulldog Rock

These two rock summits sit on a ridge above the new bridge crossing the south fork of the Kings River west of Cedar Grove. They may be most easily seen from around the vicinity of Lewis Creek bridge. Both were first climbed on June 13, 1957, by Merle Alley and George Sessions. The higher summit (Hathaway's Delight) is approached first from the west to a high-angle gully below the upper southern notch. This gully, named "Cruddy Gully" for obvious reasons when one has reached the notch, looks deceptively short and easy, but actually involves about 500 feet of fifth class climbing with one class A overhanging chockstone halfway up. From the notch, a traverse is made east to a platform below the high-angle trough leading to the summit. The register is in the south cairn. The rappel from the summit is made down the west face over a climbable route which could be used easily from an approach directly up the ridge. Class 5.2–5.5.

One more short rappel and some third class climbing down past a small irregularly-shaped pinnacle leads to the notch behind Bulldog Rock, the lower, most prominent summit on the ridge. An easy ledge leads east around to the north face of the Rock, overlooking the river. From the top of a block, direct aid is needed to reach a narrow ledge running up and to the right. At the terminus of the ledge, direct aid is used to attain the highly-sloping west face which is frictioned to the summit. To descend, rappel to the easy ledge. The rest of the ridge is climbed down and a dry watercourse east of the ridge is followed to the bridge. Class A.

Spook Spire

Above Camp 4 in Cedar Grove a 200-foot rock tower stands out from a granite cliff. It is very difficult to see from most vantage points, but at certain times of the day its shadow is visible. It was first climbed on May 17, 1958, by Merle Alley, Jerry Dixon, and George Sessions. Some fourth and fifth class climbing is done to reach the notch behind the spire. Climbing out onto a ledge on the east face, a long reach is made to connect with a crack diagonally up and left which can be nailed to the summit. Class A.

Sentinel Dome (9,115)

This peak is climbed often by hikers to obtain a view of the high country. Information of the first ascent is not obtainable.

Avalanche Peak (10,077)

First ascent in July 1895 by Prof. Bolton C. Brown and A. B. Clark. From the description of the ascent by Brown, it was just a stiff hike to the summit from the outlet of Cooper Creek.

Grand Sentinel (8,504)

First ascent in 1896 by J. N. LeConte, Helen M. Gompertz, Mr. and Mrs. W. S. Gould and party. This ascent was from the back (S) and did not involve any difficult climbing.

An interesting rock climbers' route is that used by Roy Gorin and Jerry Ganapole on July 7, 1951. Two major steps can be seen in the outline of the Grand Sentinel from the canyon floor at Zumwalt Meadows. The base of these steps is approached by working up the stream bed west of the Grand Sentinel. The lower of the two rock faces can be climbed on the edge of the buttress overlooking the 90 degree north face, with class 4 and one or two easy class 5 pitches. A walk across the wide shelf leads to the base of the upper face. From here several moderately difficult class 5 pitches lead to the summit. Climbing time from the base of the lower face is 4 hours. Total time to reach the summit from the canyon floor is 10 hours.

The Sphinx (9,146)

First ascent July 26, 1940, by Art Argiewicz and Bob Jacobs. The Sphinx is the farthest north and slightly lower of the two points comprising the mass. In order to reach the top it is necessary to climb over the higher point, down the north face about 300 feet and up to the notch between the two. The key pitch is a 200 foot face, triangular and almost devoid of holds. Above this is the 150 foot summit ridge. A delicate traverse is made across the face to the south wall, where a small ledge can be found around the corner. From here an open chimney leads to the top of the ridge and the summit. Class 4.

Palisades to Kearsarge Pass
FRED L. JONES (1953); HERVEY H. VOGE (1964)

THE AREA south of the Palisades, as far as Kearsarge Pass, does not contain many outstanding peaks, but it nevertheless is very fine High Sierra country, with much of charm and interest. There are many places where trails do not go that can be reached by knapsackers. Peaks of special note are Mount Bolton Brown, Split Mountain, Mount Baxter, Arrow Peak, and Mount Clarence King. Most, but not all, of the peaks have at least one moderately easy route. Granite predominates throughout, although dark, metamorphic rock is found on Crater Mountain, Cardinal Mountain, Split Mountain, and near Rae Lake. Map coverage is given by the Mount Pinchot and Marion Peak quadrangles, plus small portions of Mount Goddard and Big Pine quadrangles.

HISTORICAL RÉSUMÉ

Indians used Kearsarge Pass as a trading route for untold centuries before Captain John Frémont entered the region to the northwest in 1845 and traveled to 11,000 feet on the North Fork of the Kings. In 1858 J. H. Johnson was led across Kearsarge Pass by a Digger Indian. Prospectors were also active at about this time. The California Geological Survey party led by W. H. Brewer arrived in the Kings River watershed in 1864, and made further explorations in 1865.

In 1873 John Muir traveled up Bubbs Creek and went over Kearsarge Pass. In the years after 1875 sheep came to the South Fork, and in 1876 or 1877 Frank Dusy explored the Middle Fork of the Kings as far as the Palisades. In 1878 the present Split Mountain was named Southeast Palisade by George Wheeler. Taboose, Sawmill, and Pinchot passes were in use by sheepmen by 1890. Bolton C. Brown made a solo trip up the headwaters of the Middle and South forks of the Kings in 1895, and made ascents of Mount Woodworth, Mount Ruskin, and Arrow Peak. Brown explored Sixty Lake Basin and the Rae Lake region in 1899 and made a map of the area.

The early visitors to the mountains naturally paid more attention to passes than to peaks. Mather Pass was first used by stock in 1897 when a sheepman was trapped by snow in the upper Middle Fork of the Kings. Packstock were taken over Glen Pass for the first time in 1906. The Sierra Club conducted its second annual outing in 1902, taking about 200 people into the Kings Canyon. Stock were taken over Muir Pass in 1907 by George R. Davis, who then worked out of the Middle Fork to Cartridge Creek, since there was, of course, no trail down the rugged Middle Fork.

In 1908 J. N. LeConte, James Hutchinson, and Duncan McDuffie made the entire trip from Yosemite to Kings Canyon via high route, with stock. From the Middle Fork, after crossing Muir Pass, they tried to scout out a route over Mather Pass but decided that it was impassable and went up Cataract Creek, across to Cartridge Creek, over Cartridge Pass to the South Fork, over Pinchot and Glen passes, and finally down Bubbs Creek. This trip took 27 days. In 1915 work was begun on the John Muir Trail, which was finally completed in 1938.

When the trails threaded their way through the mountains, the travelers began to climb the peaks. The early trips of Brown, LeConte, Davis, Solomons, and others left relatively few conquered peaks behind. During the 1930's Sierra Club climbers made many first ascents. Norman Clyde, who began his Sierra climbing in the early 1920's while principal of the High School at Independence, has been and still is the unchallenged dean of modern Sierra mountaineers. He and a few others whose names stand out in the records have accounted for the major portion of the original climbing to date.

Approaches and Campsites

Eastern approaches are described first, from north to south, starting with Birch Creek and ending with Kearsarge Pass. Western approaches and a few words about camping follow. Note: Approach roads and trails are sometimes changed by new construction.

Birch Creek. There is no pass over the crest at Birch Creek. From

Big Pine drive west on the road to Glacier Lodge. Just past the first bridge take the branch road to the south to McMurray Meadow. Walk north along the fence to the north; about 200 yards north of the creek the trail runs west among a network of cattle trails. If necessary the trail can be picked up where it climbs up the first draw north of Birch Creek. At about 9,100 one branch of the trail crosses the ridge to the south into a basin on Birch Creek, while the other continues up the ridge to meet the first at a willow patch at about 10,000. Mediocre campsites can be found. The crest can be crossed by knapsackers between the Thumb and the next peak south.

Red Mountain Creek. This is another approach that does not lead over the crest. From Fish Springs on Highway 395 drive southwest to the old Red Mountain Fruit Ranch. Turn west through the stone portals and go past the pumice mine. Keep to the left and cross Tinemaha Creek. At the next fork turn left again. The road ends at a spring north of Red Mountain Creek. The steep, rough trail rounds the hill just above the first little rocky point above Red Mountain Creek. There are campsites on the flat just below Red Mountain Lake. The saddle to the north of Split Mountain can be reached by climbers or knapsackers by climbing above the lake to the northwest, and this saddle can be crossed to Upper Basin.

Taboose Pass (11,360+). Taboose Pass offers an approach to the Upper Basin of the South Fork of the Kings, but it is little used and has fallen into disrepair. Animals must be led over several stretches of jumbled talus blocks. It is a long, dry climb. To reach the foot of the trail turn off Highway 395 about 16 miles north of Independence on the first dirt road north of Taboose Creek. Keep to the right after passing through the drift fence and drive to the end of the rocky road. The trail is signed and leads to the north. Camp can be made in the flat below the falls at about 8,800, or at the last timber at about 10,500.

Sawmill Pass (11,347). From Highway 395 take the first dirt road north of Sawmill Creek and drive to the mouth of Sawmill Canyon. The trail goes up the low ridge north of the canyon mouth. An alternative approach is to drive up the oiled road to the Division Creek powerhouse. A trail leaves the road about one-quarter mile above the powerhouse and meets the Sawmill Canyon branch in the sandy saddle west of the red hill to the south. The trail to the pass is long and arduous, though not particularly rough. Sawmill Meadows is a good camp spot, as is Sawmill Lake, east of the pass.

Baxter Pass (12,320). Drive up the road up the North Fork of Oak Creek to the end. The trail is steep, long, and rough, but there are good campsites at Summit Meadow on the southeast side of the pass, and also at Baxter Lakes on the northwest.

Kearsarge Pass (11,823). From Independence a good road leads to Onion Valley at 8,900 feet, where the trail to the pass starts. This is an excellent and easy trail. Camps can be found at elevations of about 11,000 on either side of the pass.

Western approaches. From Cedar Grove on the South Fork the path follows up the stream. At the Bubbs Creek junction the right hand trail can be followed up Bubbs Creek to Bullfrog Lake, or the left hand one can be taken up Paradise Valley and Woods Creek. From Kings Canyon at Copper Creek a trail can be followed to Granite Pass. It is also possible to approach up the Middle Fork of the Kings, by way of Tehipite Valley, but this approach is quite lengthy.

Campsites. Places with wood and water can be found along most streams up to about 11,400 feet, which is the average timberline for this area.

<h2 style="text-align:center">PRINCIPAL PASSES</h2>

Besides the passes mentioned under approaches, there are a number of others within the area. Mather Pass, Pinchot Pass, Glen Pass, and Granite Pass are crossed by good trails. Cartridge Pass (11,680+) was for long the Muir Trail route between the Middle and South Forks of the Kings, but since the Muir Trail has been rerouted over Mather Pass, Cartridge has fallen into disrepair. Parties use it for stock each year, but it is considered rather rough. Gardiner Pass provides a rough route in current use by packers into Gardiner Basin from Charlotte Lake; the pass lies west of Mount Gardiner.

The remaining routes of this section are recommended only for knapsackers or hikers, although some have been traversed with stock.

Cataract Creek Pass (11,520+). This pass connects Amphitheater and Dumbbell lakes. The trail along Cataract Creek is said to be the worst section. From Amphitheater Lake climb to the pass just east of Observation Peak.

Dumbbell Lakes Pass (11,680+). This is an old sheep route from the head of Cartridge Creek into Dumbbell Lakes. The pass is just west of Peak 12,672.

Upper Basin Pass (12,320+). LeConte and Lindley pioneered a route eastward out of the head of Cartridge Creek into Upper Basin. It is for knapsackers only, and passes just south of Vennacher Needle.

Red Pass (11,600+). Red Pass lies between Marion Peak and Red

Point. It provides a route between Marion Lake and the South Fork of Cartridge Creek, and can be used on a cross-country route from Dougherty Meadow via Horseshoe Lakes, Windy Ridge, and Red Pass to Marion Lake, as was done by the 1935 High Trip.

Arrow Pass (*11,600+*). The notch about three-quarters of a mile southeast of Arrow Peak may be used to go from the creek southwest of Bench Lake to Arrow Creek. It was once used by sheepmen, and constitutes part of a knapsack route between Upper Basin and Paradise Valley.

Explorer Pass (*12,080+*). This leads from Bench Lake to the Lake just east of Window Peak, and on to Woods Creek. From Bench Lake proceed southwest about ¾ mile, then turn southeast and go up the valley toward Peak 12,773 (1.2 NE of Pyramid Peak). Ascend a chute (class 3 with snow) that leads to the ridge between the little peak (12,240+) southwest of 12,773 and the lowest saddle still further west. Proceed southeastward, passing between the little peak (12,240+) and a peak (12,400+) 0.4 mile north of Pyramid Peak. Descend in a southeasterly direction to the stream leading to the lake east of Window Peak.

Muro Blanco. The Muro Blanco can hardly be termed a pass, but it does offer an unconventional route between Upper Basin and Paradise Valley. The descent may be made by knapsackers by following along the river bottom. Although stock have been taken over the same route during periods of low water, the route is decidedly not recommended for animals. The ascent by knapsackers is difficult, and the party should consider that it may be turned back.

Baxter Col (*12,380+*). Between Mount Baxter and Peak 13,183 to the west is a notch which, though up to class 3 on the north, provides a handy route between Woods and Baxter lakes.

Rae Lake—Sixty Lake Basin passes. A route passable to stock lies between Peak 11,942 and Peak 12,553. A ducked trail departs from the Muir Trail on the west side of Rae Lake and crosses the intervening ridge south of Fin Dome.

Sixty Lake Col (*11,600+*). This pass crosses the ridge between Gardiner Basin and Sixty Lake Basin about one mile south of Mount Cotter. It is rough, but is passable to burros.

Knapsack route from Onion Valley to Rae Lakes. It is possible to go from Onion Valley to Rae Lakes in one day by crossing the Woods Creek–Bubbs Creek divide just west of the crest, near Mount Gould and Dragon Peak. Follow the trail to Kearsarge Pass, then go up the west side of the crest toward Gould. An old trail winds up to the top of the ridge between Gould and Rixford and ends on the crest about one-half mile north of Gould at an elevation of about 12,800. This point can also be reached by climbing westward from the southern Golden Trout Lake. Descend down talus to the three lakes just south of Dragon Lake, then follow the stream to Dragon Lake, where a trail leading to Rae Lakes is found. In the reverse direction, take the stream that falls into Dragon Lake from the south and follow it to the eastern-most of the three lakes south of Dragon Lake. From this lake climb the southernmost talus slope which looks negotiable to the ridge, follow the ridge to Mount Gould, and descend to the Kearsarge Pass trail or to the pass itself. This route is class 2 to 3, and may be done in five hours from Rae Lakes to Onion Valley.

North Dragon Pass (*12,400+*). Class 2–3. This pass also leads from Onion Valley to Rae Lakes, and is shorter than the Mount Gould route. From Onion Valley follow the trail toward Golden Trout Lake. Take the right branch to the northern lakes which lie just east of Dragon Peak. Ascend toward the col north of Dragon Peak. This col is not the pass. When part way up to the col traverse to the right (N) and go around the right (E) side of a square-topped peak north of the col, crossing the ridge that runs eastward about where the peak rises from the ridge. Continue north along the east side of the main crest past a minor peak and descend to the west on scree toward Dragon Lake.

Peaks of the Main Crest (North to South)

Peak 13,520+ (*1 N of Mount Bolton Brown; formerly 13,474*)

First ascent June 14, 1930, by Norman Clyde. It is a long, class 3 climb from Glacier Lodge. The peak is more accessible from the basin to the west via a chute leading toward the summit, which is at the north end of the jagged crest. Class 3.

Mount Bolton Brown (*13,538*)

Route 1. Northwest ridge. Class 2. First ascent August 14, 1922, by Chester Versteeg and Rudolph Berls. From the pass to the west proceed along the top of the ridge. A narrow, 100 foot chimney is climbed to reach the top.

Route 2. Southwest slope. Class 3. First descent August 14, 1922, by Chester Versteeg and Rudolph Berls. Descend the slope to the basin below.

Route 3. North slope. Class 2. First ascent October 6, 1948, by Fred L. Jones. From the basin to the north ascend the slope to the top of the ridge west of the summit. Cross to the south side and proceed to the summit.

Mount Prater (13,329)

Route 1. South ridge. Class 1. First ascent unknown. Climb from the saddle to the south, which is reached from Lake 11,599 to west. A short knife-edge ridge just south of the summit presents no great difficulty.

Route 2. North ridge. Class 3. First ascent October 6, 1948, by Fred L. Jones from the basin at the northernmost tip of the South Fork of the Kings. Ascend the largest chute to south of the pinnacles south of Mount Bolton Brown. Cross to the plateau on the east side of the crest, then ascend over the boulders at the south end of the plateau to the summit of the north peak of Mount Prater. A class 3 notch separates the two peaks.

Split Mountain (14,058)

This peak was formerly known as the Southeast Palisade. Information collected by Chester Versteeg reveals that Split Mountain was climbed in July 1887 by Frank Saulque and four others, probably by Route 1.

Route 1. North ridge. Class 2. First recorded ascent July 23, 1902, by Joseph N. LeConte, Helen G. LeConte and Curtis M. Lindley. From Lake 11,599 proceed east to the saddle north of the peak. The U.S. Geological Survey took horses and mules to the saddle in 1943. Ascend the easy north slope to the summit.

Route 2. Northwest shoulder. Class 2. First ascent by Norman Clyde date unknown. He states only that the shoulder is class 2.

Route 3. West face. Class 3. First descent by Norman Clyde, date unknown. He came directly down the west face, keeping to the ribs instead of the chutes due to drop-offs. Clyde states that the peak can be climbed by this route. It is a class 3, with class 4 if the best route isn't chosen.

Route 4. From east. Class 3. From Red Mountain Lake east of Split Mountain go northwest to the ridge east of the saddle. Ascend this, which is rubbly, to the saddle. The last few hundred feet of the ridge are class 3. Red Mountain Lake is reached by a trail following the north slope of the creek from the road end.

The first gendarme south of the summit affords several hundred feet of class 3. First ascended by Norman Clyde and Jules Eichorn, date unknown.

Cardinal Mountain (13,397)

Class 2. First ascent August 11, 1922, by George Downing, Jr. From Taboose Pass ascend either the southwest spur or the chute slightly to east. A narrow, pinnacled stretch, which must be traversed if the southwest spur is followed, is bypassed by using the chute.

Cardinal Mountain can be easily ascended from Stecker's Bench on the north side of Taboose Creek, to which a trail leads from the end of the road on Red Mountain Creek.

Striped Mountain (13,120+)

First ascent July, 1905, by George R. Davis, route unknown.

Route 1. From Taboose Pass. Class 2. From Taboose Pass proceed southeast to a lake north of the mountain and ascend either the northeast or east slopes. This is probably the route of first ascent.

Route 2. West ridge. Class 2. First ascent August 1, 1948 by Fred L. Jones. In climbing by this route follow the drainage above the twin lakes west of Striped Mountain, keeping well up on the north slope. Any of several chutes on the southwest face of the mountain lead to the summit plateau, though some are more difficult than others.

Route 3. From Woods Creek. Class 3. First ascent August 11, 1948, by Fred L. Jones. From the lake east of Mount Pinchot ascend the west slope of the crest to the junction of the ridge running east between two forks of Goodale Creek. Descend a steep, narrow chute to the head of the north fork of Goodale Creek. Ascend an easy chute to the saddle between Goodale and Striped mountains from which either can easily be climbed. The route is class 3 to Goodale Creek and class 2 from there.

Mount Perkins (12,591)

Class 2. First ascent before 1910 by a U.S. Geological Survey party. The west slope and the crest to north and south are easily climbable.

Colosseum Mountain (12,473)

Route 1. Southwest slope. Class 1. First ascent August 5, 1922, by Chester Versteeg. From Woods Lake climb to the highest lake to north, ascend the southwest slope of Colosseum Mountain over gravelly sand.

Route 2. West ridge. Class 1. From the basin to the northwest ascend to the saddle west of the peak, then go east to the summit.

Route 3. Northwest chute. Class 2. From the basin to the northwest ascend the gully north of the summit and climb out near the top.

Route 4. North ridge. Class 4. From the crest to the north traverse over several sheer-sided notches to the summit. This route is generally chosen in error.

Peak 12,080+ (0.7 S of Colosseum Mountain; formerly 12,101)

Class 2. First ascent in 1935 by Marjory Farquhar, Helen LeConte, Peter Grubb, C. Burkett, et al. It is an easy ascent from the west. Has been called Woods Pinnacles.

Mount Baxter (13,125)

First ascent in 1905 by George R. Davis, route unknown.

Route 1. North ridge. Class 2. Ascend the north ridge from the saddle east of Stocking Lake. Cross the area south of the saddle to the large chute above. Bear to the east at the top of this and wind back and forth across the ridge. This is probably the route of first ascent. The north ridge can also be climbed from the east (class 3) from the head of Sawmill Creek.

Route 2. From the northwest. Class 3. From Stocking Lake northwest of Mount Baxter climb to the saddle west of the peak, then ascend the west slope of Mount Baxter to the summit. The route to the saddle is class 3, the upper slope class 2. The basin above the lake is subject to heavy rockfall during the summer and due caution should be exercised.

Route 3. From southwest. Class 2. From the upper Baxter Lake climb northeast to the small lake above. The large talus chute northeast of the lake offers the shortest route to the summit plateau. However the rocks are loose and delicately balanced. An alternate class 2 route from the lake, via the west slope of the basin, to the saddle west of Mount Baxter (see Route 2) provides surer footing.

Route 4. Northeast ridge. Class 3. First descent July 25, 1948, by Fred L. Jones. In climbing by this route, which is a traverse from Peak 12,400+ one mile to the east, descend the north side of the ridge and work around and over the first point to the west. Cross a knife-edge to the next point, and drop into the notch to west. Ascend one of the chimneys leading to the slope above. Ascend the large chute to near the summit of the sharp point above. Traverse the blocks on the north side of the ridge to the summit plateau of Mount Baxter.

Route 5. South ridge. Class 3. First descent August 5, 1948, by Fred L. Jones. In ascending from the upper Baxter Lake climb northeast toward the notch in the crest one mile south of Mount Baxter. Cross the crest to the east side and traverse the ribs and chutes, keeping as high as possible, until the top of the crest can be followed to the summit plateau.

Route 6. Southeast slope. Class 2. Go up the Baxter Pass Trail to about 8,800 feet, cross over to the north branch of the North Fork of Oak Creek, and ascend the southeast slope of Mount Baxter. There is good camping at about 10,000 feet.

Route 7. North face. Class 3. Ascend a wide chute that terminates about 300 yards east of the summit.

Peak 13,070 (0.5 N of Diamond Peak; formerly 13,051)

First ascent 1925 by Norman Clyde, route unknown. It can easily be ascended by long class 2 climbs west from the Baxter Pass trail or on a traverse from Diamond Peak. A class 3 route was followed from Baxter Pass, on August 6, 1948, by Fred L. Jones. Climb along the crest to west. Traverse the ribs and chutes on the south side keeping high, until beneath the summit. Several fairly difficult pitches lead to the top.

Diamond Peak (13,126)

First recorded ascent August 1922 by Norman Clyde, route unknown. He thinks that there was a cairn there.

Route 1. West slope. Class 2. This route is a long climb from Rae Lakes. It is the most often used and probably was the route of first ascent.

Route 2. From Black Mountain. Class 2. First recorded ascent August 20, 1948, by Fred L. Jones. From Black Mountain descend into the basin to the north, then cross the crest to the west side through a notch. Ascend the south slope of Diamond Peak.

Route 3. Northeast couloir. Class 3. The northeast face of the mountain is split by two snow couloirs. Approach from the Baxter Pass Trail and ascend the eastern couloir. This route was descended May 30, 1960, by Henry Mandolf, Charles Bell, and Rowland Radcliffe.

The plateau south of Diamond Peak can be reached from the head of the southern branch of the North Fork of Oak Creek, via the southeast slope. This is a fine snow climb in the spring (Andy Smatko).

Black Mountain (13,289)

First ascent in 1905 by George Davis, route unknown.

Route 1. South slope. Class 2. Take the trail from Rae Lakes to Dragon Lake and ascend the south slope from it.

Route 2. From Diamond Peak. Class 2. Follow the reverse of Route 2 for Diamond Peak.

Route 3. East ridge. Class 2. First descent August 19, 1948, by Fred L. Jones. The large blocks directly below the summit present the only difficulty. The summit of the east ridge can be reached from the North Fork of Oak Creek, Charlie Canyon, or the South Fork of Oak Creek.

Dragon Peak (12,955)

First ascent in 1920 by either Fred Parker and J. E. Rother, or by Norman Clyde.

Route 1. From east. Class 3. From the east climb to the col immediately to the south, then go along the crest to the peak and up the west face.

Route 2. South ridge. Class 3. Traverse from Mount Gould along the connecting ridge and knife-edge to a point south of the top. Ascend the couloir on the southeast face to the ridge and proceed over blocks to the top.

Route 3. From southwest. Clyde states that the best route is from the lakes to the southwest, though he gives no details of the route.

The summit is a gendarme and is class 3. See Mount Gould for the route of the trail to the plateau to south, which gives access to Dragon Peak.

Mount Gould (13,005)

Route 1. South ridge. Class 1, except for class 3 summit blocks. First ascent July 2, 1890, by Joseph N. LeConte, Hubert P. Dyer, Fred S. Pheby and C. B. Lakeman from Kearsarge Pass via the south slope.

Route 2. Southeast ridge. Class 1. From east of Kearsarge Pass ascend the southeast ridge keeping to south of the ridge top.

Route 3. From the north. Class 1. The plateau to the north is readily reached on a traverse from Mount Rixford or Dragon Peak and it is an easy climb to the summit. A trail leaving the Kearsarge Pass trail a short distance west of the Kearsarge Lakes turn-off winds up the slope to north and proceeds to the north end of the plateau. Both Mound Gould and Dragon Peak are then easily reached.

Peaks West of the Crest

MIDDLE FORK TO SOUTH FORK OF KINGS, EAST OF GRANITE PASS

Peak 12,851 (1 SW of Cardinal Mountain; formerly 12,806)

Class 1. First ascent August 5, 1945, by A. J. Reyman via the southeast ridge.

Peak 13,080+ (0.7 NE of Mather Pass; formerly 13,046)

First recorded ascent August 16, 1922, by Chester Versteeg from Mather Pass along the north side of the ridge. He found a cairn.

Peak 12,680+ (1.8 SW of Mather Pass; formerly 12,674)

First ascent August 12, 1922, by Chester Versteeg, Mrs. Versteeg, Val Ellery, and Rudolph Berls, from the pass north of the peak.

Peak 12,840+ (1.7 NW of Mather Pass)

First ascent prior to 1955. Class 2-3 by the southwest slope.

Peak 12,920+ (1.3 W of Mather Pass).

First ascent September 9, 1955, by Frank Orme, Alan Lohse, and Robin McKeown. Class 2 by the southwest ridge.

Observation Peak (12,322)

First ascent July 25, 1902, by Joseph N. LeConte and Curtis W. Lindley from Dumbbell Lakes. It was climbed in 1926 by Marjory Hurd via the northwest ridge. The east ridge is class 2 from the saddle southwest of Amphitheater Lake (W. Hayes).

Mount Shakespeare (12,151)

First ascent July 20, 1930, by Francis P. Farquhar, Mary Lou Michaels, Doris Drust, Lorna Kilgariff and Robert L. Lipman.

Peak 12,174 (1 SW of Observation Peak)

First ascent September 11, 1955, by Frank Orme and Robin McKeown. Class 2 by the southeast slope.

Windy Cliff (11,132)

No record of ascent is available.

Peak 11,265 (1.8 NW of Observation Peak)

This peak was a USGS benchmark so it has been climbed.

Peak 12,860 (0.7 E of Dumbbell Lakes; formerly 12,835)

Class 3. First ascent August 12, 1945, by Art Reyman from Lake Basin. Ascend open benches and approach from the southwest. Go beyond the lake lying southeast of the peak and ascend the difficult couloir on the east face. Several routes develop as the climb progresses, all being rather difficult and exposed, but a way is open to the summit.

Peak 12,320+ (1.7 N of Marion Lakes formerly 12,316)

Class 2. First ascent August 12, 1945 by Art Reyman from Lake Basin up the south slope. No specific route is needed to reach the summit.

Peak 12,811 (0.8 N of Mount Ruskin; formerly 12,775)

Class 2. First ascent August 13, 1945, by Art Reyman from Lake Basin via the west slope.

Peak 12,080+ (0.5 NE of Mount Ruskin)

Class 4. First ascent July 22, 1939, by Bruce Meyer, Charlotte Mauk and David Brower. They climbed the east face and the arête from the notch to west. They roped down to the south from the west notch. It has been called the Saddlehorn.

Mt. Ruskin (12,920)

Route 1. Northwest ridge. First ascent August 7, 1895, by Bolton C. Brown. From Cartridge Pass he climbed the ridge running north to the junction of it and the ridge running southeast to Ruskin, then out it. The ridge became steep and narrow so he dropped down to the southwest. The other side is a sheer precipice. He then crossed the fluted west face and ascended the south spur. This last portion was termed by Brown to be the most aerial climbing he had ever attempted. Probably class 3.

Route 2. West slope. Class 3. First ascent August 13, 1945, by Art Reyman. Ascend the west slope to the couloir on the west face; ascend this to class 3 rocks which lead to the summit.

Route 3. East ridge. Class 3. Climbed in 1961 by A. J. Smatko, Arkel Erb, and Tom Ross.

Peak 12,162 (0.3 W of Cartridge Pass; formerly 12,139)

Class 1. Ascended prior to 1930. It is an easy short climb from Cartridge Pass.

Peak 11,553 (0.3 E of Marion Lake)

First ascent August 6, 1895, by Bolton C. Brown from Cartridge Creek (presumably via the west slope). He ascended the south side to Marion Lake. On July 22, 1902, Joseph N. LeConte and party climbed it by circling Marion Lake. They termed the climb an easy scramble.

Peak 12,361 (1 NE of Marion Peak; formerly 12,368)

Class 2. First recorded ascent August 11, 1945, by Art Reyman. He found what may have been a cairn. Traverse from Marion Peak and ascend the south slope.

Marion Peak (12,719)

Route 1. East slope. First ascent July 22, 1902, by J. N. LeConte and Curtis Lindley. From Marion Lake ascend the east slope to the summit. The east and southeast slopes are class 2.

Route 2. Northwest ridge. Class 3. First ascent August 11, 1945, by Art Reyman. From the knapsack pass to the northwest follow the knife-edge ridge, then go over difficult rocks to the summit.

Red Point (11,840+)

Class 1. First ascent August 11, 1945, by Art Reyman. From Marion Lake ascend to Red Pass, then go up the south ridge.

Peak 12,524 (0.7 N of State Peak)

First ascent probably in 1935 by a Sierra Club party which "climbed peaks of Cirque Crest."

Peak 11,150 (Windy Point)

First ascent unknown, but as it is a USGS benchmark it was climbed by a survey party. It can be reached by following Windy Ridge to its northwest end. A fine view is obtained from this point.

Windy Peak (8,867)

No record of ascent is available.

State Peak (12,620)

First ascent probably in 1935 by a Sierra Club party which "climbed peaks of Cirque Crest." Class 2–3 by west slope and southwest ridge, from State Lakes. The south and east slopes, from the lakes just south of the peak, are class 2.

Dougherty Peak (12,244)

First ascent in 1935 by a Sierra Club party. Class 2 from the north via State Lakes.

Goat Crest (12,059)

No record of ascent is available.

Kid Peak (11,458)

First ascent July 2, 1940, by a Sierra Club party of 18 led by Norman Clyde and David Brower from Paradise Valley.

Goat Mountain (12,207)

Class 2. First ascent apparently July 22, 1864, by James T. Gardiner and Charles F. Hoffmann from Granite Basin. It has been ascended several times from Copper Creek via the south ridge; also from Grouse Lake.

West of the Crest

SOUTH FORK OF KINGS RIVER TO BUBBS CREEK

Peak 12,720+ (1 NW of Mount Pinchot)

First ascent July 23, 1939, by Madi Bacon and Tom Noble.

Mount Pinchot (13,495)

Class 2–3. First ascent in 1905 by either Charles F. Urquhart of the USGS, or George Davis, both of whom climbed it in that year. It is easily climbable from almost any direction.

Mount Wynne (13,179)

First ascent in 1935 by a Sierra Club party. It is climbable from almost any direction. The traverse from Mount Pinchot is class 3.

Crater Mountain (12,874)

Class 2. First ascent July 19, 1922, by W. H. Ink, Meyers Butte, Frank Baxter and Capt. Wallace. The best routes are from the east or northeast. This peak is not a crater as the name implies.

Peak 12,968 (1.3 NW of Crater Mountain; formerly 12,938)

First recorded ascent July 25, 1939, by Art Argiewicz and party from the cirque southeast of Bench Lake. They found evidence of prior ascent.

Peak 12,000+ (0.5 SE of Bench Lake; formerly 12,044)

First ascent August 12, 1922, by W. Sloane and J. Sloane.

Arrow Peak (*12,958*)

Route 1. Northeast spur. Class 3. First ascent August 8, 1895, by Bolton C. Brown. He climbed the northeast spur from the base to the top. It is a simple ascent, but most of it is serious climbing. There are some narrow, knife-edge spots. Brown descended the southeast spur and returned to the South Fork of the Kings.

Route 2. Southwest ridge. First ascent June 1902 by Joseph N. LeConte, Tracey Kelley and Robert Pike from the head of Arrow Creek. They ascended the south slope to the top of the ridge. A false summit one quarter mile south of the peak is separated from it by a knife-edge ridge.

Route 3. Southeast ridge. Class 2. First ascent possibly August 20, 1930, by Walter A. Starr, Jr. from Bench Lake. From the west end of Bench Lake head for the rock slide at the pass southeast of the peak. Ascend this and then go westerly over talus to the summit.

Arrow Ridge (*12,188*)

Class 1. First ascent August 8, 1945, by Art Reyman on a traverse from Arrow Peak.

Pyramid Peak (*12,777*)

Class 3. First ascent July 21, 1942, by Art Reyman on a traverse from Window Peak. The ridge narrows to a class 3 knife-edge. The climb can more readily be made by climbing to the notch just south of the peak from the east or from the west (class 2), and following the south ridge to the summit (class 3). The west ridge appears to be class 2.

Peak 12,350 (*1 SE of Pyramid Peak*)

First ascent June 27, 1940, by Jed Garthwaite, Jim Quick, and Howard Leach. Class 2–3 by west slopes or south ridge.

Window Peak (*12,085*)

First ascent July 5, 1940, by Art Argiewicz and Bob Jacobs. Their route is not known. The window measures seven by five feet. The peak has been climbed from Castle Domes via the broken connecting ridge. Another route has been followed by Art Reyman on a descent via the north ridge to Pyramid Peak. The east face is a class 3.

Castle Domes (*11,360+*)

The highest dome is an old benchmark, so the first ascent was probably made in early years by a USGS survey party. The first ascent of the second most prominent dome was made July 5, 1940, by Art Argiewicz and Bob Jacobs. From Woods Creek the east slope and the northeast ridge afford a class 1 route. It can be climbed on a traverse of the connecting ridge from Window Peak.

Peak 12,372 (*1 W of Colosseum Mountain; formerly 12,332*)

Class 1. First ascent August 25, 1935, by Norman Clyde. The southeast slope is class 1. Class 3 from the saddle west of Colosseum Mountain.

Peak 12,349 (*2.7 W of Mount Baxter; formerly 12,329*)

Class 2. First recorded ascent July 4, 1940, by Jim Harkins, Bob Jacobs and Don Heyneman. They found evidence that it had been climbed before. Their route is not known. It can easily be climbed from the saddle to the southeast.

Peak 12,804 (*1.7 NW of Mount Baxter; formerly 12,786*)

Route 1. East ridge. Class 2. First ascent July 1935 by a Sierra Club party led by Norman Clyde via the southeast ridge.

Route 2. From northwest. Class 2. First ascent July 21, 1948, by Fred L. Jones from Woods Lake. Ascend the ridge leading to the east edge of the plateau west of the peak, then go up the west slope to the summit. The descent was made by a class 2 route via the west ridge to the saddle east of Peak 12,349.

Peak 12,852 (*1.7 W of Mount Baxter; formerly 12,885*)

Class 2. First ascent July 1935 by a Sierra Club party led by Norman Clyde on a traverse along the north ridge from Mount Baxter. They continued on to Peak 12,804.

Peak 13,183 (*0.8 W of Mount Baxter; formerly 13,167*)

Class 2. First ascent July 1935 by a Sierra Club party led by Norman Clyde on a traverse from Mount Baxter. The east ridge has been reached by Fred L. Jones via the saddle to east from both the north and south. The route to the saddle from the north is class 3 and from the south class 2. Clyde continued the traverse down the west ridge, also class 2.

King Spur (*12,160+*; *1.2 N of Mount Clarence King*)

Date of first ascent unknown. First ascents on the two most northerly points of the ridge were made from the north on July 6, 1940, by Jim Harkins, Bob Jacobs, Art Argiewicz and Bruce Meyer. Ropes were used on the summit monoliths.

Mount Clarence King (*12,905*)

In July 1895 Bolton C. Brown attempted the north and east arêtes, being stopped by vertical cliffs on both. On the east he reached to within one or two hundred feet of the summit. The following year he successfully climbed the south face.

Route 1. South face. Class 3–4. First ascent 1896, probably in August, by Bolton C. Brown via the south face. From the head of Gardiner Creek or from Sixty Lake Basin proceed to the saddle south of the peak. From Sixty Lake Basin the route follows either a ledge in the cliff or a rockslide further south; from the saddle go north up the slope. Walter Starr's choice of the best route is as follows: at the top of this slope, next to the eastern drop-off, is a small hole under the rocks just large enough to squirm up through. This hole is in line with the summit, Mount Cotter and Mount Stanford. The last 50 feet is class 4. Ropes should be used. The summit is composed of big slabs. Those not small enough to go through the hole can climb a large slanting block about 20 feet below the top and to the west of the hole.

Route 2. East ridge. Class 4. Climbed August 1948 by Fred Davenport and Standish Mitchell. The first barrier on the ridge can be passed by a series of narrow cracks and ledges on the south face. Farther on, the ridge is blocked by a large wafer and a traverse on the north side is used.

Mount Cotter (*12,721*)

Class 2–3. First ascent August 6, 1922, by Bob Fitzsimons from Sixty Lake Basin. Go up the south ridge or southeast slope.

The north peak of Cotter was first climbed on July 8, 1940, by a Sierra Club party led by David Brower on a traverse of the north ridge. An exposed 20-foot wall which had to be descended was the only obstacle. Ropes are needed. Probably class 4.

Mount Gardiner (*12,907*)

Two of the most prominent Sierra mountaineers of all time, Joseph

N. LeConte and Bolton C. Brown, met by chance on the lower summit of the peak in July 1896 and joined forces to share in its first ascent.

Route 1. South slope. Class 4. First ascent July 1896 by Joseph N. LeConte and Bolton C. Brown. The south slope from Charlotte Creek to the summit of the lower peak is an easy ascent. A knife-edge ridge (class 4) separates the summit of the highest peak.

Route 2. Southeast ridge. On July 7, 1940, Paul Estes and Jack Pointeki traversed the southeast ridge between Mount Gardiner and Peak 12,560+, though they didn't specify which way.

Route 3. Northeast face. First ascent July 9, 1940, by a party led by Norman Clyde. They ascended the glacier to the summit.

Peak 12,560+ (1 SE of Mount Gardiner; formerly 12,565)

First ascent July 7, 1940, by Paul Estes and Jack Pointeki. They traversed between it and Mount Gardiner.

Peak 12,553 (2 E of Mount Gardiner)

First ascent in 1899 by Bolton C. Brown. A map of his route shows that he crossed the summit using the south and north slopes, though his direction of travel isn't indicated.

Fin Dome (11,693)

First ascent 1910 by James Rennie, route unknown, though probably similar to Route 1.

Route 1. West face. Class 3. Ducks starting from the top of the talus fan on the southwest side lead to the easiest route on the west face, directly under the dome. It is a high-angle, zig-zagging trail of sand, gravel and small blocks between large slabs and boulders. If one didn't stay on the easiest route ropes would be needed. There are several good routes for ropes.

Route 2. Class 4. First ascent July 7, 1940, by Sierra Club party led by David Brower. Traversing the south ridge they established a class 4 route. Details are not known.

Mount Rixford (12,890)

First ascent in 1897 by Dr. Emmet Rixford and two others. Their route is unknown. Several routes have been used: from Bullfrog Lake, class 1 by the west ridge; from Mount Gould, mostly class 2 but the sharp ridge up Mount Rixford from the east may be class 3. The northeast face has been descended by Bolton Brown, who described it as dangerous.

Painted Lady (*12,126*)

First ascent July 1931 by Robert Owen.

Mount Bago (*11,869*)

Class 1. First ascent either July 11, 1896, by Joseph N. LeConte and W. S. Gould, or July, 1896, by Bolton C. Brown and Lucy Brown. Both parties were in the area at the same time. Ascend from Charlotte Lake.

East of the Crest

Birch Mountain (*13,665*)

First ascent in 1887 by J. W. Bledsoe. The best route is from Birch Lake up the chute leading southwest to the col west of the peak, then east to the top. This route is probably class 1 or 2 at most. The north face affords class 3 routes among the many ribs and chutes. The south slope is class 1 or 2. Clyde has descended the east slope on snow in the spring.

Mount Tinemaha (*12,561*)

First recorded ascent July 1, 1937, by Chester Versteeg. He climbed from Tinemaha Creek to the top of the ridge west of the peak, then went east on it to the summit. It can also be climbed from the main crest north of Split Mountain via the southerly slope of the ridge. The west end of this ridge and several steep ribs are class 3. From Red Lake the gravelly southwest slope gives a class 2 route. The south and east ridges are class 3.

Goodale Mountain (*12,790*)

Route 1. From the west. Class 2, except for class 3 summit rocks. First recorded ascent July 23, 1939, by Norman Clyde, Allan A. MacRae, and Albion J. Whitney. Apparently they climbed it from the saddle to the west. This saddle can be reached easily from Taboose Pass.

Route 2. From Woods Creek. Class 3. First ascent August 1, 1948, by Fred L. Jones. For details see Route 3 up Striped Mountain. From the saddle to the east the class 2 west slope is followed.

Route 3. East slope. Class 1. The east slope of Goodale Mountain can be climbed from the road ends between Taboose and Goodale creeks and apparently has been by deer hunters.

Peak 11,765 (1.3 E of Mount Perkins)

Class 2. First recorded ascent July 31, 1948, by Fred L. Jones. A cairn was found but no record. The top of the connecting ridge was followed from the crest.

It was ascended May 11, 1951, by Fred L. Jones via Division Creek from Scotty Spring. The lower part of Division Creek canyon is class 3 in places, the upper part class 2. The peak was descended via the big chute on the northeast face, which is class 2.

Sawmill Point (9,416)

Class 3. First recorded ascent January 11, 1953, by A. J. Reyman and Fred L. Jones via the northeast ridge. Leave the Sawmill Pass trail above the red cinder cone north of Sawmill Creek. Ascend the spur above to the east edge of the summit ridge. At the notch directly east of the summit cross to the north side and regain the top of the summit ridge just west of the summit. Climb east to the top. Two old cairns were found, but no record. An easier ascent can be made by following the trail into Sawmill Creek until under the peak on the north side.

Lookout Point (10,144)

First ascent 1926 by Norman Clyde.

Peak 11,520+ (1 SW of Lookout Point; formerly 11,511)

Class 2. First ascent October 31, 1926, by Norman Clyde, probably from Sawmill Lake, as was the second ascent, also by Clyde in 1935. He descended into Black Canyon. The peak was ascended July 26, 1948, by Fred L. Jones on a traverse from Peak 12,400+ by going west of that peak, then dropping to the head of the basin to the north and crossing it to the top of the ridge south of 11,520+. The route was class 2.

Peak 12,400+ (1 NE of Mount Baxter; formerly 12,411)

Class 2. First ascent September 4, 1935, by Norman Clyde from Sawmill Pass by going southeast across the intervening cirque. The peak was climbed from Mount Baxter on July 25, 1948, by Fred L. Jones by keeping to the top or north side of the intervening ridge (see Route 4 up Mount Baxter). The route is class 3. The peak was climbed from Thibaut Creek on October 16, 1948, by Fred L. Jones by keeping to the top or south side of the ridge between Thibaut Creek and Black Canyon. The route is class 3. The descent into Thibaut Creek was made via a class 2 chute from the summit.

"Indian Rock" (*12,160+*)

This locally named prominence lies on the ridge between Black Canyon and Thibaut Creek about three-tenths of a mile southeast of Peak 12,400+. Looking southerly from Highway 395 just north of Aberdeen, it is the prominent tooth on the skyline directly over the highway.

Class 3. First ascent October 16, 1948, by Fred L. Jones. From the head of Thibaut Creek ascend the chute to the base of the northwest face and then go directly up this to the broad top.

Peak 11,844 (*1 E of Mount Baxter; formerly 11,810*)

Class 3. First ascent September 16, 1935, by Norman Clyde. From Thibaut Creek he ascended the crest of the ridge to east of the peak and climbed west to the summit. It is mostly class 2. An easier ascent is west from Thibaut Creek and up the easy northwest slope. Clyde descended south into the basin at the head of the Little North Fork of Oak Creek. The route is class 1.

Peak 13,045 (*1 NE of Black Mountain; formerly 13,031*)

First ascent probably September 14, 1935, by Norman Clyde who prior to and after that date was climbing in the near vicinity, though his allusion to the main crest is obviously incorrect: "On Peak 13,031, on main crest, at an altitude of 11,500 feet picked up a pair of weathered (mountain sheep) horns. No recent evidence except a bed and droppings on the saddle west of peak."

The next recorded ascent was August 19, 1948, by Fred L. Jones on a traverse from Black Mountain. The route was class 2.

Peak 12,720+ (*¾ W of Kearsarge Peak*)

First ascent in 1925 by Norman Clyde: "peak west of Kearsarge." It is easy from the east, though a deep notch to the west is difficult.

Kearsarge Peak (*12,598*)

First recorded ascent in 1925 by Norman Clyde. This peak is traversed nearly to the summit by mining trails and is an easy class 1 ascent by them. It has been descended by a more varied route by Art Reyman, Mary DeDecker, Joan DeDecker and Carol DeDecker. Take the steep chute due south of the second or third rocky point from the summit, which ends in a fall below the mine. Climb out of the chute to the north above this and descend by the South Fork of Independence Creek trail to Onion Valley.

Kearsarge Pass to Army
and Franklin Passes

IN THIS southern part of the Sierra the loftiest peaks are found, but a little farther south the range declines in both height and ruggedness. For this reason the Guide does not discuss peaks south of Army Pass on the main crest nor south of Franklin Pass on the Great Western Divide, although there are a few worthy peaks in the excluded area.

Much excellent climbing is to be found here. The east wall of the Sierra near Mount Whitney is one of the outstanding regions for climbing in the United States. The Kings-Kern Divide contains many fine peaks in a small area. The Kaweahs have a reputation for challenging faces of friable rock, contrasting with the granite peaks to the north and west in the Great Western Divide.

Most of this section, south of the Kings-Kern Divide, and west of the main crest, is within Sequoia National Park, and therefore boasts some fine trails, including the southern end of the Muir Trail, the Whitney Trail, and the High Sierra Trail which runs eastward from Giant Forest. The trails are described in more detail in the individual areas below, which are as follows:

The Kings-Kern Divide and the Adjacent Crests. Included are the main crest from Kearsarge Pass to Shepherd Pass, the Kings-Kern Divide, and the northern end of the Great Western Divide.

The Whitney Region. This covers the main crest from Shepherd Pass to Army Pass and adjacent peaks east of the Kern River.

The Kaweahs and the Great Western Divide. This describes the Great Western Divide south from the point where it is joined by the Kings-Kern Divide to Franklin Pass, the Kaweah Peaks ridge, and adjacent peaks to the west.

The Kings-Kern Divide
and the Adjacent Crests

HERVEY H. VOGE (1953); ANDREW J. SMATKO (1964)

THE RUGGED ridge of the Kings-Kern Divide connects the main crest of the Sierra with the northern part of the Great Western Divide like the bar in a giant letter *H*. To the south of this bar lies the high plateau where the Kern River starts, while on the north the tributaries of the South Fork of the Kings River flow northward in several canyons between the subsidiary ridges which jut out from the divide. The Muir Trail crosses the Kings-Kern Divide at Foresters Pass. Maps for this area are the Mount Whitney and Mount Pinchot quadrangles.

The Kings-Kern region has much to offer climbers of various tastes. The main peaks range from easy to moderate by the standard routes, and are without exception very fine viewpoints. The precipitous Kearsarge Pinnacles, the crags north of Mount Ericsson, and many of the north and east faces of the larger peaks present real challenges to rock climbers.

HISTORICAL

Recorded climbing started in 1864 with the explorations of the party of the California State Geological Survey. This party was led by William H. Brewer and included Charles Hoffman, Clarence King, and Richard Cotter. Brewer and Hoffman ascended and named Mount Brewer, while King and Cotter made their way from Roaring River across the Great Western and Kings-Kern divides to Mount Tyndall and back in the classic trip described in King's *Mountaineering in the Sierra Nevada*. King's narrative relates climbing adventures in the dramatic style of the nineteenth century, and two of the most exciting passages concern the Kings-Kern Divide. The first of these describes the crossing of the divide, from north to south, somewhere between Thunder Mountain and Mount Jordan, in the course of which crossing the adventurous climbers at one time pulled themselves up by a lasso thrown over a partially loose spike of rock thirty feet above, and at another time descended by rope-downs when neither forward nor return progress was certain. The other dramatic episode occurred when the two climbers, on the return journey from Mount Tyndall, passed around the south end of what is now called Lake Reflection. Here they encountered a sheer bluff which could only be passed by ascending a steep tongue of icy snow and climbing a cliff at its head. After an unsuccessful attempt by King, Cotter led up the cliff and seated himself at the top. He called down to King and said, "Don't be afraid to bear your weight on the rope." Thus reassured King made the climb unaided, only to discover that Cotter had a very precarious perch and that the least pull would have dragged him over.

John Muir climbed several unidentified peaks near the Kings-Kern Divide in 1873. The region was more thoroughly explored by Bolton Coit Brown, J. N. LeConte, and others in 1896 and thereafter, and by E. T. Parsons in 1903. (The early history of the Kings River Sierra has been described by Francis P. Fraquhar, *SCB*, 1941, 28). In later years many have climbed these peaks, Norman Clyde alone having at one time or another visited most of the major summits.

GEOGRAPHY

The arbitrary region here considered extends about eight miles along the crest from Kearsarge Pass to Shepherd Pass, westward along the Kings-Kern Divide to the Great Western Divide, and north along the latter divide to its terminus. The rock is mostly granite, but some dark, metamorphic rock is found on Center Peak, the Videttes, and in a few other areas. The granite varies from firm material in some places to other badly decomposed rock in others. Sketch 25 is a map of the area.

APPROACHES

From Independence. Kearsarge Pass (11,823). From the end of the road in Onion Valley at 9,300 feet a good horse trail leads over Kearsarge Pass to Bullfrog Lake. Just below Bullfrog Lake this lateral joins the Muir Trail, which may be followed south to the upper regions of Bubbs Creek, Center Basin, and the Kings-Kern Divide at Foresters Pass. East Lake may be reached by following west down Bubbs Creek (leaving the Muir Trail at Vidette Meadow) to just below the juncture with East Creek at a spot called Junction Meadow, whence a trail leading up East Creek climbs southward.

Shepherd Pass (12,000+). The Shepherd Pass trail starts at an elevation of about 6,500 feet at the end of a road which leaves U.S. 395 at Independence. The rather poor trail leads over Shepherd Pass to the Tyndall Creek plateau just south of the Kings-Kern Divide. Knapsackers may turn north at an elevation of about 10,500 on the east side of the pass and follow the old Junction Pass trail across Junction Pass (13,200) into Center Basin. The Junction Pass trail is not recommended for animals.

From Kings Canyon. The Bubbs Creek trail leaves the Kings River Canyon at 4,800 feet and follows the creek until the Muir Trail is reached at 9,700 feet in Vidette Meadow. At Junction Meadow, at an elevation of about 8,500 feet, the trail to East Lake leaves the Bubbs Creek trail and goes south up East Creek.

From the north. The Muir Trail leads over Glen Pass (11,978) and to the foot of Bullfrog Lake, from which point various routes may be followed as described for the approach over Kearsarge Pass.

From the south. The Muir Trail traverses the high plateau east of the Kern River and crosses the Kings-Kern Divide at Forester Pass (13,200). From the pass the trail descends to the headwaters of Bubbs Creek and Vidette Meadow.

From the west. Several routes to the high peaks are possible from the west. Either the trail up Sphinx Creek or that from Big Meadow may be followed to Moraine Meadow, Scaffold Meadow or the head-waters of the Roaring River. These trails are described in more detail in Starr's *Guide* (1951). Knapsack routes lead from these points via Brewer Creek or Longley Pass to East Lake or Lake Reflection.

CAMPSITES

Camps suitable for knapsackers may be found up to about 11,300 feet elevation in nearly all the valleys. Popular camping spots for those traveling with animals are situated at Bullfrog Lake, along Bubbs Creek from Vidette Meadow to the lower part of Center Basin, on East Creek from East Lake to just below Lake Reflection, and on the south side of the divide along Tyndall and Milestone creeks.

PASSES

Besides the main trail passes mentioned under approaches, several others are of interest to climbers and knapsackers.

Junction Pass (*13,200*). Class 1. This pass crosses the main crest and connects Center Basin to the head of Shepherd Creek. It was once the main horse trail for north-south travel in this region, but is no longer maintained. Parts have been obscured by slides, and the trail is not well marked, so that knapsackers following it should pay close attention to the topographic map.

Harrison Pass (*12,600+*). Class 2. This pass across the Kings-Kern Divide leads from East Lake to Lake South America. It has occasionally been crossed by pack animals, but like Junction Pass is only recommended for foot travel. The trail is not clearly marked over the higher portion of the north side, but the place of crossing the divide is not especially critical. Steep and sometimes icy snow may be met on the north side, but the south side in this region is very easy walking.

Lucys Foot Pass (*12,400+*). In 1896 Bolton Coit Brown and his wife Lucy crossed the Kings-Kern Divide just west of Mount Ericsson, and since that time the pass has borne her name. There is no trail, and considerable rough talus is encountered, but the route is class 2.

Millys Foot Pass (*12,240+*). Perhaps the most direct route from Lake Reflection to the broad flats of the Upper Kern is the saddle just north of Mount Genevra. This was crossed in July 1953 by Mildred Jentsch and Sylvia Kershaw. The cliff on the northwest side is not as difficult as it appears, for a cleft passes diagonally up through it. The route is class 2 except near the very top where the chute or cleft narrows and is blocked by a large chockstone. Climb a 10–15 foot class 3 pitch on either side of the chockstone to the top of the Kings-Kern Divide.

Andys Foot Pass (*13,600+*). Class 2–3. By means of this pass a cross-country route can be made from upper Bubbs Creek southwest of Center Peak to the Kern Basin near Lake South America. Proceed southwest to the saddle just southeast of Gregorys Monument. From the saddle go west several hundred feet and work down to the southwest to the Harrison Pass Trail. Snow is likely to be found on the north side of this pass.

University Pass (*12,640+*). Class 2. This is a climber's pass from Onion Valley to Center Basin; it is the lowest point between University Peak and Peak 12,910. There is a steep snow gully on the northeast side and a long rocky chute on the southwest side. This pass is quite steep and rough. In late summer when snow is gone the boulder fields on the northeast side are quite tedious.

Brewer Creek to East Lake Pass (*12,640+*). Class 2. This pass crosses the ridge between Mount Brewer and South Guard, and leads from Brewer Creek to East Lake. It is for foot travel only. The routes are about the same as for Mount Brewer, Routes 1 and 2, except that the summit of Brewer is bypassed.

Longley Pass (*12,400+*). Class 1. This foot pass leads from the stream below South Guard Lake on the west to Lake Reflection on the east side of the Great Western Divide, and passes just south of South Guard. On the west it is quite easy, and on the east not difficult except for a possible, seasonal, steep snow bank. There is a trail part of the way on the east side.

Deerhorn Saddle (*12,560+*). Class 2. The saddle east of Deerhorn Mountain provides a feasible knapsack route from the basin north of Harrison Pass to Vidette Creek.

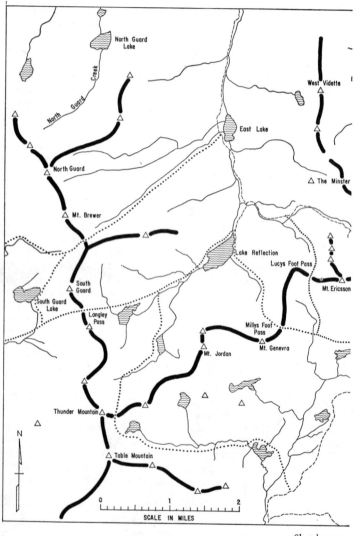

North Guard Lake

North Guard Creek

West Vidette

East Lake

The Minster

North Guard

Mt. Brewer

Lake Reflection

Lucys Foot Pass

South Guard

Mt. Ericsson

South Guard Lake

Longley Pass

Millys Foot Pass

Mt. Jordan

Mt. Genevra

Thunder Mountain

Table Mountain

N

0   1   2

SCALE IN MILES

Sketch 25.

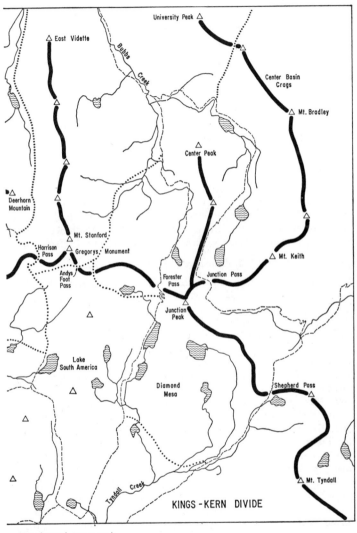

University Peak △

△ East Vidette

Bubbs Creek

△

Center Basin Crags

△ Mt. Bradley

△
Deerhorn Mountain

△ Center Peak

△

△

△ Mt. Stanford
Harrison Pass
△ Gregorys Monument
Andys Foot Pass

△

Forester Pass

Junction Pass

△ Mt. Keith

△

Junction Peak

△

Lake South America

△

Diamond Mesa

Shepherd Pass △

△

△

Tyndall Creek

△ Mt. Tyndall

KINGS - KERN DIVIDE

(See legend, page 14.)

The descriptions of routes and records are arranged in the following order:

Peaks of the main crest (north to south)
Peak east of the main crest
Peaks of the Great Western Divide (north to south)
Peaks west of the Great Western Divide
Peaks of the Kings-Kern Divide (west to east)
Peaks north of the Kings-Kern Divide
Peaks south of the Kings-Kern Divide

Peaks of the Main Crest (North to South)

Nameless Pyramid (0.2 S of Kearsarge Pass)

A small pyramid of rather monolithic granite stands on the main crest south of Kearsarge Pass and above Pothole Lake. It was first ascended in July 1952 by Ted Matthes, Frank Tarver, and Phillip Berry. The approach by the ridge from the pass, or from the northeast, or from the west, is class 3. The northern side of the pyramid is class 4 to 5.

Peak 12,400+ (0.7 S of Kearsarge Pass; formerly 12,423)

Ascended by Norman Clyde, 1926. Class 2 up the east ridge from between Heart and Bench lakes (Tom Ross).

University Peak (13,632)

Route 1. From the northwest. Class 2. First ascent July 12, 1896, by J. N. LeConte, Helen M. Gompertz, Estelle Miller, and Belle Miller. From the environs of Bullfrog Lake proceed southeast up the basin between the Kearsarge Pinnacles and the main crest to the upper Kearsarge Lake and continue toward a low gap in the ridge west of University Peak, passing over rough, giant talus and some snowbanks (seasonal) to the gap. From the gap the easiest route is to traverse around and up on the sandy southwest slope of the peak. It is also feasible to proceed from the gap to the ridge running northwest from the summit and to follow the ridge to the top; this variation (Walter Starr, Jr.) is class 2–3.

Route 2. South face. Class 1. From Center Basin the long, rather easy slope to the summit may be climbed by a number of routes.

Route 3. North face. About class 3. First known ascent by Norman Clyde, prior to 1928. From the group of lakes at the northern base, at about 10,500 feet (Slim Lake) climb up a steep, rocky slope, several thousand feet in length, to the eastern end of a knife-edge which can be followed to the summit with comparative ease.

Route 4. Southeast face. About class 3. Climbed by Norman Clyde, September 29, 1928. He described it as a good but not very difficult rock scramble.

Route 5. Southeast ridge. Class 2. From University Pass (see above, section on passes) the ridge may be followed easily if one stays somewhat on the south side.

Route 6. Northeast ridge. It is reported that this ridge was climbed in 1947. Class 3 to 4.

Sketch 26. The Center Basin Crags from the southwest.

Center Basin Crags (*about 12,500*)

The sharp crags standing on the main crest between Peak 12,910 and Mount Bradley have been numbered from north to south. Crag 1 is a fairly broad one, while Crags 2, 3, and 4 are sharper and are grouped together. Crag 5 is less steep. (See Sketch 26)

Crag 1. South arête. Class 5. First ascent August 29, 1953, by Phil Berry and party.

Crags 2, 3, and 4. First ascended in July 1940 in a class 4 traverse by David R. Brower and L. Bruce Meyer. A long rope-down was used at the end. Crags 3 and 4 were ascended again in August 1953 by Brower and Phil Berry. They proceeded from Center Basin toward the notch south of Crag 4 and then crossed northward to the notch between Crags 3 and 4; from this point both crags were climbed. Class 5.

Crag 5. The north ridge is class 2. First ascent by unidentified party.

Mount Bradley (13,289)

Route 1 West face. Class 2. First ascent July 5, 1898, by Mr. and Mrs. R. M. Price, J. Shinn, and Lalla Harris. The summit can probably be reached by any one of a number of chutes leading up from Center Basin to the main ridge. The easiest way is to climb straight up the talus chute below the main summit. When the chute forks about three-forths of the way up, take the branch to the right, which leads to the saddle between the two summits. From the saddle go around behind (E of) the main summit, which is the left or northerly one, and ascend a narrow, easy chute to the top. The party of the first ascent took four hours from camp in lower Center Basin to the summit.

Route 2. Northwest ridge. Probably class 3 to 4. This ridge was followed on August 31, 1948, by Fred L. Jones.

Route 3. East ridge. Probably class 2. Climbed October 27, 1948, by the east ridge from Symmes Creek by Fred L. Jones.

Route 4. North slope. Class 2. Probably the easiest route of ascent from the east side. Go up Pinyon Creek to its head, and then climb directly south up the long nivated slope to the summit.

Peak 13,280+ (0.7 NE of Mount Keith; formerly 13,370)

All but the last 15 feet were climbed in 1940 by Paul Estes. The summit monolith was first ascended in August 1963 by Sy Ossofsky and Arkel Erb, who used a shoulder stand and one piton.

Route 1. Southeast slopes and south ridge. Class 2. From Shepherd Creek go to the saddle south of the peak and thence along the west side of the south ridge to the summit monolith.

Route 2. West slope. Class 2. From upper Center Basin go up easy chutes and rock to the crest just north of the summit.

Mount Keith (13,977)

Route 1. Northwest face. Class 1 to 2. First ascent July 6, 1898, by R. M. Price, J. E. Price, J. C. Shinn, and C. B. Bradley. Time from camp in Center Basin to the top was four hours.

Route 2. Southwest ridge. Class 2 to 3. The sharp ridge from Junction Pass was followed by two Sierra Club parties in 1916, and it was thought that this route had not been used in any previous ascents.

Route 3. South face. About class 2. According to Norman Clyde the ascent from about 10,000 feet on the Shepherd Pass trail is comparatively easy.

Route 4. Northeast shoulder. Class 2. From the open cirque between

Mount Keith and peak 13,280+ to the northeast, climb up class 2 slopes to the summit.

Junction Peak (13,888)

Route 1. South ridge. Class 3. First ascent August 8, 1899, by E. B. Copeland and E. N. Henderson. Ascend the west wall of Diamond Mesa near the lower (southern) end and proceed north along the sandy plateau and along or somewhat to the west of an easy knife-edge leading to the summit.

Route 2. West ridge. Class 3. From Forester Pass follow the ridge eastward, passing over or to the south of one small subsidiary peak. On the main peak stay to the south of the northwest ridge, and proceed southward and upward from one chute to another as convenient.

Route 3. Southeast ridge. On August 21, 1929, A. R. Ellingwood followed the ridge from Shepherd Pass to the summit. Class 4.

Route 4. East Couloir. Class 3–4. In 1956 Carl Heller, Bob Stein, and Kermit Ross descended the northerly of two couloirs on the east face.

Peak East of the Main Crest

Independence Peak (11,744)

This may be climbed by the north slope from Onion Valley. Norman Clyde ascended the peak three times in 1926 and twice in 1927. Class 2–3. From near Robinson Lake above Onion Valley climb the western slopes and follow the southwest ridge to the summit. Alternatively, the north ridge provides class 3 climbing on solid rock.

Peaks of the Great Western Divide (North to South)

Cross Mountain (11,920+)

Climbed in 1929 by Walter L. Huber. Class 1–2 from the west, via Sphinx Creek. The east slopes from Cross Creek are of about the same difficulty. The northern summit is higher.

Peak 12,893 (1 NW of North Guard; formerly 12,871)

First ascent July 17, 1932, by Sierra Club parties, including Norman Clyde, Thomas Rawles, Lincoln O'Brien, and eleven others, from Sphinx Lakes. The climbers said that it was a splendid peak and that the highest point was a large slab almost overhanging the steep east face. The northwest ridge is easy class 4; the south ridge is class 3. The saddle at the foot of the south ridge can be gained from the head of North Guard Creek, or from Sphinx Creek.

North Guard (13,327)

First ascent July 12, 1925, by Norman Clyde. The summit is a large, sloping obelisk, which overhangs the east face.

Route 1. South ridge or slopes. Class 3. From the north fork of Brewer Creek proceed to the saddle between Brewer and North Guard, or up the south slopes of the peak.

Route 2. East and north faces. Class 4. Climbed May 28, 1934, by David R. Brower and Hervey Voge. From East Lake proceed up Ouzel Creek and tributaries to the northeast flank of the mountain and ascend this wall to the prominent shoulder or col north-northeast of the summit. From the col climb a thirty-foot V crack on the nose of the ridge to a platform, and from this platform go to the right (W) on broken ledges on the north face and ascend a second difficult crack to the easier rocks leading to the summit.

A subsidiary peak north-northeast from North Guard, about 13,100, was climbed from Ouzel Creek August 10, 1948, by James Koontz and two others.

Mount Brewer (13,570)

Route 1. West slopes and south ridge. Class 1. First ascent by W. H. Brewer and C. F. Hoffman, July 2, 1864. From Roaring River or Moraine Creek go up Brewer Creek to the notch just south of Mount Brewer and follow the easy ridge of broken rock to the summit.

Route 2. East slopes and south ridge. Class 2. First ascent by Bolton C. Brown and A. B. Clark, 1895. From East Lake proceed up Ouzel Creek, taking the middle fork which leads almost directly toward Mount Brewer. From this fork, in one of several possible places, climb the ridge to the south. Alternatively, the ridge may be climbed over rounded slabs at its foot from the junction of the first fork of Ouzel Creek shown on the map. This ridge joins the main south ridge of Mount Brewer at about the southern edge of the summit pyramid. Where this subsidiary eastern ridge joins the peak, work to the left (S) through a small notch to the main south ridge, and proceed northward up this to the summit. Time from East Lake to the top is about four hours.

Route 3. Northwest slopes. Class 2. Climb from the north fork of Brewer Creek. A convenient approach to this route from Kings Canyon is up the Bubbs Creek Trail, then up the Sphinx Creek Trail, then up Sphinx Creek to Lake 10,520 and beyond. An easy pass is crossed northeast of Peak 12,393 to the north fork of Brewer Creek.

Route 4. Northeast couloir and north ridge. Class 2 to 3. Ascended August 4, 1940, by Oliver Kehrlein, August and Grete Frugé, E. Hanson, L. West, R. Leggett, and A. Mulay. From the east side of the mountain ascend a steep couloir filled with snow and (or) ice which leads to the base of the main pyramid of the mountain on the north side, and then climb the north ridge or face to the top.

Route 5. Northeast face. Class 5.7. First ascent September 1963 by Kenneth Boche and Russell McLean. The route starts in the first chimney to the right of the small overhangs on the rib leading directly up the face to the summit. Climb 200 feet up the chimney to an overhang. Here traverse right into the next chimney. Pass a chockstone on the left. Then, keeping to the right, ascend 40 feet to some slabs, which can be climbed for 400 feet. Then climb to the right and reach the crest to the right of the summit. About 25 pitons are needed.

South Guard (13,224)

This peak may have been climbed by Clarence King and Richard Cotter on July 4, 1864. Clarence King wrote, in *Mountaineering in the Sierra Nevada,* that from the notch just south of Mount Brewer "with very great difficulty we climbed a peak which surmounted our wall just to the south of the pass...." From this peak they attempted to follow the Great Western Divide southward, but soon descended to the east.

Route 1. South slope. Class 2. Proceed from Longley Pass up the south slope. In the approach to Longley Pass from the east, a snow cornice may be encountered. This can be passed by class 2–3 rocks at the north end.

Route 2. North ridge. Class 2. From the saddle southeast of Mount Brewer, at the head of Ouzel Creek, the ridge may be followed over class 2 blocks to South Guard.

Peak 12,960+ (0.3 S of Longley Pass; formerly 13,021)

First ascent by Norman Clyde in 1925.

Climbed August 8, 1940, by Oliver Kehrlein and five others from Lake Reflection by ascending the east side of the Great Western Divide somewhat north of Peak 12,960+, and traversing along the divide, from north to south. Several minor summits were climbed before Peak 12,960+ was reached. Class 2 from the region of Longley Pass by northwest slope or west ridge.

Thunder Mountain (13,588)

First ascent August 1905 by G. K. Davis of the U. S. Geological Survey. The second ascent was made in July 1927 by Norman Clyde.

Route 1. Southeast slope and east ridge. Class 3. From Lake 12,280 southeast of the peak ascend the slope to the ridge east of the summit. Traverse just below the ridge line on the north side to the notch south of the higher (N) summit. Cross the notch on an airy bridge and climb a class 3 wall to the top.

Route 2. Northeast slope and east ridge. Class 3. From the lake basin southwest of Lake Reflection climb to the saddle between Thunder Mountain and Peak 13,231 to the east. Proceed along the ridge as in Route 1.

Peaks West of the Great Western Divide

Peak 12,683 (0.5 W of South Guard Lake; formerly 12,680)

First ascent July 1959 by Phil Arnot, Shel Arnot, Harry Pancoast, Dale Nelson, and Charlie Backus by the south slope from Cunningham Creek. Class 2. The north summit is the higher.

Peak 12,560+ (1.5 W of Thunder Mountain; formerly 12,620)

First ascent in 1940 by Sierra Club party of six, by the south slope from Table Creek. Class 2.

Second ascent July 1958 by Phil Arnot and party of four via the north face to the west ridge and thence to the summit. Class 3-4.

Peaks of the Kings-Kern Divide (West to East)

Peak 13,231 (0.7 E of Thunder Mountain; formerly 13,241)

First ascent unrecorded. Second ascent by the east face, August 1939 by Fritz Lippmann, Dave Nelson, Don Woods, and Edward Koskinen. The west ridge and southwest face appear to be class 3.

Peak 13,090 (0.5 S of Mount Jordan; formerly 13,102)

First ascent July 1931 by Norman Clyde. Probably class 3 by the north ridge from Mount Jordan or by the southeast ridge.

Mount Jordan (*13,344*)

First ascent by Norman Clyde, July 15, 1925, evidently of the lower north peak.

Route 1. East slope. Class 2-3. In 1936 two Sierra Club parties, led by Lewis Clark and Carl Jensen, made the ascent. They found a cairn on the northern summit and also climbed the interesting southernmost pinnacle, which is the higher. It bore no evidence of any previous ascent. From the lake southeast of Mount Jordan climb to the north, then veer northwest and finally west to the saddle between the north and south summits. The ridge between the two is easy class 3. The spectacular block on the south summit can be climbed on its east face (class 4); it can also be attained by means of a delicate five-foot leap.

Route 2. North face. Class 3. Climbed August 3, 1940, by Art Argiewicz and six others from Reflection Lake and a basin to the southeast of the lake. From Lake Reflection go east of Peak 12,070 to an elongated lake northeast of Jordan. Then proceed southwest to the north face, climb the north face, and traverse the ridge to the southern summit.

Route 3. West face. Descended August 3, 1940, by Art Argiewicz and party. About class 2, except for summit.

Mount Genevra (*13,055*)

First ascent July 15, 1925, by Norman Clyde, who also climbed it in 1927. A Sierra Club party led by Lewis Clark and Carl Jensen made the ascent from Milestone camp in 1936.

Route 1. East slope. Class 2, except for summit blocks which are class 3. Ascended August 6, 1939, by Dave Nelson, Earl Jessen, and Hal Leich.

Route 2. North ridge. Class 2. On August 3, 1940, Robert Schonborn led a party of six to the top from East Lake by way of Lucys Foot Pass and the north ridge. As an alternative from Lake Reflection a good class 2 route leads to Millys Foot Pass (12,240+) just north of Mount Genevra.

Route 3. North face. Class 3. Ascended July 19, 1951, by Bill Bade, Barbara Lilley, and Franklin Barnett up the north face by way of a snow chute leading to the ridge just west of the summit.

Route 4. Southwest slope and west ridge. Class 2. Climbed by Andy Smatko, Bill Sanders, Frede Jensen, and Peter Hunt. Descent was made via the narrow chute (ordinarily snow-filled) directly south from the summit.

Mount Ericsson (13,608)

Route 1. West ridge. Class 2. First ascent August 1, 1896, by Bolton C. Brown and Lucy Brown. From Lucys Foot Pass follow the easy ridge to the summit.

Route 2. East ridge. Class 3. Descended August 1, 1896, by Bolton C. Brown and Lucy Brown. From Harrison Pass climb the east ridge.

Route 3. South ridge. Class 3. Climbed by Lewis Clark and Carl Jensen in 1936.

Route 4. Northwest couloir. Class 4. Climbed in July 1946 by Norman Clyde, Robert Breckenfeld, Jules Eichorn, Joe Brower, and Danny Kaplan. From Lake Reflection ascend toward Lucys Foot Pass. Climb the rocky chute which heads between Mount Ericsson and the first crag to the north. About one hundred feet below the head of this chute turn right (S) and ascend a steep, icy couloir which leads to the Kings-Kern Divide somewhat west of the summit of Ericsson. An ice axe is necessary in the couloir. From the divide climb the west ridge or the southwest slopes to the top.

Gregorys Monument (13,920+)

Route 1. West or southwest slopes. Class 1. First ascent July 1894 by Warren Gregory, Emmet and Loring Rixford, and W. Sanderson. This peak is the south and lower peak of Mount Stanford and is separated from the latter by a jagged, class 3 ridge about one-fourth of a mile long. Technically speaking, the many who have ascended only to this point have not climbed Mount Stanford.

Route 2. North ridge. Class 3. Follow the ridge from Mount Stanford. See routes on the latter in the section on peaks north of the Kings-Kern Divide.

Route 3. East face. Class 3 to 4. Descended July 23, 1929, by Walter Starr, Jr., who wrote: "Left summit at 4:30 and descended to Center Basin via the first chute (lowest gap next to the peak) on the Junction Peak side. Bad rock climb down to ledge. From ledge descended steep snow chute, and from bottom snow in talus along stream to Center Basin and down Bubbs Creek. Arrived at Vidette Meadow 7:45 P.M."

Peak 13,760+ (1.1 NW of Junction Peak; formerly 13,826)

This is a high point on the divide between Junction Peak and Gregorys Monument. First ascent June 3, 1934, by David R. Brower and Hervey Voge. Class 3. From the lake on the south side of Forester Pass they ascended the southeast face of the peak to the ridge between

Gregorys Monument and the peak proper, reaching the ridge at nearly its lowest point. They then proceeded eastward along the west arête to the top. Descent was by way of a shallow chute which led down the southeast face from the ridge just east of the summit, and included a rappel of about twenty feet.

Peaks North of the Kings-Kern Divide

Peak 12,960+ (0.9 SE of Mount Brewer; formerly 12,964)

On some older maps this peak is called South Guard. However the current map shows South Guard (13,224) one mile southeast and on the Great Western Divide, which seems more appropriate.

Route 1. Northeast ridge. Class 2–3.

First ascent July 26, 1916, by Walter L. Huber, Florence Burrell, Inezetta Holt, and James Rennie. They followed the south fork of Ouzel Creek to the snowfield of its upper basin, and finding the snow too hard for secure footing, climbed the rocky northeast ridge of the peak, described as a very thin knife-edge of very loose rock. This ridge led them to the summit. To avoid the slow ridge, descent was made by ledges of the north face to the snow, and down the snow.

Route 2. South face. Class 2–3. From the lake to the south climb to the ridge west of the summit and go east along the ridge.

Peak 12,620 (1.5 NW of East Lake; formerly 12,610)

Traversed May 26, 1934, by David R. Brower and Hervey Voge who proceeded from Ouzel Creek to the saddle between the peak and North Guard and then ascended the southwest ridge. Descent was by the south face. Both routes are class 2.

Peak 11,520+ (0.5 SW of East Lake; formerly 11,597)

This is actually a long ridge which extends northeastward from South Guard; it offers interesting and convenient climbing.

Route 1. Southwest ridge. Class 3. David R. Brower and Hervey Voge, May 28, 1934. From the upper portion of the south fork of Ouzel Creek climb to the ridge and follow it eastward, weaving among small towers, blocks, and knife-edges.

Route 2. South face. Class 3. David R. Brower and Hervey Voge, May 28, 1934. An entertaining climb, just below the difficulty requiring a rope.

Route 3. North face. Climbed August 3, 1940, by parties led by Alan MacRae and Oliver Kehrlein.

Peak 11,609 (*1.2 S of East Lake; formerly 11,593*)

This peak is called The Noonmark on David Starr Jordan's map of 1899. The north face of this cleaver-shaped peak was climbed on July 31, 1940, by Oliver Kehrlein and six others. The saddle southwest of the summit can be gained by the southeast slopes from Lake Reflection.

Peak 12,070 (*0.5 S of Lake Reflection; formerly 12,047*)

This peak is called Crag Reflection on Jordan's map. Ascended prior to 1952 by M. Roth and Calkins Fletcher. Class 3 from the saddle to the south.

Ericsson Crags

There are three main crags on the north ridge of Mount Ericsson. Crag 1 is that closest to Ericsson, and Crag 3 is that farthest away. These crags are most readily accessible by way of the rocky chutes which lead up to the ridge from the west. The crags offer challenging climbing and there are many possible routes and minor pinnacles that have not yet been explored.

Crag 1. (*About 13,000.*) Southeast face. First ascent August 4, 1939, by Edward Koskinen, Don Woods, and DeWitt Allen. Ascend the chute which goes up from the west between Crag 1 and Ericsson. About two-thirds of the way up this chute branches. Take the left or north branch, which will lead to a broad shoulder on the ridge just south of the top-most portion of Crag 1. A smaller and rather difficult crag (climbed in 1939 by Voge, Waller, and Woods) separates this shoulder from the north face of Mount Ericsson. From the shoulder a rather open chimney leads up the southeast face of the crag, but at the bottom the chimney ends in an overhanging crack. The climbable portion of the chimney can be reached by a delicate, downward traverse from a little arête just to the left (W) of the crack. The route then leads up the chimney, over several large steps, and finally up the northwest side of the summit block.

Crag 1W. This is a formidable looking crag quite a distance out on the ridge running west from Crag 1. There are no records of any attempts. The most feasible route appears to be on the north and north-west faces.

Crag 2. (*About 12,950.*) Class 3 to 4. First ascent August 3, 1939, by David R. Brower and Hervey Voge. Ascend the main rocky chute coming down to the west between Crags 2 and 3. From this climb the next to the highest chute which enters this main chute from the south and which leads to the northwest face of Crag 2. Take the right (W) branch of this next-to-highest subsidiary chute and climb out of it just to the left (N) of some caves by means of a class 4 pitch. From there rather easy slopes lead to the top.

Crag 3. (About 12,900.) Class 3 to 4. First ascent prior to 1939. Ascend the main chute coming down to the west between Crags 2 and 3. When nearly to the top of this chute cross a rib to the left (N) by a band of broken rock and continue up the next chute to the north. Leave this by means of a rather delicate chimney which leads to the crest of the south ridge of the crag. Proceed along the east side of the ridge to a little arête running east from the top of the crag. Climb up the arête to the main ridge and follow this to the top. The climb can also be made by way of the southwest slope from the main chute.

Peak 12,225 (0.7 NE of East Lake; formerly 12,222)

First ascent September 19, 1926, by Norman Clyde. Class 2 up south slopes and the southeast ridge from the lake to the south.

Peak 12,160+ (1.1 W of East Vidette; formerly called West Vidette)

First ascent August 1920 by Norman Clyde and Louis Schichter. This peak is class 1 to 2 from the southeast from Vidette Creek. The north face may offer interesting climbing.

West Vidette (12,560+)

This new position for the West Vidette accords better with the description of C. B. Bradley, who named the Videttes, than does the position on the old map. Bradley spoke of "two of these promontories, standing guard, as it were, the one at the entrance to the valley and the other just within it...." Formerly this was called West Spur Peak 12,500+. First ascent in 1926 by Norman Clyde.

Class 2 by east slopes and south ridge, from Lake 10,820 on Vidette Creek. Ascend to the saddle south of the peak and follow the ridge to the summit.

West Spur Peak 12,640+ (1.3 E of East Lake; formerly 12,685)

On July 14, 1940, Dick Goldsmith and Anna Shinn stopped 50 feet from the top. On August 8, 1940, William Morrison and three others made the ascent from the west, from East Lake.

A northeast approach from Lake 10,820 on Vidette Creek was used by Arkel Erb, Andy Smatko, Tom Ross, Frede Jensen, David Oyler, and Mike McNicholas. Climb to the saddle north of the peak and follow the ridge south. Class 1–2.

The Minster (12,240+)

This is a jagged ridge of grotesque spires extending westward from Deerhorn Mountain. A complete east to west traverse was made on August 3, 1939, by Ted Waller, Don Woods, and Edward Koskinen, who found no records of previous visits on any of the spires.

Deerhorn Mountain (13,265)

The twin peaks of Deerhorn make it an easily recognized landmark. The southeast peak is slightly higher. The first recorded ascent was made on July 8, 1927, by Norman Clyde, who found no cairn on the southeast peak, but possibly one on the northwest peak. Various routes have been used; those listed below are not necessarily arranged in chronological order.

Route 1. Southwest chute. Class 3 to 4. Ascend the chute which heads between the twin peaks of Deerhorn. The most difficult portions are near the bottom and near the top. From the notch the southeast peak may be climbed by its north face or its northwest arête. This peak has a small, steep top, and in 1939 a party of three was so cramped there that they lost the can containing earlier names down the north face.

Route 2. West ridge. Class 3. From the trail to Harrison Pass, at about 11,000 feet, ascend the southwest slopes of the ridge to a point a little east of the lowest point on the ridge between The Minster and the west gendarmes of Deerhorn. Proceed eastward on the ridge, staying more on the north side than on the south. Ascend the northwest peak of Deerhorn on cluttered ledges. Descend to the notch between the two peaks, and climb the southeast peak by its north face. This route was followed by Norman Clyde, Hervey Voge, and Ted Waller on August 5, 1939.

Route 3. Northwest basin and west ridge. Class 3. Climb into the basin almost due east of East Lake and proceed from its upper end to the west ridge of Deerhorn, which may be traversed as noted above to the summits. Route done by W. Morrison, R. Kauffman, and Norman Roth on August 5, 1940.

Route 4. Southwest face. Class 3 to 4. From the Harrison Pass trail at about 11,000 feet climb the southwest face of the mountain, aiming for a point just west of and about 300 feet below the northwest peak. From here work around to the north and climb to the top of the northwest peak. The traverse may then be made to the southeast peak. It is also possible to climb directly up the west face of the northwest peak, which for 300 to 400 feet is quite airy but not really difficult. This route was made by Norman Clyde, Jules Eichorn, Robert Breckenfeld, and others, in July 1946.

Route 5. North buttress. Class 3. This buttress leads from upper Vidette Creek directly to the northwest peak of Deerhorn. It was climbed by Norman Clyde.

Route 6. Northeast ridge. Class 4. Climbed by Arkel Erb, Andy Smatko, Frede Jensen, Tom Ross, David Oyler, and Mike McNicholas. From near the base of the snow chute that comes down northeast between the two summits, climb up the northeast ridge of the higher (southeastern) peak. The crest of the ridge is reached about halfway up. Continue on the ridge to about 60 feet below the summit. Here an exposed class 4 pitch leads to easier rocks and the single block constituting the summit.

Subsidiary Peaks of Deerhorn Mountain

To the east of Deerhorn there are two sharp subsidiary peaks. No records exist regarding the double-pointed peaklet nearest the main southeast peak. The next peaklet to the east was climbed August 3, 1939, by DeWitt Allen and Fritz Lippmann by the southwest chute. They used a piton a number of times for safety in the wet chute.

An arête running north of Deerhorn somewhat west of the northwest peak was traversed by Norman Clyde, David R. Brower, and eight others on July 13, 1940. No record was found of previous ascent of peaks on the arête.

East Vidette (12,350)

First ascent by a Sierra Club party in 1910.

Route 1. East ridge. Class 3. A variation of this route is the ascent of the north side of the east ridge and the traversing of the upper part of the ridge to the summit.

Route 2. North side. Class 3-4 up north or northwest face.

Route 3. West slope. Class 4. Climbed from Vidette Creek by Arkel Erb and Mike McNicholas by a steep, shallow chute heading 300 yards south of the summit, then along a ridge to the summit. The rock is unsound on this route.

East Spur Peak 12,735 (formerly 12,722)

Climbed for the first time by Jim Harkins and Pat Goldsworthy, July 14, 1940.

Peak 12,160+ (1.4 W of Center Peak; formerly 12,288)

First ascent by Andy Smatko, Gordon MacCleod, and Tom Ross on June 9, 1963. Class 2.

Peak 13,414 (0.7 E of Deerhorn; formerly 13,440)

Climbed by Boynton and Edith Kaiser, August 7, 1948. This peak may possibly have been traversed by Norman Clyde and David R. Brower on August 4, 1939, during a descent from Mount Stanford. It was climbed from Vidette Creek by the Kaisers, who went up the northwest slope, staying somewhat northeast of the ridge leading from 13,414 to the low pass to the west. An alternate route (class 2) is the west slope from the Deerhorn Saddle.

Mount Stanford (13,963)

This peak is separated from Gregorys Monument (see peaks of the Kings-Kern Divide) by a knife-edge ridge about one-fourth of a mile long.

Route 1. South ridge. Class 3. From Gregorys Monument follow the ridge, with minor deviations to one side or the other. The crossing takes about 20 minutes. First ascent August 1, 1896, by Bolton C. Brown.

Route 2. West face. Class 3. First descent August 1, 1896, by Bolton C. Brown, who went down the chute where the knife-edge from Gregorys Monument joined the peak of Stanford (just S of the final peak). He went down the chute for about one thousand feet and then proceeded downward and toward the south from chute to chute to the cliff base near a small lake below Harrison Pass.

Route 3. West face and north ridge. About class 3. The west face may be ascended to the ridge north of the summit and the ridge followed southward to the summit. This route was followed by Art Argiewicz and three others in August 1940.

Route 4. North ridge. About class 3. This route was descended by David R. Brower and Norman Clyde, August 4, 1939. They traversed the north ridge from the summit to the saddle east of Deerhorn. For the ascent, go east from Deerhorn Saddle to the ridge, and then south along the ridge, deviating to west or east as expedient. Class 3.

Route 5. East face. About class 3. A steep couloir or chute usually filled with snow descends almost directly from the summit of Stanford toward the basin west of Center Peak. The face to the south of this chute may be ascended to the summit, or the chute itself may be followed, if one keeps to the north side. These climbs were made in August 1947 by James R. Harkins and several others. In 1948 Beckett Howorth and party ascended the "east ridge."

Route 6. East arête and north ridge. Class 3. Ascended in 1953 by High Trip party. About one-half mile north of the summit an arête extends eastward. Climb this to its junction with the main mass, and ascend a chimney leading to the north ridge.

Kearsarge Pinnacles *(about 11,600 to 12,000+)*

These sharp little pinnacles are numbered consecutively from southeast to northwest, numbers 1 through 12, after the 1939 system of Edward Koskinen. Several numbering systems have been applied in the past, and the numbers on the summits, if any, may differ from those given here. The minor summits are not numbered. The pinnacles may be identified from the accompanying Sketch 27. From the north the notches 3–4, 5–6, and 9–10 are rather readily reached, while 4–5 and 8–9 are harder.

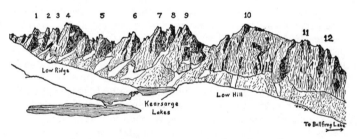

Sketch 27. The Kearsarge Pinnacles from the north.

Pinnacle 1. First ascent July 28, 1935, by May Pridham, Miles Werner, and Pan Coffin.

Pinnacle 2. First ascent as for Pinnacle 1.

Pinnacle 3. First ascent August 1, 1939, by Ted Waller, Don Woods, David Nelson, and Edward Koskinen.

Pinnacle 4. First recorded ascent as for Pinnacle 3.

Pinnacle 5. Records unknown.

Pinnacle 6. Climbed August 18, 1954, by Dwight Ericsson from the 5–6 notch. Class 3. Evidence of previous ascent was found.

Pinnacle 7. This pinnacle has been climbed numerous times.

Pinnacle 8. Class 5. Best climbed from the south notch (7–8 notch). First ascent in July 1932 by Glen Dawson, Thomas Rawles and Hans Leschke.

Pinnacle 9. First recorded climb July 25, 1924, by R. Howard. It is easy class 4 from the northeast. Climb up the chute to the high V-notch between 8 and 9, go around to the south side of the ridge, and climb up the face, reaching the lower summit first. An ice axe may be needed in the chute. Or climb from the 9–10 notch.

Pinnacles 10, 11, 12. All have been climbed many times. First ascent probably by Glen Dawson, Owen Ward, and Hans Leschke in 1932. They may be approached from the northwest end of the ridge, from the north, or from the 9–10 notch.

Besides the ascents mentioned above, climbs of unidentified pinnacles were made earlier. In 1932 Jack Riegelhuth climbed up the nearest chimney from Vidette Meadow to the top of "the highest pinnacle." On July 28, 1935, a Sierra Club party including Peter Grubb and Neil Ruge climbed "a few" of the northwestern pinnacles.

Center Peak (*12,760*)

First ascent July 5, 1898, by C. G. Bradley, by an unknown route. Two hours to the top from the meadow at the foot.

Route 1. North face. Class 3. David R. Brower and Hervey Voge, May 22, 1934. Three chutes discharge prominent talus fans into Center Basin northwest of the peak. Take the center chute and climb well up within the mountain wall; then turn to the right (SW) up a chute which leads up to the northwest buttress of the peak. Follow along the buttress to a saddle, and there cross to the west side of the northwest ridge and climb upward close to the ridgetop to within two hundred feet of the summit; then cross to the north face for a short way, back to the west, and then to the top.

Route 2. East face. Class 1 to 2. This face may be reached in several places from about 11,500 feet in Center Basin.

Route 3. Northwest face. Class 3. Ascended by Phil Berry and Frank Tarver, July 26, 1952. South of the talus fans mentioned under Route 1, and about 100 yards south of the sheerest part of the face, proceed directly up the face to a tunnel at the top of the face. From the tunnel ledges lead to the summit.

Peaks South of the Kings-Kern Divide

Peak 12,513 (1 S of Mount Genevra; formerly 12,492)

This peak was climbed from the south in August 1939 by Fritz Lippmann, Dave Nelson, Don Woods, and Ed Koskinen. Class 3.

Peak 13,832 (1.2 SE of Mt. Stanford; formerly 13,844)

First ascent by Norman Clyde, June 22, 1926.
Route 1. East ridge. Class 3. Climbed June 8, 1963, by Andy Smatko, Arkel Erb, Tom Ross, and Gordon MacCleod. *Route 2. Southeast slopes.* Class 2. *Route 3. West face.* Class 3 by choice of several chutes.

Peak 13,030 (0.5 SE of Lake South America; formerly 13,028)

Climbed July 10, 1939, by Jack Sturgeon. Class 2 by the north ridge and by the south ridge or southeast slopes; southwest slopes, class 3.

Diamond Mesa

Strictly speaking there is no summit of the Mesa, since it rises continuously toward Junction Peak. It was climbed July 10, 1898, by Bolton C. Brown and a companion in an attempt on Junction. It may be ascended by the west face, especially near the southern end, and may also be reached by following the ridge from Junction Peak. There is a meadow and a stream on the Mesa's lower end. The northern end of the Mesa narrows to a class 3 knife-edge that leads to Junction Peak.

The Whitney Region

JOHN D. and RUTH MENDENHALL, ARTHUR B. JOHNSON, BRAEME GIGAS, and HOWARD KOSTER (1941); JOHN D. and RUTH MENDENHALL (1953); HERVEY H. VOGE (1964)

THE WHITNEY REGION, that portion of the crest of the Sierra Nevada lying between Shepherd Pass and Army Pass, is a spectacular display of mountain sculpture. Rising west of Lone Pine, in Owens Valley, and following the northeast border of Sequoia National Park, this jagged thirteen-mile escarpment includes six of California's thirteen peaks exceeding 14,000 feet in elevation: Mounts Tyndall, Williamson, Russell, Muir, Langley, and the culminating summit, 14,495-foot Mount Whitney, highest peak in the United States excluding Alaska. The 10,000-foot scarp of the Mount Whitney fault block forms impressive eastern precipices. Deep glacier-cut canyons, glacial cirques plucked out among the peaks, moraine deposits in the valleys, sharp ridges, myriad glacial lakes, alpine trails and passes, beautiful timberline campsites—these provide a wilderness of variety for the climber. Indeed, one of the finest rock climbing areas in the Sierra is concentrated in the six miles between Mount Russell and Mount Langley.

In 1864, members of a California State Geological Survey party, Clarence King and Richard Cotter, viewed the region from the north and gave to the highest point the name of their chief, Whitney. Years later, after two unsuccessful attempts, King reached the summit, only to learn that he had been preceeded a few weeks by several parties from Owens Valley. A. H. Johnson, C. D. Begole, and John Lucas had, on August 18, 1873, been the first to reach the top. During the years following, the summit rocks have known the tread of countless climbers, singly, in groups, in mass ascents. They have been visited by world travelers, by trail builders, by survey parties. The trail to the summit was completed in 1904, and a stone shelter was erected on the peak in 1909.

Mount Whitney has naturally received the greatest share of attention, both from climbers and from historians. Little, therefore, is known of the early history of the other 14,000-foot peaks of the region, except for Mount Tyndall. This first came to attention in 1864 when King and Cotter made their famous ascent so dramatically described in King's *Mountaineering in the Sierra Nevada*. Of recent years, dating specifically from the introduction of modern roped climbing on the East Face of Mount Whitney in 1931, the mountaineering approach to the region has been somewhat altered.

TOPOGRAPHY AND ITS RELATION TO CLIMBING

A mountain mass of fault-block origin usually possesses a precipitous face contrasting with a gentle approach. This characteristic is exhibited to a striking degree in the region surrounding Mount Whitney, for the general contour rises gently from the west, only to break off in huge cliffs toward Owens Valley on the east. Accordingly, the majority of the difficult climbs are found east of the crest. For details of topography refer to the Mount Whitney and Lone Pine quadrangles of the United

States Geological Survey map, or the Sequoia-Kings Canyon National Parks topographical map. A sketch map (Sketch 28) shows knapsack routes and some local names not on the USGS maps.

In general, the most exposed faces are quite firm: eternal vigilance, however, must be exercised to avoid mishap. The general dependability of the cliffs does not extend to the chutes. Some members of an inexpert or careless party may readily find themselves subjected to a deadly barrage, usually caused by the climbers above. In addition, rockfalls and snow avalanches occur from natural causes, and any leader conducting his party without due regard for this contingency is guilty of negligence or poor judgment. Unsettled weather, accompanied by hail storms, often occurs during the summer, and will, of course, affect climbing conditions. Climbers are also reminded that many of the routes involve a length of time and altitude well in excess of that normally encountered in the Sierra. The Whitney Region contains no glaciers, and ice equipment is unnecessary in late summer and fall. One must remember that the climbs are classified upon the basis of most favorable conditions, and that the season or adverse weather can raise the class of an ascent by one or two numbers.

APPROACHES AND CLIMBING CENTERS

The Whitney Region is most accessible by Inyo National Forest trails from the east; here the grandeur of the range is an inspiring sight, the most lofty summits towering well over 10,000 feet above Owens Valley.

From Independence. From U.S. 395 at the south end of Independence, drive to the Symmes Creek road end (5,900). Follow the arduous trail which starts up Symmes Creek, and leads over to and up Shepherd Creek, where one can camp at timberline (10,400) below Shepherd Pass (12,030). Mounts Williamson and Tyndall can be climbed from the pass.

From Manzanar. Take a dirt road just north of Manzanar, and follow to the second road branching right. This passes through a gate, and just beyond take the right-hand road. Drive to a level spot below a very steep hill (impractical for standard cars). Walk one-half mile to the end of the road. Hike up a faint trail on the south side of George Creek to a waterfall about halfway to timberline. Cross below the waterfall and continue up the north side. Just below timberline, the stream forks. If Williamson is the objective, ascend north (right) branch to timber-

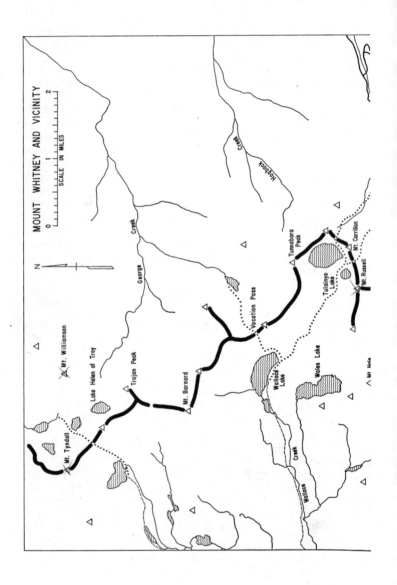

MOUNT WHITNEY AND VICINITY

SCALE IN MILES
0   1   2

N

Mt. Williamson

Lake Helen of Troy

George Creek

Mt. Tyndall

Trojan Peak

Mt. Barnard

Vacation Pass

Tunnabora Peak

Hogback Creek

Tulainyo Lake

Mt. Carillon

Mt. Russell

Wallace Lake

Wales Lake

Mt. Hale

Wallace Creek

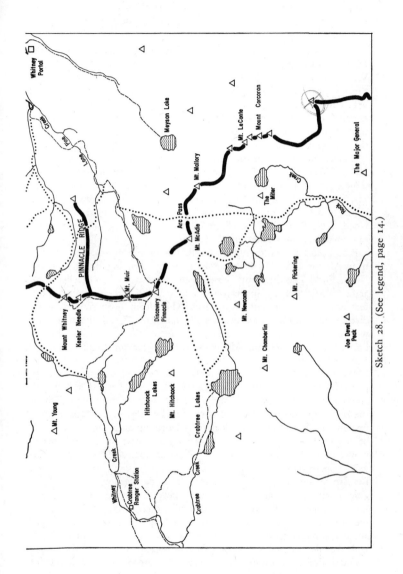

Sketch 28. (See legend, page 14.)

line camp. If Barnard is to be climbed, go up south (left) fork to camp just below a small lake.

From Lone Pine. Drive up Lone Pine Creek to Whitney Portal (8,361), where a Forest Service campground is maintained. The Mount Whitney horse trail leads up the Middle Fork to Bighorn Park (10,365), Mirror Lake (10,650), and continues to the summit of Mount Whitney by way of Whitney Trail Crest (13,600+). Trail Crest is northwest of Whitney Pass (13,335) which was crossed by the old trail. The junction with the John Muir Trail is met just on the west side of Trail Crest.

Convenient bases for the East Face and Mountaineers routes on Mount Whitney are at East Face Lake (12,640; called Iceberg Lake on some maps), or on the North Fork of Lone Pine Creek to the southeast and at a slightly lower elevation. These sites lack firewood. Some climbers prefer to camp at Mirror Lake, which is supplied with firewood, cross Pinnacle Pass, climb Whitney's East Face, and return via the horse trail in a long day.

East Face Lake or the upper North Fork campsites may be reached from Mirror Lake via Pinnacle Pass, or by climbing directly up the North Fork. The first route possesses the advantage of an excellent trail as far as Mirror Lake, but involves a subsequent trailless climb of 1,600 feet and a steep descent of 300 feet. The North Fork route is more direct and primitive, but occasionally obscure. Ascend the foot trail, which starts at the highest point of the road. Where the trail joins the horse trail, turn left for Mirror Lake or right for the North Fork near-by.

North Fork Route: Proceed up the south side of the stream for approximately one-half mile after leaving the trail. Beyond a large triangular rock, cross the fork and ascend a steep, narrow slope. This is the first break in the cliffs, and is marked by large pines. After approximately 100 feet of climbing, a narrow ledge running downstream will be found. Follow this up and to the right almost to the end, where it will be possible to turn left and follow another shelf upstream. This way (Ebersbacher Ledges) replaces the route south of the stream. Remain on the north side of the fork to Clyde Meadow, a lovely bowl graced with a tarn amid foxtail pines. Beyond the meadow, recross to the south side of the main stream and ascend large talus blocks. At the crest of the slope, recross to the north side and ascend to a point about three-quarters of a mile east of the great walls of Whitney. Gravel will provide reasonably comfortable campsites.

If it is desired to camp at East Face Lake, proceed onward to a point just beyond a stream coming from the right (N). Turn right and ascend the steep but rather firm rocks (less tiring than the talus farther upstream). East Face Lake is a short distance beyond the crest.

From Cottonwood Creek. Drive up the Lone Pine-Carroll Creek road and ascend Cottonwood Creek via trail. Numerous campsites will be found in the vicinity of Cottonwood Lakes. Mount Langley is easily climbed from this trail, which leads over Army Pass.

Other Approaches. Entry into the region from Kings Canyon National Park is gained via Forester Pass (John Muir Trail), or over Colby Pass and down the Kern-Kaweah. From the Giant Forest, climb via the High Sierra Trail over Kaweah Gap and across the Big Arroyo. A long pack-in can be made up the Kern River from the south.

Principal Passes

The Whitney Region is crossed by three passes having stock trails. These are Shepherd and Army Passes, bounding the region to the north and south, and Whitney Trail Crest south of Mount Whitney. Other passes are undeveloped, and are suitable only for experienced knapsack parties (see map, Sketch 30).

Tyndall Col (12,960+). Class 2. Connects the Bowl (west of Mount Williamson) with Wright Creek.

Vacation Pass (12,640). Class 2-3. Provides a route from a lake on the southern fork of George Creek to Wallace Lake. Cross somewhat north of the lowest point.

Russell-Carillon Pass. Class 3. This is a rough, steep route across the lowest part of the saddle (13,280+) between Mount Russell and Mount Carillon, and leads from Clyde Meadow on the North Fork of Lone Pine Creek to Wallace Lake by way of Lake Tulainyo. From Clyde Meadow climb a steep scree slope in a northwesterly direction to the easy slopes below the saddle. On the north side descend a class 3 wall. (An alternate route crosses the crest north of Mount Carillon.)

Whitney-Russell Pass (13,040+). Class 2. The notch provides convenient passage between the North Fork of Lone Pine Creek and Whitney Creek. *East to west:* Ascend talus northwest of East Face Lake, and climb into the notch at the corner of the wall north of the lake. *West to east:* From the bowl at the head of Whitney Creek, climb talus, keeping right to the higher (S) of two notches through headwall. The lower (N) notch is steep on the east side, but can be crossed (class 3).

Discovery Pass. Class 2. This provides a shortcut from the Whitney Trail to Crabtree Creek. Leave the Whitney Trail on the east side of

Trail Crest, pass south of Discovery Pinnacle, and proceed southwest on the south side of the ridge toward the large lake (11,312) on Crabtree Creek.

Arc Pass (13,000). Class 1. This saddle offers a direct route between Consultation Lake and upper Rock Creek. *North to south:* Pass the lake on the east and climb the talus to the south, keeping high up to the left until it is convenient to follow a ledge back to the right into the pass. *South to north:* From Sky Blue Lake, ascend talus to the northeast into a small cirque; thence directly north into the pass.

Tuttle Pass (12,800). Class 1. This route involves a long trek along the south fork of Tuttle Creek, and is recommended only for sturdy knapsackers.

Crabtree Pass (12,560+). Class 2. A convenient link between Crabtree Creek and Rock Creek recess.

Pinnacle Pass (12,240). Class 3. *South to north:* Pass north of Mirror Lake and ascend a broad, sloping canyon to northwest, keeping near the base of cliffs to north. After three-quarters of a mile, ledges on the right lead up to the pass, 1,600 feet above Mirror Lake, just right of a prominent pinnacle visible from Mirror Lake. The first part of the descent, eastward, is moderately difficult rock work; below, descend diagonally west. The lower portion and the basin floor are composed of very rough talus. Proceed diagonally toward Mount Whitney to the right side of canyon. Camp on sheltered gravel beds, or ascend to the East Face Lake plateau by going to a gully a short distance beyond the point where a stream comes down the right slope. *North to south:* From the North Fork canyon, ascend talus at the first place where it rises appreciably against the south wall. At the high point of the talus (300 feet above the stream), follow ledges right and upward into the pass.

Principal Peaks (North to South)

Mount Tyndall (14,018)

Route 1. North face. Class 3. First ascent July 6, 1864, by Clarence King and Richard Cotter. From a point between Shepherd Pass and the saddle leading to the Bowl, ascend the rib in the middle of the face (or the gully to its right) over granite slabs, to the arête. Proceed east among the gendarmes to the summit.

Route 2. Northwest ridge. Class 2. Leaving the Shepherd Pass trail, climb the ridge at the junction of north and northwest faces. Ascend to the arête of Route 1 and follow it to the summit. *Variation:* Climb one of several gullies to the south of the northwest ridge, traverse the south face of the north peak 100 feet below its crest, and ascend to the arête, thence to the summit.

Route 3. Southwest slopes. Class 2. First descent July 6, 1864, by Clarence King and Richard Cotter. Climb the talus above the highest lake on Wright Creek.

Route 4. East face. Class 4. First ascent August 13, 1935, by William F. Loomis and Marjory Farquhar. Climb the first prominent open chute on the east face of the north ridge. The principal difficulty is entering the chute.

Route 5. Southeast ridge. Class 4. First ascent August 11, 1939, by Ted Waller and Fritz Lippmann. The ascent from the east of the southeast wall of the third large chute southeast of Tyndall involves 500 feet of class 4 climbing. The rest of the route follows the nivated southwest slope of the ridge to the top.

West Peak of Tyndall (13,540). Class 2 via the south slope. First ascent unrecorded. The oddly sculptured northwest face offers varied scrambles of class 3–5 difficulty, all on excellent granite.

Mount Williamson (14,384)

Apart from the crest, Williamson offers one of the finest views of the eastern escarpment, and is one of the most imposing peaks to be seen from Owens Valley. Although first described as "an inaccessible cluster of granite needles," the summit has now been reached by many routes. The mountain is so complex that it is easy to get off the route and into difficulty. Accordingly it is well to have a rope available, even though the actual climbing problem on most of the routes is moderate in degree. Williamson from the northwest, with marked routes, is shown on Sketch 29.

Route 1. Southeast ridge from George Creek. Class 2. First ascent in 1884 by W. L. Hunter and C. Mulholland. A nine-hour, almost trailless climb up George Creek (see Manzanar approach) brings one to a timberline campsite (about 11,500) on the north fork of the creek. From here ascend north-northeast to the gradual slope of the south-east ridge, following this to the base of the steeper slope. Here it is possible to cross the east slope past a small lake and then go diagonally upwards; but "much the easier climb is to keep on ... the backbone of the ridge ... There is not very much difficulty in either direction." (A. W. Carroll)

Variation: From Bairs Creek. Class 3. Climbed in 1958 by Dick Jali,

John Harding, and Dick Cowley. Follow the South Fork of Bairs Creek to the cirque at its head, and climb a chute up to the southeast ridge, which is then climbed to the summit as in Route 1.

Sketch 29. Mount Williamson from the northwest.

2	Route 2	R	Red talus
B	Black stains on rock	NNN	Northwest buttress
S	Summit	NF	North face
SL	Small lake	V	Variation on Route 2

Route 2. West face. Class 3. First ascent by this approach was in July 1896, by Professor Bolton Coit Brown and Mrs. Lucy Brown. The 1,800-foot west face of Williamson has provided varied routes to the summit, and, to less experienced climbers, many cul-de-sacs. After ap-

proaching from Shepherd Pass, follow the top of the low ridge which separates two lakes in the floor of the Bowl. Proceed along the ridge, avoiding a cliff by passing to the right. After passing the rise in the center of the basin, and beyond the second of two lakes to the right of the ridge, move straight toward the summit of Williamson. Ascend to the right on talus toward black marks on rock caused by snow water, and enter the chute above. This is a large chute or gully to the left of a lower buttress, which resembles an inverted shield with a rectangular column superimposed on top of it. Ascend the chute, which soon branches above; continue up the left branch. Near the top avoid a broad slope to the left. Climb a chimney to the right and emerge on top of a high plateau on the northwest ridge which slopes gently toward the summit.

Variations: Another, perhaps more frequently used, route lies well to the south. From the Bowl climb up red talus. Ascend the southernmost of abundantly scree-filled chutes, keeping to firmer rock along either wall, to the notch in the southwest ridge. Cross into an open chute in the upper south face, and climb ledges in zigzag route marked with ducks to the nivated summit slope. Several other variations have been worked out by Norman Clyde and others, sometimes unintentionally. The southwest arête may be followed to the summit, but this is almost class 4. The west face chutes north of Route 2 have been used frequently, but involve much more scree and route-finding. The abundant scree in these chutes can simplify the descent—provided one chooses the correct chute.

Route 3. Northeast ridge. Class 4. First ascent 1925, by Homer D. Erwin. This involves an arduous trailless approach up Williamson Creek. From timberline ascend a chute heading on the nivated slope on the northeast ridge of Williamson and follow the ridge over Peak 14,125 and Peak 14,160+ (see East Peak of Williamson) to summit. Norman Clyde has followed the northeast ridge from Owens Valley—an 8,000-foot, waterless climb from the mouth of the Shepherd Creek gorge.

A winter ascent of the northeast ridge was made by Warren J. Harding and John Ohrenschall, December 29, 1954, through January 2, 1955. The 3½ day climb was mostly class 4, but some class A pitons were used getting out of the notches between the summit peaklets. Descent was via George Creek.

Route 4. North face. Class 4–5. Climbed July 6, 1957, by John and Ruth Mendenhall, using ice axes and one piton. Proceed more or less up the middle of the face, climbing first a snow gully, then a chimney in a buttress, then steep, firm granite, and then an icy chute, coming out on the summit plateau between the northeast peak and the main peak.

East Peak of Williamson (*14,160+*; *formerly 14,211*). Class 4. First ascent by Leroy Jeffers. From the summit of Williamson descend northeast along the summit plateau; drop 200 feet to the notch below the plateau by traversing diagonally down the southeast side of the notch; ascend a chute to the crest of the sharp peak arête; and drop 100 feet down the opposite side, whence a minimum class 4 pitch leads to the summit. Variations of this route are possible, the purpose of all of them being to avoid following the spectacular arête itself. The same applies to the ascent of Peak 14,125 to the northeast.

Trojan Peak (*13,950*)

Route 1. Minimum class 3. First ascent June 26, 1926, by Norman Clyde, via west side.

Route 2. Maximum class 2, by north ridge from saddle south of Williamson.

Route 3. Class 2, from south.

Mount Barnard (*13,990*)

Class 1. First ascent, September 25, 1892, by John and William Hunter and C. Mulholland. This is a high granitic plateau rising from the south. The east summit (13,680+) lies at the crest of the great eastern ramparts, which form an impressive 2,200-foot cliff. Mount Barnard can be easily ascended from Wright or Wallace creeks, via the southwest ridge or the south slopes. The northwest slope and the north ridge offer convenient class 2 routes to the summit, and involve less scree. From the northeast an ascent may be made by a broad couloir above George Creek to the wide plateau. Climb class 2 slope to summit.

Peak 12,723 (*1.5 E of Mount Barnard*)

Class 2 by the south slope, from the south fork of George Creek. The north face (class 4) was climbed in July 1963 by Arkel Erb and Sy Ossofsky.

Tunnabora Peak (*13,565*)

Route 1. South slope. First ascent August 1905, by George R. Davis. Class 2 from the headwaters of Wallace Creek.

Route 2. Northwest face. Climbed from a southerly fork of George

Creek, via Marmot Lake and a chute that led to the west ridge a short distance from the summit, by B. Bingham, B. Lilley, and F. Bressel, 1958.

Mount Carillon (13,552)

Class 2 via west ridge or south slope. This peak lies northeast of Mount Russell and one-third mile southeast of Tulainyo Lake. First ascent 1925, by Norman Clyde.

Mount Russell (14,086)

This peak presents a formidable appearance from almost any direction, and was one of the last of the major Sierra peaks to be climbed. The south wall is deeply fluted, consisting of four buttresses separated by deep couloirs. The outer ribs rise to nearly identical heights, making the summit a twin-horned arête. The north face is more regular, being cut by a series of horizontal ledges with steep smooth rises. The west summit is slightly higher than the east peak.

Route 1. East arête. Class 3. First ascent June 24, 1926, by Norman Clyde. From Tulainyo Lake, ascend the 500-foot wall to the south. Continue along a ledge on the north side under the crest of the arête, to the summit of the east horn.

Route 2. North arête. Class 3. First descent June 24, 1926, by Norman Clyde. From the moraine bench just west of Tulainyo Lake, follow up the rib that leads into the north arête. Difficulties of the arête can be turned by keeping right along the ends of the north face ledges.

Route 3. West arête. Minimum class 3. First descent July 1927 by Norman Clyde.

Route 4. Southwest face–west arête. Class 4. First descent July 1932 by Jules Eichorn, Glen Dawson, Walter Brem and Hans Leschke. From near the head of Whitney Creek, climb the narrow couloir just left of the buttress that rises sheer to the summit of the west horn. This couloir heads on the west arête; proceed thence by Route 3 to summit.

Route 5. South face–west chute. Class 4. First ascent July 1932 by Jules Eichorn, Glen Dawson, Walter Brem and Hans Leschke. From the head of Whitney Creek, or Whitney-Russell Pass, follow up the talus into a wide chute occupying the center of the south face. Halfway up, the chute divides. Take the left (W) branch to near the end, whence ascend the right wall. Attain the arête, which terminates in the summit ridge just east of the west horn.

Route 6. South face–east chute. First ascent was made in 1928 by A. E. Gunther. From the branch in the chute of Route 5, continue up the right (E) couloir to the headwall. There are three variations from here. *Gunther variation:* Class 3. Climb the second chimney right (S) of the headwall to the crest of southeast arête, thence on to east side of arête and up blocks to summit of east horn. *Chimney variation:* Class 4. First ascent July 29, 1932, by James Wright. Climb the first chimney on the right (at corner), passing over loose overhang near top, to a shelf on the east face of the southeast arête, thence by Gunther variation. *Face variation:* Class 3. First ascent August 7, 1931, by Howard Sloan, Frank Noel, and William Murray. Climb the headwall by a ledge leading diagonally up the face to the left, ending at midpoint of the summit arête.

Route 7. Southeast face–east arête. Class 3. First ascent June 19, 1927, by Homer D. Erwin and Fred Lueders, Jr. From Clyde Meadow, go up the right (N) canyon of the North Fork of Lone Pine Creek. Near the head, a long talus slope leads east into a short but prominent chimney, which ends at a high mesa. Cross the plateau westerly to the east arête of Russell proper. From this point, the way is a variation of Route 1.

Route 8. North face. Class 3–4. Climbed by J. H. Czock, Mildred Czock, and Mary Luck, about 1935. From the small lake at the base proceed up the east side of the face over easy rock to the first ledge that leads out into the middle of the north face. Follow the ledge to the middle of the face and climb directly up to the summit ridge midway between the two peaks (Jim Koontz).

Mount Hale (13,440+)

Class 1. First ascent July 24, 1934, by J. H. and Mildred Czock via the south slopes.

Peak 12,800+ (W of Wales Lake; formerly 12,808)

Class 2. First ascent September 5, 1935, by Chester Versteeg via the north ridge, from northwest.

Mount Young (13,177)

This peak is a long, rounded granite mass with a sheer north wall broken by avalanche chutes. An excellent view is obtained of the Whitney crest, the Kaweahs, the Great Western Divide, and the Kings-Kern Divide.

South slopes. Class 1. First ascent September 7, 1881, by Frederick Wales, William Wallace and J. Wright. Ascend from Crabtree Creek into the low saddle visible from the trail. Proceed to the summit over talus.

Mount Whitney (*14,495*)

This peak provides an exceptionally wide range of climbing difficulty. One route is a horseback trail (Route 1, class 1), and entails nothing more than time and stamina. Scrambles, difficult to various degrees, may be made from the west and north (Routes 2 and 3). Block climbing and couloir scrambling are found on the Mountaineer's Route (Route 4). Hardy and thoroughly experienced rock climbers can attack difficult and exposed routes up the East Face (Routes 5 and 6) and from the southeast (Route 7). The accompanying Sketch 30 shows East Face routes.

Route 1. The trail. Class 1. The path leaves the Whitney Pass trail about 300 yards from Trail Crest on the west side of the crest. The way swings high on the west slope of the pinnacles, skirting the notches that give impressive views down the great eastern precipices. The final peak is surmounted from the southwest. Trail distance from the roadhead to the summit is 10.5 miles (Bob and Jerri Lee).

Route 2. West slopes. Class 2. First ascent August 18, 1873, by A. H. Johnson, C. P. Begole and John Lucas. Leave the lower lake in the glacial basin at the west foot of the mountain. Climb steep talus and pass through any of the numerous chutes. Then proceed directly to the summit.

Route 3. North slopes. Class 2–3. From near the head of Whitney Creek, or from Whitney-Russell Pass, climb west over talus and large blocks. Keeping well under the wall of the north arête, ascend into any of the shallow chutes leading to a 50-foot wall of broken blocks. Pass through the wall and climb directly to summit. *Note:* Avoid the lower portion of the west half of the north face, for it is covered by steep, smooth glacial slabs, involving class 4 climbing.

Route 4. (Mountaineer's Route). Northeast side. Class 2–3. First ascent generally credited to John Muir on October 21, 1873. A large couloir separates the north arête from the great East Buttress. This couloir leads directly from East Face Lake to a notch, the junction of the north arête with the main massif. From the junction, go left directly up 400 or 500 feet of steep large blocks (often icy) to a large cairn on the crest. The summit is 200 yards southeast. This route involves some rockfall danger, and it is best to stay on the north side of the bottom of the couloir when feasible.

Route 5. East buttress. Class 4, with one class 5 pitch. First ascent September 5, 1937, by Robert K. Brinton, Glen Dawson, Richard Jones, Howard Koster and Muir Dawson. From East Face Lake, climb the

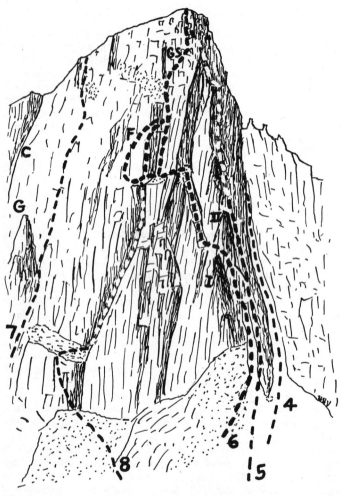

Sketch 30. East Face of Mount Whitney, showing Routes 4, 5, 6, 7, and 8

I	First Tower	C	Whitney-Keeler Couloir
II	Second Tower	G	Gendarme
F	Fresh Air Traverse	GS	Grand Staircase

talus and ledge to the left of Route 4 for 500 feet, reaching a notch between the First Tower and Second Tower on the face of the east buttress. Rope here and work right, up the face of the Second Tower. Turn it to the right 15 feet below its summit, thus gaining the second notch. On the first pitch above the notch, two pitons are needed for safety. Above this point, the route roughly follows the arête of the east buttress to a point below the "Peewee," a huge, precariously-placed block of granite over halfway up the buttress. Climb past the right side of the block. Ascend directly ahead, or swing right, up to the summit blocks.

Route 6. East face route. Class 4, with two class 5 pitches, or one class 5 and one class A pitch. First ascent August 16, 1931, by Robert L. M. Underhill, Glen Dawson, Jules Eichorn and Norman Clyde. From East Face Lake follow Route 5 to notch behind First Tower. Rope up for the exposed Tower Traverse, class 4 (first ascent August 17, 1934, by Jules Eichorn and Marjory Bridge [Farquhar]). Traverse left (S) face of Second Tower by narrow out-sloping ledge leading steeply upward for 25 feet. The shelf then traverses for 25 feet (piton advisable) to the bottom of a 15-foot crack. This is followed by a series of scree-covered ledges, the Washboard. Climb the Washboard to a cliff at the upper end, and move left, up an easy pitch. Descend to a wide ledge leading right and into the angle formed by the Great Buttress and the face proper. Mount about twenty-five feet on easy rocks. Three routes present themselves, namely (left to right): *Fresh Air Traverse, Shaky-Leg Crack,* and *Direct Crack.*

Fresh Air Traverse, minimum class 5, 100 feet. Traverse left (S) around a large rectangular block, cross a gap in the ledge requiring a long step, and work out about 20 feet to the left. At this point climb upward over a rather smooth face to a steep, broken chimney leading gradually back to the right. Ascend the chimney and traverse right at the head. The lead ends almost directly above the start. The climber is now in the angle at the foot of the Grand Staircase, a series of shelves.

Shaky-Leg Crack, class 5, strenuous. First ascent June 9, 1936, by Morgan Harris, James N. Smith and Neil Ruge. Climb a few feet above the beginning of the Fresh Air Traverse. The belayer should be anchored on a narrow, partly overhung ledge. A shoulder-stand may be advisable, and the difficult crack above merits at least two safety pitons.

Direct Crack, class A. First ascent July 4, 1953, by John D. Mendenhall. The crack splits the wall about forty feet south of the right-hand cliffs, and requires about four pitons.

Above any of these three variations, climb the Grand Staircase to the wall at its head, and move left into a narrow squeeze chimney or crack (one piton advisable). A register will be found after the pitch is conquered. Traverse upward and right until easy rocks lead to the summit above. *Ortenburger Variation:* ascend blocks above the register to the ridge, thence north to summit.

Route 7. Southeast face. Minimum class 5. First ascent October 11, 1941, by John D. and Ruth Mendenhall. North of the base of the long couloir separating Whitney and Keeler Needle rises a buttress capped by an impressive gendarme. The buttress is separated from the eastern precipices of Whitney by an overhanging chimney. Ascend the buttress on easy class 4 rocks until one can traverse into and cross the chimney above the overhang. The thousand feet of rock remaining requires but two anchor pitons. The couloir between Whitney and Keeler is dangerously unsound, having claimed three lives.

Route 8. East face direct. Class 5.7 and A3. Grade V. First ascent July 4-6, 1959, by Denis Rutovitz and Andrzej Ehrenfeucht. This climb closely follows the enormous crack that splits the east face and joins Route 6 near the Fresh Air Traverse. Ascend talus to the base of the crack, make a 300-foot left-ascending traverse to the base of a 100-foot open-book chimney, and climb the chimney to a broad terrace. Go right along the terrace to the main crack and climb the face to the right of the crack for five leads. Then climb in the crack or on its faces to the great overhang. Here bolts are used to reach a crack on the right-hand face, up which the route continues (A3). A system of giant steps is then climbed by means of chimneys and faces until the Fresh Air Traverse and Route 6 is reached, some 16 leads from the base. Follow one of the Route 6 variations to the summit.

Keeler Needle (14,240+)

This is the first needle south of Mt. Whitney. *West side.* Class 1. First ascent unknown. A short climb over small blocks from the Mount Whitney trail.

East face. Class 5. First ascended July 1960 by Warren J. Harding, Glen Denny, Rob McKnight, and "Desert Frank." The ascent took 3½ days.

Day Needle (14,080+)

This is the second needle south of Mt. Whitney. *West side.* Class 1. First ascent unknown. From the Mount Whitney trail, climb easy blocks to the summit.

Third Needle (14,080+)

Route 1. West side. Class 1. First ascent unknown. Make a short climb over easy blocks from the Mount Whitney trail to the summit.

Route 2. East buttress. Class 4 and 5, with one class A pitch. First ascent September 5, 1948, by John D. Mendenhall, Ruby Wacker and John Altseimer. Walk up glaciated slabs west of Mirror Lake, south of Pinnacle Ridge. Ascend easy blocks where the ridge ends against the east buttress of the Third Needle. Rope up and ascend the south edge of the rib to about 13,600 feet elevation, where one crosses to the east face and climbs the class A chimney. Some distance above, traverse right into a rotten, bottomless chimney. The rib eases off, and one shifts from the south to the north side via a convenient cleft. A providential ledge leads to easy rocks just north of the summit.

Route 3. East face. Class 4, with one class 5 traverse. First ascent September 3, 1939, by John D. Mendenhall and Ruth Dyar (Mendenhall). Follow Route 2 to roping-up point. Class 3 climbing leads upward and to the left into an easy gully, which is capped by an abrupt overhang above the halfway point. Turn the difficulty by a short class 5 traverse to the right. Climb directly to the summit of the ridge by class 4 rocks, emerging upon the watershed between Third Needle and Day Needle. Routes 2 and 3 are recommended for those desiring roped routes combined with maximum accessibility.

Pinnacle Ridge (13,040+)

This serrated ridge separates the middle and north forks of Lone Pine Creek. A class 4 traverse of the ridge can be made in either direction (John D. Mendenhall and Nelson P. Nies, July 10, 1935). The views are among the finest in the entire Sierra, for the eastern battlements of Mount Whitney tower above, and Thor Peak dominates the view to the east.

Pinnacle Pass Needle (12,300). Northwest of Pinnacle Pass. Maximum class 4. First ascent September 7, 1936, by Robert K. Brinton, Glen Dawson and William Rice. Ascend a severe crack on the corner facing Whitney. Traverse a short arête to the summit.

Thor Peak (12,300)

This spectacular wall, separating the middle and north forks of Lone Pine Creek, towers to the north of Bighorn Park. The south face provides interesting climbs. Routes 1, 4, and 5 are shown on Sketch 31 of Thor's south wall.

Sketch 31. South wall of Thor Peak.

    1, 4, 5 Routes
        P Pink Perch
        V Variation, Route 4

Route 1. Southwest side. Class 2. First ascent by Norman Clyde. Climb ledges north of Mirror Lake to a sloping, sandy plateau southwest of the peak. Mount talus and scree to the notch south of the peak, and traverse to the northeast side, thence to the summit.

Route 2. West arête. Class 2. First descent September 7, 1936, by Robert K. Brinton, Glen Dawson and William Rice. A pleasant route to the summit over large granite blocks.

Route 3. Southeast chimney. Class 4. First ascent September 7, 1936, by William Rice, Robert K. Brinton and Glen Dawson. Climb to trees on the wall north of Bighorn Park. From a point near the highest trees, traverse left along a ledge. Ascend a difficult vertical chimney. Follow ledge back to right. Mount cracks and ledges to a large red-tinged pinnacle standing out from the wall. Between the pinnacle and the main face, traverse right to a gully sloping up to left. A well-defined ledge to left leads to summit.

Route 4. South face. Class 5. First ascent September 4, 1937, by Howard Koster, Arthur B. Johnson and James N. Smith. Follow the Mount

Whitney trail above Bighorn Park to top of switchbacks. A broad, brush-covered talus fan leads up to the right. Mount into a crack separating the main peak from Mirror Point to the southwest. Ascend the crack for two pitches, and traverse east along a series of ledges. Climb via a crack to the "Pink Perch," a high reddish ledge. Descend a crack eastward for a hundred feet. Two or three delicate steps place one in a vertical crack a few feet out on the face. Climb two pitches upward in the crack to a shelf behind a gendarme. Turn to the right and make a delicate face climb of 15 feet; easier going completes a 70-foot lead. Climb another pitch on fine, high-angle blocks, then traverse west high above the Pink Perch. Follow a series of ledges, which lead up into a recess under a 10-foot wall of cornice blocks, and emerge upon the arête a few hundred feet east of the summit.

Variation. Class 4. First descent September 3, 1940, by Carl Jensen, Howard Koster, Wayland Gilbert and Elsie Strand. The Pink Perch may also be reached by a small gully from the east. Take the trail from Bighorn. At top of switchbacks, leave trail and go up broad gully to where a wide ledge comes in from the right. Follow this ledge about two-thirds its length, then take a steep narrow gully leading diagonally left across the face directly to the Pink Perch.

Route 5. Direct crack, south wall. Class 5.9. First ascent July 1962 by Tom Condon and Ron Dickenson. Follow Route 4 until it is intersected by the second crack from the left skyline. Ascend this crack to its top, then work slightly left and then directly up to the summit.

Route 6. Northeast slope. Class 2. Leave the Whitney Trail below Lone Pine Lake and go up through brush and open slopes (Bob and Jerry Lee and Kathy Merrick, 1959).

Mirror Point. This is the southern buttress of Thor Peak, rising immediately north of Mirror Lake.

Route 1. West side. Class 1.

Route 2. Southeast face. Maximum class 4. First ascent September 6, 1936, by William Rice and Robert K. Brinton. Mount the talus slope northwest of Bighorn Park (northeast of Mirror Lake) to an apron. Climb up and around the apron to the left, ascending series of cracks above. The most difficult pitch is an overhanging 20-foot crack. The route works gradually to the left (S).

Mount Muir (14,015)

This peak provides a most impressive view of the entire region.

Route 1. West face. Class 3. First ascent unknown. A monument of rocks stands in a shallow chute at the point where one leaves the Mount

Whitney trail. The summit, 400 feet above, is plainly visible. Climb over loose talus and blocks, and head for the ridge to the right, at the point where the talus blends into the summit rocks. Traverse to the left and up a short crack to the small summit cap.

Route 2. East buttress, north side. Minimum class 4. First ascent July 11, 1935, by Nelson P. Nies and John D. Mendenhall. The route lies up the well-defined buttress that interrupts the sweep of the east wall. Rapid climbing will be encountered by maintaining a course just to the right of the ridge. When approximately halfway up the rib, swing left into a well-fractured chute that climbs back to the right, between two gendarmes. Behind the gendarmes, turn left and ascend large blocks to notch beneath summit. Keep slightly to left and attain summit via steep trough.

Route 3. East buttress, south side. Class 4. First ascent September 1, 1935, by Arthur B. Johnson and William Rice. From near the start of Route 2, climb the face of the buttress for a few pitches. Where the blocks become difficult, traverse down a ledge into a gully under the south face of the arête. Follow the trough to its head, where a 70-foot vertical crack appears in the very corner. Ascend the crack and steep blocks to the arête. Work right and up under gendarme to a fractured chute, and rejoin Route 2.

Wotan's Throne (12,720+)

This point rises in cliffs from the southwest shore of Mirror Lake. *Northwest arête.* Class 2. First ascent 1933, by Norman Clyde. From flats north of Consultation Lake there is a prominent class 2 couloir leading directly to the summit. *East Chimney.* Class 2. First ascent by Chester Versteeg July 10, 1937. Climb the northernmost of three short chimneys that breach the southeast wall of summit rocks.

Discovery Pinnacle (13,680+)

Immediately south of Whitney Trail Crest. First ascent September, 1873, by Clarence King and Knowles. Class 2 from the south.

Mount Hitchcock (13,184+)

Class 1. This has a long, ascending nivated slope rising from the southwest. The northeast side is a steep, impressive cliff. The first ascent was claimed by Frederick Wales, September 1881. Ascend the west shoulder from Crabtree Meadows and proceed along the plateau to the summit.

Mount McAdie (*13,680+*)

The mountain consists of three summits. The north peak is the highest, with the middle next in elevation.

North peak, Route 1. East face. Class 3. First ascent 1922 by Norman Clyde. From the slopes north of Arc Pass climb nearly to the summit of the middle peak. Descend to the col between the middle and north summits, traverse to the west side of the north peak, and climb upwards.

North peak, Route 2. West side. Class 3-4. Ascent July 1954 by Jim Koontz, Hervey Voge, Norv LaVene, Claire Millikan, Mike Loughman, Ro Lenel, and Bent Graust. Climb up the rock rib north of the chute that heads between the north and middle peaks. The ascent may also be made by way of the chute and the wall north of the col.

Middle peak. Class 2. First ascent June 1928 by Norman Clyde. From the slopes north of Arc Pass, ascend directly to the summit.

South peak. Class 2. First ascent June 12, 1936, by Oliver Kehrlein, Chester Versteeg and Tyler Van Degrift. From Arc Pass, ascend chimney on southeast face to summit. A class 3 traverse of a knife-edge enables one to attain the middle summit.

Mount Mallory (*13,850*)

Route 1. Class 2. First ascent June, 1925, by Norman Clyde. From Mount Irvine, go around the east shoulder of Mount Mallory to the easy south slope.

Route 2. From south of Arc Pass. Class 2. From south of Arc Pass, go up one of several chutes just to the north of the prominent peak on the edge of the LeConte plateau. Then follow Route 1.

Route 3. West side. Class 3. First ascent July 18, 1936, by Oliver Kehrlein, Chester Versteeg and Tyler Van Degrift. Ascend a wide couloir from Arc Pass to a point northwest of summit. Mount talus blocks to a horizontal crack running north to south. Class 3 rocks lead from upper end of crack to summit.

Route 4. Traverse from the north peak. Class 3. First ascent July 26, 1931, by Howard Sloan. Traverse from the head of the chute between Irvine and Mallory along the crestline, over the north peak, and into the notch between the north and main peaks. Thence climb to the summit. A variation is to climb about halfway up the north peak, and traverse by a series of easy ledges across its east face, onto the arête a hundred feet above the notch, and thence into the notch and up the north arête of the main peak.

Route 5. East side. Class 2 from Upper Meysan Lake. Climb a chute south of the east arête to the LeConte plateau and ascend the south-east slope to the top. An east side approach can also be made via Tuttle Creek.

Mount Irvine (*13,770*)

This ragged granite peak can be climbed by any of the chutes leading from Arc Pass to the high plateau east of crest, from which the summit is easily accessible.

Route 1. Class 1. First ascent June, 1925, by Norman Clyde. From Arc Pass, ascend a deep chute to the ridge to the east. Cross the ridge, descending slightly. Go around to the southeast side and ascend final easy rocks to summit.

Route 2. Class 1. The peak can be climbed directly from the Middle Fork of Lone Pine Creek.

Route 3. West face. Class 2–3. Ascend the fourth chute south of Consultation Lake (Charles House, 1957).

Mount Candlelight (*12,000+, 0.5 SE of Lone Pine Lake*)

This peak presents an imposing face as seen from Whitney Portal.

Route 1. Class 1. First ascent August 31, 1940, by Chester Versteeg. From Lower Meysan Lake, east of the peak, ascend a scree slope south of the prominent rock face to the saddle, thence to the summit.

Route 2. Class 3. Ascend the rock face directly above Lower Meysan Lake, up a chimney. Traverse left on a broad ledge for 25 feet, and follow an orange-colored dike to within 10 feet of top. Traverse right on a narrow ledge for 10 feet, then ascend 500 feet of scree to the summit.

The north face (above Whitney Portal Campground) offers interesting class 5 climbs, as yet unrecorded.

Lone Pine Peak (*12,944*)

This is an imposing summit when seen from Lone Pine; from the west and northwest, the northeast arête presents an interesting profile.

Route 1. Class 1. First ascent 1925, by Norman Clyde. Climb up the north fork of Tuttle Creek to a point west-southwest of the peak and ascend a talus slope to the high plateau, which presents a steep front to the east. Follow the plateau to the summit.

Route 2. North-northeast ridge. Long class 5 (6 pitons). First ascent September, 1952, by A. C. Lembeck and Ray W. Van Aken. From Whitney Portal drive east to summer home tract. Follow Meysan Lake trail, and take left branch where it divides. This trail drops to stream. Ascend north talus of Lone Pine Peak, bearing easterly. Cross under the ridge, gain the ridge's crest, and follow (class 3) to first large step (visible from Lone Pine). Ascend step, bearing to right (1 piton). The next pitch is strenuous (2 pitons). Climb an overhanging slab with layback to a platform, which is followed by a smooth chimney (3 pitons). Easy class 3 and 4 climbing over towers leads to the final summit blocks.

Route 3. Northwest face. Ascent was made by way of a chute from Meysan Lake, by Murray Bruch and Fred Johnson, July 1947.

Route 4. East face. Class 4. Ascent July 1952 by Warren Harding. Go up the second chute south of the ridge south of Whitney Portal (the NNE ridge), and climb class 4 pitches to 400 feet below the summit. From this point rappel 200 feet into the chute to the south and ascend this.

Mount Newcomb (13,410)

Route 1. Southwest slope. Class 2. First ascent August 1936 by Max Eckenburg and Bob Rumohr.

Route 2. East ridge. Class 2–3. Descended by Andy Smatko, Frede Jensen and Graham Stephenson.

Route 3. Northwest wall. Class 2–3. From the largest lake on Crab-tree Creek ascend one of several feasible chutes between Chamberlin and Newcomb.

Mount Chamberlin (13,169)

Route 1. West slope. Class 1–2. First ascent by J. H. Czock. May be reached from Lake 11,312 to the north, by way of the low saddle west of Chamberlin (Arkel Erb, 1963).

Route 2. East ridge. Class 2–3 from Mount Newcomb (see Mount Newcomb, Route 3). Climbed by B. Lilley; also by Andy Smatko, Frede Jensen, and Graham Stephenson.

Route 3. South slope. Class 1–2.

Mount Pickering (13,485)

First ascent July 1936 by Chester Versteeg, Tyler Van Degrift, and Oliver Kehrlein. The peak is class 2 from Primrose Lake via southeast slopes. Other routes of about equal difficulty are: from the lake west of Sky Blue Lake to the saddle east of the peak, and then up the east ridge; or, from the lakelet northwest of Erin Lake up the south slope; or, from the lake at the head of Perrin Creek to the saddle between Joe Devel and Pickering and up the southwest ridge.

Joe Devel Peak (13,325)

Class 2. First ascent September 20, 1875, by Wheeler Survey party, route unknown. Climbed July 7, 1937, by Owen L. Williams via the southeast arête. Records from 1875 to 1908 were found. The ascent is class 2 from the south, southwest, or the northeast ridge (see Mount Pickering). [The spelling should probably be *Devel.*]

Mount Guyot (12,300)

Class 1. This mountain lies west of the main crest and affords a fine view of both the Whitney Region and the Great Western Divide. First ascent 1881 by William Wallace.

The Miter (12,770)

South face. Class 3. First ascent July 18, 1938, by R. S. Fink. From Rock Creek, ascend a low ridge just south of Iridescent Lake and follow this to a saddle on the south side of the mountain. Climb many ledges, bearing slightly to the west. Then go in an easterly direction on the upper slope. Class 3. According to Donald Clarke, a chute northwest of the peak is class 3.

Mount LeConte (13,960)

Route 1. Northwest ridge. Class 3. First ascent June 1935 by Norman Clyde. "Followed ridge running southeast from Mount Mallory; thence on ridge around to southwest shoulder of mountain, encountered 20-foot drop, retraced shelf for 100 yards, dropped down to and came up chimney, passing below 20-foot drop, thence to summit." The head of the chute near the summit is the most difficult part of the climb. This route is still used by parties approaching the peak from the north.

Route 2. Northeast face. Class 3. First ascent September 7, 1952, by Steve Wilkie, Barbara Lilley, Wes Cowan, George Wallerstein and June Kilbourne. From Meysan Lake, ascend a loose, narrow chute to the plateau between LeConte and Mallory (also readily accessible from northwest). Cross the plateau to the cairn at the base of LeConte. Traverse easterly 200 yards. Now on the northeast face but short of the east arête, ascend directly to the summit.

Route 3. East arête. Class 3. First recorded ascent June 12, 1937, by Gary Leech, Bill Blanchard and Hubert North. Follow Route 2 to the cairn. Traverse for 450 or 500 yards to a chimney on the east face and follow up the chimney to a point near the summit; leave the chimney and complete the climb on the east arête.

Route 4. From the west. Class 4. First ascent July 17, 1936, by Oliver Kehrlein, Tyler Van Degrift and Chester Versteeg. Climb talus fan about 200 yards north of the east end of Iridescent Lake, the only lake in the recess; thence up a long couloir to a point below crest. Traverse to the northwest for 60 feet, at which point climb directly east toward the summit about 400 feet distant.

Route 5. From the west. Class 3. Follow Route 4, except that the traverse northwest is followed until a difficult chute in the north face leads to the summit.

Corcoran Mountain (*13,600+*)

This is one-half mile south of Mount LeConte, and the most northerly of three summits just south of LeConte.

Route 1. From the north. Class 2–3. First ascent 1933, by Howard S. Gates. Climb from Iridescent Lake up a chute to the saddle in the crest north of peak; thence up easy rocks to the summit. The northern saddle may also be reached from the east side, via Tuttle Creek. Go north past the base of the east arête of Corcoran and cross the high sloping basin to the saddle (class 2).

Route 2. From the south. Class 2. First ascent July 20, 1938, by R. S. Fink. Ascend west side of the main crest to the notch just south of the peak, thence up the south ridge.

Mount Langley (*14,042*)

According to Clarence King, first ascent prior to 1871. Second ascent 1871, by Clarence King and Paul Pinson.

Route 1. From Army Pass on the south. Class 1.

Route 2. From Rock Creek on the west. Class 2. Climb a wide chute, one-half mile south of a point directly west of the summit, to a level bench. Thence follow an easy arête in a northeasterly direction to the summit. The west face farther north is class 3.

Route 3. North face. Class 3. First recorded ascent August 1937 by Howard S. Gates and Nelson P. Nies. From a bench south of Tuttle Creek, climb to the base, thence southwest to a chimney blocked at the head. Climb out of the chimney to the south ledge, thence traverse southeast, then southwest to a ridge. Follow the ridge to the summit.

Route 4. East-southeast ridge. Class 3. From the northernmost large Cottonwood Lake, ascend talus to the westernmost of two saddles in the east-southeast ridge. Follow the crest of the broad ridge and plateau to the summit.

Route 5. Northeast chute. Class 2–3. From timberline on the south fork of Tuttle Creek, ascend south toward the east ridge about one-half mile east of the summit. Further up one can go diagonally right toward the junction of the east ridge and the main peak (Donald V. Clarke).

Route 6. East slope. Class 2. Follow an old trail up Diaz Creek. From the head of the creek work up eastern slopes to the summit.

The Major General (12,400+)

Rising northwest of Army Pass, this peak was first ascended by Chester and Elizabeth Versteeg August 8, 1937. From Rock Creek, climb shallow couloir slightly northwest of summit, thence up rock mass. Final pinnacle is short class 3.

The Kaweahs and the Great Western Divide

MILDRED JENTSCH and A. J. REYMAN (1953);
CARL HELLER (1964)

HISTORY AND GEOGRAPHY

The French and Spanish sheepherders were undoubtedly the earliest mountaineers in this region. They drove their flocks up the grassy canyons of the Kern and Kings rivers and tended them on the mountain slopes of the large basins of the tributary streams. The earliest known ascent was on Sawtooth Peak (then called Miner's Peak) in 1871 by Joseph W. Lovelace while deer hunting. In 1881 Mount Kaweah was climbed by James A. Wright, Wm. B. Wallace and Rev. F. H. Wales. Wallace did much of the early exploration of the Kings-Kern Divide and the headwaters of the Kaweahs in his search for gold, silver, and copper during the 1879 mining excitement in Mineral King.

It was not until July 1896 that Prof. Wm. R. Dudley ascended Sawtooth Peak and perceived the fact that the Kaweahs were not along the main crest of the Great Western Divide. He also traced the Kaweah River and discovered that its drainage did not include the Kaweah Peaks. Upon further excursions in 1897 he climbed Mount Kaweah, believed to be 14,140 feet, and named Kern-Kaweah River, Milestone Bowl, Red Spur and Picket Guard Peak. The Divide itself has had several designations since 1865 when the Whitney survey referred to it as the western ridge. John Muir in 1891 called it Greenhorn Ridge and LeConte in 1893 regarded it as the Great Western Ridge. In 1896 it had two names—Western Divide according to W. R. Dudley and Great Western Divide according to LeConte's map.

A map of this area is shown in Sketch 32. Topographic maps are: Triple Divide Peak, Mount Whitney, Mineral King, and Kern Peak. Study of the maps shows that the Great Western Divide is a high ridge to the west of the main divide of the Sierra. It stretches in a large reverse "S" from Table Mountain at the northeast to Florence Peak at the southwest. Kern Ridge and Kaweah Ridge extend east from the Great Western Divide toward the Kern River, the eastern boundary of this area. To the west more gentle terrain is cut by the tributaries of the Kaweah River.

The Great Western Divide consists mainly of the granitic rocks common in the Sierra. The Kaweahs consist of black and red volcanic rock which is extremely loose-jointed. Climbing here requires extra caution owing to the hazard of loose holds and falling rock.

The main ridge in this area, the Great Western Divide, is a lofty chain of boldly carved peaks varying in shape from spire-like Milestone Mountain to flat-topped Table Mountain and pyramidal Sawtooth Peak. Each canyon leads up to a magnificent amphitheater, or cirque, with steep granite walls frequently a thousand feet or more high. In these barren wastes of rock and snow are found many small glacial tarns. The canyons, in sculptured forms and polished rocks, give convincing evidence of the vigorous action of the glaciers they once contained. The Kaweah Group is formed as a jagged spur jutting from the Great Western Divide just south of Triple Divide Peak. The Kaweah group of peaks exhibits a color change from black to red which further enhances the spectacular quality of its sky-piercing crags and minarets.

Approaches

From the west. From Mineral King (7,760), a small mountain village situated 60 miles east and a little north of Visalia, there are five well-constructed trails that lead east and north to the high peaks by various passes. *Timber Gap* (9,400) renders the country to the north accessible after a two-mile switchback trail from Mineral King. A good horse trail leads north to Redwood Meadow and thence north and east over a long, steep ascent through rugged rock walls of the majestic Hamilton Lakes region to Kaweah Gap (10,640). *Black Rock Pass* (11,600) is reached by a trail which leaves the Timber Gap trail in Cliff Creek Canyon to proceed eastward into Little Five Lakes and the Big Arroyo. This pass affords a magnificent view of Kaweah Peaks, Big

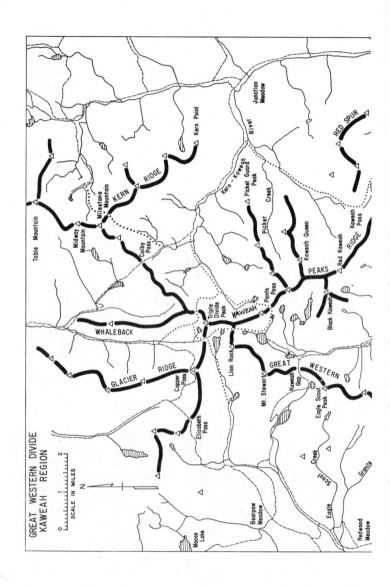

GREAT WESTERN DIVIDE
KAWEAH REGION

SCALE IN MILES
0   1   2

Table Mountain

KERN RIDGE

Kern Point

Milestone Mountain

Midway Mountain

Colby Pass

Junction Meadow

RED SPUR

Kern - Kaweah River

Picket Creek

Picket Guard Peak

Kaweah Queen

Red Kaweah

KAWEAH PEAKS

Black Kaweah

KAWEAH RIDGE Pass

WHALEBACK

Triple Divide Peak

Lippincott Pass

KAWEAH

GLACIER RIDGE

Copper Pass

Lion Rock

Mt. Stewart

GREAT WESTERN

Elizabeth Pass

Kaweah Gap

Eagle Scout Peak

Eagle Scout Creek

Granite Creek

Moose Lake

Bearpaw Meadow

Redwood Meadow

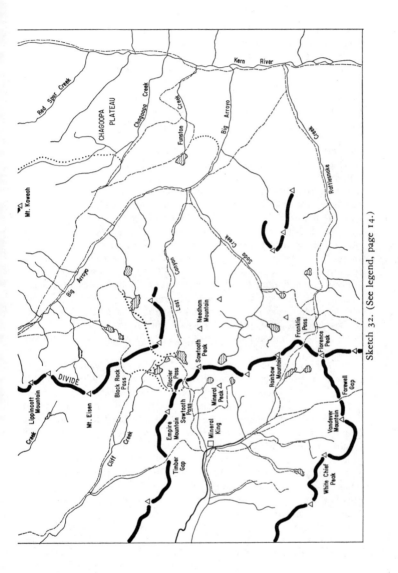

Sketch 32. (See legend, page 14.)

Arroyo and Chagoopa Plateau. The trail is steep and rough. The west side rewards the traveler with views of Upper Cliff Creek, Sawtooth Peak and Columbine Lake. *Sawtooth Pass* (11,680), 4.0 miles from Mineral King, is approached from the west by a rocky trail that becomes a steep descent to beautiful Columbine Lake on the east. It is recommended for foot travel only. The choice of direction from Columbine Lake may be either east down Lost Canyon or north over a knapsack route (see below, Glacier Pass) to the Black Rock Pass trail and thence to Little Five Lakes. *Franklin Pass* (11,680) cuts over the divide and serves to join Mineral King (5.1 miles north and west of the pass) with Rattlesnake Creek. The pass is through scree and rocks and is reminiscent of sandy desert travel for a short distance. A trail junction one mile east of the pass renders the areas to the south, east, and northeast accessible. The trail cutting past Little Claire Lake to Soda Creek from Rattlesnake Creek presents a little difficulty to animals on the steep south bank of Soda Creek. *Farewell Gap* (10,587) is 6.0 from Mineral King. It is gentle and green and is the gateway into the more southerly reaches of the Great Western Divide. Livermore calls this a friendly pass.

From Giant Forest (6,500), 52 miles from Visalia and 95 miles from Fresno, a park road leads two miles from headquarters to Crescent Meadow where the High Sierra Trail starts. This trail goes eastward to Bearpaw Meadow, passes along and literally through sheer granite walls of the Hamilton Lakes region, and over Kaweah Gap into the Big Arroyo.

From the roadhead on the Middle Fork of the Kaweah River, six miles above the Ash Mountain Park Headquarters, a trail contours to meet the Timber Gap trail north of Redwood Meadow.

From Big Meadow (7,659), about two miles east of General Grant Grove Section and about four miles above the northern boundary of Sequoia National Park, a trail leads eastward from the forest campground to Rowell Meadow and to Roaring River where the trail divides. One route follows Deadman Canyon over Elizabeth Pass (11,360), a rough, steep talus climb, to the Kaweah River. The other route follows Cloud Canyon and its southeast tributary to Colby Pass (12,000). This pass is rough and steep on both sides. Copper Pass connects Cloud Canyon and Deadman Canyon.

From Cedar Grove (4,631), on the South Fork of the Kings River, a trail climbs up the south wall of the canyon to Summit Meadow and joins at Rowell Meadow the Big Meadow Trail, which may be followed to either Elizabeth Pass or Colby Pass (see above). Another trail from

Cedar Grove may be followed up Bubbs Creek to the Sphinx Creek trail, and so to Scaffold Meadow on Roaring River; thence up Cloud or Deadman Canyon.

From the north. The Muir Trail leads over Forester Pass and descends to Tyndall Creek where a lateral may be taken north to Milestone Basin or south to Junction Meadow.

From the east. From Lone Pine on US 395 a road extends to Whitney Portal, the starting point of the Mount Whitney Trail. The trail leads over Whitney Trail Crest (13,600) and joins the High Sierra Trail which leads to the Kern River Canyon. Further south, Siberian Pass and Army Pass give passage to the east flank of the Kern Canyon.

From the south. There are long approaches from Kernville and Fairview on the Kern River and slightly shorter ones from Balch Park, Wishon Camp, and Camp Nelson over various routes.

CAMPSITES FOR CLIMBING AND EXPLORING

At the head of the *Big Arroyo* in the timber below Kaweah Gap is a good vantage spot for climbing Mount Stewart, Eagle Scout Peak, Kaweah Peaks, Black Kaweah, Red Kaweah, Lippincott Mountain, and other peaks, unnamed. From here many charming lakes and recesses may be explored also.

From *Little Five Lakes* one gets a fine view of the Kaweah ridge and one can find delightful camping areas. Lippincott Mountain, Mount Eisen and peaks south of Big Five Lakes furnish interesting climbing.

A camp at timberline in *Lost Canyon* may be a base for a third or fourth class ascent of Needham Mountain. Sawtooth Peak is within easy range, as is "Two Fingers" peak.

Florence Peak and Rainbow Mountain west of Little Claire Lake and the undesignated one east of it can be reached readily from the upper regions of *Rattlesnake Creek* or *Little Claire Lake*. The latter is a scenic spot for parties without animals, and the mountains about it reward the explorer with very curious rock and fox-tail pine formations.

Moraine Lake is a popular and convenient campsite. From it one gets a view of the large lake with the impressive back drop of Mount Kaweah. From the rim of the canyon a panorama of the Big Arroyo and its drainage basin presents itself. Mount Kaweah may be ascended from here.

From the environs of *Mineral King* itself, Sawtooth Peak, Mineral Peak, and Florence Peak may be reached. Mineral King has some public campgrounds.

Camps with pasture for stock may be found at Junction Meadow and Upper Funston Meadow on the Kern River, on the Kern-Kaweah River in many meadows along its entire length, along Milestone Creek, in Cloud Canyon, in Deadman Canyon, along Big Arroyo, and at Moraine Lake.

KNAPSACK PASSES

These are mostly without formal trail, and should not be attempted with animals. Approximate routes are indicated on the map (Sketch 32).

Triple Divide Pass. Class 2. This leads from Glacier Lake at the head of Cloud Canyon to Gallats Lake on the Kern-Kaweah River. From Glacier Lake proceed to the saddle (12,160) northeast of Triple Divide Peak. From the saddle contour around to the right (SE) and descend almost due south to a lake. The left (N) side of the Kern-Kaweah River can be followed to Gallats Lake.

Lion Lake Pass (11,600). Class 2. This leads from Cloud Canyon to Lion Lake through the pass just west of Triple Divide Peak.

Lion Rock Pass (11,680+). Class 3. The first or second pass east of Lion Rock can be used in going from Lion Lake to Nine Lake Basin to the south.

Kern-Kaweah Col (12,000+). Class 2–3. This is a rough knapsack pass from Nine Lake Basin to the upper Kern-Kaweah River. It has been dubbed Pants Pass by mountaineers because of the destructive effect on trousers when descending. The pass is east-northeast of the large (10,730) lake on the stream draining the northwest side of Nine Lake Basin. From this lake a small peak is seen to the northeast. North of this peak is a fairly low notch that is easily approached from the west, but which connects with a steep, rocky, class 3 chimney that descends between cliffs on the east. The recommended pass lies south of the little peak; it is a little higher and steeper on the west, but still quite feasible, and much better on the east side. From the east this pass is reached from a lake (11,380) about a mile north of the cirque at the head of the Kern-Kaweah River. The steep chimney leading to the lower pass is easily identified, and the better pass is south of this.

Kaweah Pass (12,400). Class 2. This leads cross country from the High Sierra Trail on Chagoopa Plateau to the Colby Pass Trail on the Kern-Kaweah River. Leave the High Sierra Trail at about 10,000 feet elevation, proceed northward over the Chagoopa Plateau, and follow Chagoopa Creek to the low gap just east of Mount Kaweah. Descend at the lowest point, go west of a lake and then through the Kaweah Basin south of the two smaller lakes and north of the larger lakes. Cross the granite bluff north of the large lake and work across to Picket Creek, which is descended on the west side. The Colby Pass trail on the Kern-Kaweah River is met about three miles west of Junction Meadow.

Glacier Pass (*11,040+*). Class 3. Connects the Sawtooth Pass Trail with the Black Rock Pass Trail north of Cliff Creek. The pass is west of a little peak north of Sawtooth Pass. An ice axe is desirable.

Cyclamen Lake Shortcut (*11,040+*). Class 3. From Columbine Lake proceed north on the east side of Cyclamen Lake to the saddle 0.3 mile north of peak 11,772 (northeast of Cyclamen Lake). From the saddle descend to Big Five Lakes or contour north on the east side of the ridge to Little Five Lakes and the Black Rock Pass Trail.

Routes and Records for the Principal Peaks

The descriptions of routes and records are arranged in the following order:

Peaks of the Great Western Divide (*north to south*)
Peaks of the Kaweah Group (*northwest to southeast*)
Peaks east of the Great Western Divide (*north to south*)
Peaks west of the Great Western Divide (*north to south*)

Peaks of the Great Western Divide (North to South)

Table Mountain (*13,630*)

The first ascent was made on August 25, 1908, by Paul Shoup, Fred Shoup, and Gilbert Hassel.

Route 1. Northeast face. Class 3. First ascent by Norman Clyde and party on July 26, 1927. The only route up this face is a steep chimney which usually contains snow and ice well into the summer.

Route 2. South side. Class 3. Ascended by Norman Clyde on July 29, 1927. This is a shelf and chimney climb of moderate difficulty. The important thing is to change shelves, for each dips at a hazardous angle after a certain point is reached.

Route 3. Southeast face. Class 3. Ascended by Norman Clyde and a party of five persons in July 1932. The ascent began in a cirque on Milestone Creek.

Midway Mountain (*13,666*)

The first ascent was made in 1912 by Francis P. Farquhar, Wm. E.

Colby, Robert M. Price, and four others. The north side of the east ridge is an ordinary rock climb with no difficulties (class 2 to 3). The west slope is about class 2.

Milestone Mountain (13,641)

First ascent on July 14, 1912, by Francis P. Farquhar, William E. Colby, and Robert M. Price. They climbed from Milestone Bowl.

Route 1. Northeastern side. Class 3. From Milestone Creek ascend just north of Milestone and cross to west face.

Route 2. South side. Class 3. Milestone Bowl route. Traverse under the south face of Milestone Mountain to the ridge whose main axis points southwesterly and then go up this ridge which trends northeasterly to the summit cairn.

Route 3. Northwest face. Class 3. The route of Walter A. Starr, Jr., September 19, 1931. From the northwest ascend talus slopes and chutes to the southwest ridge and follow this to the final spire.

Peak 13,255 (0.7 SW of Milestone Mountain)

First ascent by Francis P. Farquhar, William E. Colby, and Robert M. Price in 1912. A class 1 ascent from Colby Pass.

Peak 12,600 (0.5 SW of Colby Pass)

Route 1. Northeast ridge. Class 3. First ascent by Jules Eichorn, Kenneth May, and A. Tagliapietra in 1936.

Route 2. Southwest ridge. Class 2. Ascended by Carl P. Jensen and Howard Gates in 1936 while traversing the ridge.

Peak 12,640+ (0.7 NE of Triple Divide Peak)

First ascent on July 21, 1926, by George R. Bunn and R. C. Lewis. Class 3 by southwest slope.

Triple Divide Peak (12,634)

First ascent in 1920 by J. S. Hutchinson and Charles A. Noble by Route 1.

Route 1. East Ridge. About class 2. From the saddle to the northeast ascend the east ridge.

Route 2. South Ridge. Easy class 3. Don Clarke climbed to the south ridge just east of Lion Rock. His route followed the ridge, dropping to the east side to avoid gendarmes and then went up the northeast face.

Route 3. West ridge. Class 3. Climbed by John Wedberg, Bill Engs, and others, from Lion Lake Pass, 1963.

Lion Rock (12,320+)

First ascent by Dave Winkley, William Curlett, and Earl S. Wallace, July 7, 1927.

Route 1. West slope. Class 2. From Tamarack Lake ascend the broad western slope and the west ridge to the summit.

Route 2. East chute. Class 3. From Nine Lake Basin climb north to Lion Rock Pass, enter the northern chute between the two peaks and ascend the southeast face of the north peak to the summit.

Mount Stewart (12,205)

First ascent by Norman Clyde, August 14, 1932.

Route 1. From Kaweah Gap. Class 2. Traverse over talus. Time required from the Gap is about two to three hours.

Route 2. From Nine Lake Basin. Class 2. Ascend a grassy gully at the north end of the first lake in the basin. Time is about three to four hours.

Eagle Scout Peak (12,040)

First ascent on July 15, 1926, by Francis P. Farquhar and Eagle Scouts Frederick Armstrong, Eugene Howell, and Coe Swift. The peak was named on this ascent. It is a class 2 from the Big Arroyo, and the time is about 2 hours.

Peak 12,250 (0.6 N. of Lippincott Mountain)

First ascent unknown. A. J. Reyman found a cairn on the summit on August 1, 1951. The east ridge is class 2. Ascend the low notch from the lake basin northeast of the peak and walk along the east ridge to the rocky summit.

Lippincott Mountain (12,260)

First ascent by Norman Clyde in 1922.

Route 1. Southeast slope. Class 2. An easy ascent from either the Big Arroyo or the Little Five Lakes.

Route 2. East ridge. Class 2. Ascend the east ridge from the basin north of the peak and walk along the east ridge to the summit over large blocks.

Mount Eisen (*12,160*)

First recorded ascent on July 15, 1949, by Howard Parker, Mildred Jentsch, Ralph Youngberg, and Martha Ann McDuffie.

Route 1. From Little Five Lakes. Class 3. Go around the large lake of the north branch of Little Five Lakes. Contour on the north side on granite to the highest shelf which has a lakelet. Proceed to the south notch between the two peaks, and thence north to the peak. Caution: The lowest notch is reached by a high-angle scree slope and the rocks are very loose; therefore avoid this route. There is a possible fourth class route on the east face.

Route 2. West side. Class 1. Walk over scree and talus.

Route 3. Southeast ridge. Class 2. Follow the ridge from near the top of Black Rock Pass.

Sawtooth Peak (*12,343*)

First ascent was made by Joseph W. Lovelace while deer hunting in 1871. It is climbed several times each year by virtue of its accessibility and rewarding view. Follow Sawtooth Pass Trail and continue up the northwest ridge to the summit. Class 2.

Peak 12,045 (*1.3 S of Sawtooth Peak*)

First ascent unknown. A. J. Reyman found a mineral claim monument on the south slope below the summit on August 11, 1951.

Route 1. South slope. Class 2. An easy ascent from Franklin Lakes via the south slope.

Route 2. Via Crystal Lake Trail. Class 2.

Rainbow Mountain (*12,000+*)

First ascent on July 15, 1942, by Oliver Kehrlein, Jack Allen, and "Black Bart" Evans.

Route 1. Southeast ridge. Class 2 from Franklin Pass.

Route 2. Southwest slope. Class 2 from Franklin Lake.

Florence Peak (*12,432*)

First ascent unknown.

Route 1. From Franklin Pass. Class 2.

Route 2. From Rattlesnake Creek. Ascend over huge talus blocks near the top. Class 4. About two hours.

Peaks of the Kaweah Group (Northwest to Southeast)

Peak 12,480+ (1.9 N of Black Kaweah; formerly 12,547)

First ascent by Norman Clyde in July 1922.

Peak 13,140 (1 N of Black Kaweah)

First ascent on July 11, 1924, by G. A. Gaines, C. A. Gaines, and H. H. Bliss.
Class 2 from anywhere in Nine Lake Basin.

Kaweah Queen (13,360+; 0.8 NE of Black Kaweah)

First ascent by Gerald A. Gaines, C. A. Gaines, and H. H. Bliss, July 11, 1924.
Route 1. Southwest slope. Class 2. A loose rock climb from Nine Lake Basin.
Route 2. Northwest ridge. Class 2. A traverse from Peak 13,140 over loose rock.

Black Kaweah (13,765)

First ascent by Duncan McDuffie, Ovis I. Brown, and J. S. Hutchinson on August 11, 1920, by Route 1. All routes are on dangerous loose-jointed rock.
Route 1. West ridge. A long class 3 with much loose rock. Ascend the ridge from the south and proceed eastward. Keep on the south side but below the crest of the ridge until just below the summit. Ascend a wide chute to the ridge and summit.
Route 2. Southwest face. Class 4. First ascent July 26, 1921, by Philip E. Smith, Marian Simpson, and Irene Smith. Ascend to the lake in the cirque below the peak and continue up the high angle slope of loose rock at the base of the mountain. Here two chutes, inclined at an angle of about 60° go up toward the summit. Enter the right hand chute and after about 100 feet cross over to the left chute which can be followed nearly to the summit. Snow or ice are likely obstacles in the chute. About two or three hours are required to the top.
Route 3. Southwest ridge. Class 4. Climbed by A. R. Ellingwood and Carl Blaurock, August, 1928. Ascend the southwest ridge from the Big Arroyo and keep to the crest until the west ridge is reached. Climb the west ridge to the summit.

Route 4. East ridge. Class 4. First climbed by Neil Ruge and James Smith in June 1935. Ascend from the south to the ridge between Black and Red Kaweahs at the second small notch toward Red Kaweah. Work under Pyramidal Pinnacle on the northeast to lowest point on ridge. Then climb the ridge westward, only descending to avoid gendarmes. Near the top of the Black Kaweah a sloping ledge is visible. Go to this ledge, crossing several couloirs. Keep to the left and climb a chute which leads to summit.

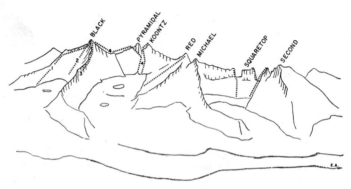

Sketch 33. The Kaweah Ridge from the southwest.

Route 5. North face of east ridge. Class 4. From the northeast side of Lake 11,705 in Nine Lake Basin ascend the face to the low point of the east ridge between Pyramidal Pinnacle and Black Kaweah. Follow Route 4 to the summit.

Pyramidal Pinnacle (*13,600*)

Route 1. Class 4. Probably first climbed August 1, 1932, by Glen Dawson and Jules Eichorn. An ascent was made in August 1953 by Jim Koontz and companions, who traversed from the southeast face of the Black Kaweah along the ridge toward the Red Kaweah and up the Pyramidal Pinnacle. Then they turned down the Black Kaweah side, traversed under the west wall of the pinnacle, and descended the chute south of the one heading between Pyramidal Pinnacle and the next pinnacle to the southeast (Koontz Pinnacle).

Route 2. Class 4. An ascent was made in August 1955 by Carl Heller and Robert Stein from Nine Lake Basin (see Black Kaweah, Route 5).

Koontz Pinnacle (*13,600+*)

Class 3. First ascent August 26, 1953, by Jim Koontz, Pete Murphy, and Fred Peters. From the west ascend the first chute south of that which descends directly from the notch between Pyramidal and Koontz pinnacles. Traverse from the chute over to the notch and climb to the summit.

Red Kaweah (*13,760+*)

First ascent in 1912 by Charles W. Michael. The west side is class 3.

Michaels Pinnacle (*13,680+; just south of the Red Kaweah*)

First ascent by C. W. Michael in 1912 by an unknown route. The second ascent was made August 28, 1953 by Jim Koontz, Pete Murphy, and Fred Peters. Class 3 to 4 from the lake to the west. They climbed to the ridge north of Squaretop and climbed over the pinnacles between Squaretop and Michaels Pinnacle. No cairns were found on the four major pinnacles on this ridge. From the southeast side of the fourth pinnacle they worked around the west side on a narrow ledge which petered out in a steep couloir. They descended this about thirty feet until it joined the next couloir and then worked back up onto the ledge and so to the col between this pinnacle and Michaels. From the col they ascended a wide talus ledge on the northeast side of the ridge to some easy rock which led back to the ridge. From here it was a walk to the summit.

Squaretop

First ascent June 26, 1935, by Jim Smith and Neil M. Ruge. Class 3 to 4 from the west via the col between this pinnacle and the one to the southeast. Climb directly to the col from the lake at the base of the ridge. Climb the southeast face on exposed ledges, about two rope lengths to a broad ledge. A chute on the right leads to a second series of ledges. Climb left on these to the summit ridge. The fairly firm rock on this face makes the climb more enjoyable than many other Kaweah climbs.

Pinnacle southeast of Squaretop

First ascent by Jim Koontz, Fred Peters, and Pete Murphy, August 27,

1953. Class 3 from the col between this pinnacle and Squaretop, climbing directly to the summit. Descent was made on the south.

Second Kaweah (13,680+)

First ascent in 1922 by Norman Clyde. The south slope is class 2. There is some question as to what is the correct summit. Three pinnacles on the northwest ridge were first climbed August 29, 1953, by Jim Koontz, Fred Peters, and Pete Murphy. Class 3.

Mount Kaweah (13,802)

First ascent in September 1881 by Judge William B. Wallace, Captain James Albert Wright, and Reverend F. H. Wales. The south slope from Chagoopa Plateau is class 1.

North ridge. Class 4. Climbed in September 1964 by Eduardo Garcia and Carlos Puente of the Andean Federation of Chile.

Peak 13,285 (1.3 NE of Mount Kaweah; formerly 13,291)

First ascent on July 17, 1936, by Jules Eichorn, Virginia Adams, Jane Younger, and Carl P. Jensen. The south slope is class 2.

Red Spur (13,183; formerly 13,186)

First ascent by Jules Eichorn, Virginia Adams, Jane Younger, and Carl P. Jensen by the southwest ridge on a traverse from peak 13,000+ in July 1936. Class 3. Stay below crest on south.

Red Spur (12,785; formerly 12,771)

Ascended in 1916 by Walter L. Huber. Class 1.

Peaks East of the Great Western Divide (North to South)

Peak 12,785 (1.4 SE of Table Mountain; formerly 12,673)

First ascent in July 1936, by Sierra Club party. Class 2 from the eastern saddle.

Peak 13,520+ (0.6 SE of Milestone Mountain; formerly 13,560)

First ascent by W. F. Dean, Otis B. Wright, Harry C. Dudley, W. R. Dudley, August 3, 1897.

Peak 13,186 (Kern Ridge)

First ascent unknown. May Pridham found a cairn but no records in July 1936.

Peak 12,789 (Kern Point)

First ascent on July 25, 1924, by William Horsfall and C. Laughlin. Class 2 from west or southwest.

Picket Guard Peak (12,302)

First ascent on August 1, 1936, by C. Dohlman, H. Manheim and B. Breeding. Class 2 from the south; class 3 by the north ridge.

Peak 11,861 (0.3 S of largest Big Five Lake; formerly 11,845)

No information is available.

Peak 11,680+ (½ SW of Peak 11,861)

The name "Two Fingers" is suggested. From a distance this peak resembles two fingers pointing skyward. At close range a large east-west fault is discovered into which one may look a long way down. The north side of the peak is precipitous, but the south side is a gentle scree slope. The two summit blocks seem to be composed of solidified scree. On an ascent made July 13, 1949, David R. Brower and Jim Harkins found a cairn but no register.

Route 1. From Little Five Lakes. Class 3. Go to the knapsack pass one mile south of Black Rock Pass and along the ridge toward the summit.

Route 2. From Big Five Lakes. Class 3. Climb up the north face.

Needham Mountain (12,467)

First ascent in July 1916, by M. R. Parsons, Agnes Vaile, H. C. Graham, and Edmund Chamberlain.

Route 1. North slope. Class 2. Climb the north slope from Lost Canyon to the notch between Needham Mountain and Sawtooth Peak. Proceed along the west slope to the summit. This route was followed on July 28, 1949, by R. R. Breckenfeld, Emily Frazer, and Donald Scanlon.

Route 2. North face. Class 3. Ascended July 28, 1949, by Howard Parker and Helen Parker. Ascend the north couloir to the ridge and traverse westward to the summit.

Route 3. North face. Class 3. Mildred Jentsch climbed from Lost Canyon July 28, 1949, directly up the face.

Route 4. Southeast slope. Class 2. Ascended by A. J. Reyman August 8, 1951, on a traverse from Peak 12,320+.

Route 5. South slope. Class 2.

Peak 12,079+ (*1.2 E of Little Claire Lake*)

First ascent by Richard Olhausen, Robert Olhausen, and B. A. Olhausen July 14, 1942. The south slope is scree and the southwest ridge from Little Claire Lake is class 1. The weathered rock and foxtail pines present interesting formations. The north face may be class 3.

Peaks West of the Great Western Divide (North to South)

Peak 12,237 (*Glacier Ridge*)

First ascent in July 1936, by E. Grubb, May Pridham, and D. Von Lobensels. Class 2 to 3.

Peak 12,416 (*Glacier Ridge*)

No records are available.

Whaleback (*11,726*)

First ascent August 5, 1936, by May Pridham and Adel Von Lobensels.

Peak 10,252 (*1.6 W of Mount Stewart*)

First ascent unknown. On July 6, 1949, Jules Eichorn, Jim Harkins, Howard Parker, Tom Kendig, and Mildred Jentsch climbed from Hamilton Lake and found a cairn below the summit. The southeast slope is class 3. Climb up a rocky, wooded ridge onto smooth granite, and thence onto a ramp on the north side to the five-foot-wide summit.

Peak 9,770 (*2 WNW of Eagle Scout Peak*)

First ascent in 1936 by D. Johnson and party.

Towers above Eagle Scout Creek.

On the north and south walls of Eagle Scout Creek there are some fine rock towers, about 9,500 to 10,000 feet, offering fourth and fifth class routes. A number were climbed by the Loma Prieta Rock Climbing Section of the Sierra Club in 1953.

Empire Mountain (11,509)

There is a mineral claim on the summit, which can be reached by a class 2 climb from Glacier Pass along the southeast ridge.

Mineral Peak (11,550)

First ascent August 3, 1937, by Chester L. Errett and Don A. McGeein. Class 2 by the northeast slope and the east ridge from Monarch Lake.

References

THE LIST below has been selected to include books that may be of particular interest to climbers. For the most part these books are concerned with early history and exploration, geology, or general descriptions and tourist information. Very little is to be found in them about Sierra climbing. A number, however, contain outstanding collections of photographs that can be very valuable to those who wish to climb or explore.

ADAMS, ANSEL. *Sierra Nevada and the John Muir Trail.* 50 plates. Archetype Press, Berkeley, 1938.

———. *My Camera in Yosemite Valley.* 24 plates. Houghton Mifflin Company, Boston, 1949.

ADAMS, ANSEL AND VIRGINIA. *Illustrated Guide to Yosemite Valley.* Rev. ed., Sierra Club, San Francisco, 1963.

BROWER, D. R. (ed.). *Manual of Ski Mountaineering.* Sierra Club, San Francisco, 1962.

———. *Going Light—with Backpack or Burro.* Sierra Club, San Francisco, 1951.

———. (ed.). *The Sierra Club, A Handbook.* Sierra Club, San Francisco, 1960.

COLBY, W. E. (ed.). *John Muir's Studies in the Sierra.* Rev. ed., Sierra Club, San Francisco, 1960.

ERICKSON, C. E. *Sunset Sportsman's Atlas: The High Sierra and Its Environs.* Lane Book Co., Menlo Park, 1955.

FARQUHAR, F. P. *Place Names of the High Sierra.* Sierra Club, San Francisco, 1926.

———. "Exploration of the Sierra Nevada," *California Historical Society Quarterly,* vol. 4, 3–58 (1925).

———. *Yosemite, the Big Trees, and the High Sierra: A Selective Bibliography.* Univ. Calif. Press, Berkeley, 1948.

———. *Up and Down California in 1860–1864: The Journal of William H. Brewer.* Yale Univ. Press, New Haven, 1930; Univ. Calif. Press, 1950.

HALL, ANSEL F. *Yosemite Valley: An Intimate Guide.* National Parks Publishing, Berkeley, 1929.

KING, CLARENCE. *Mountaineering in the Sierra Nevada.* First edition, 1872. Later edition (F. P. Farquhar, ed.), W. W. Norton, New York, 1946.

LeCONTE, J. N. *A Journal of Ramblings through the High Sierra* (in 1870). Sierra Club, San Francisco, 1930.

LEONARD, R. M., et al. *Belaying the Leader. An Omnibus on Climbing Safety.* Sierra Club, San Francisco, 1956.

MANNING, H. (ed.). *Mountaineering: The Freedom of the Hills.* The Mountaineers, Seattle, 1961.

MATTHES, F. E. *Geologic History of the Yosemite Valley.* (U.S.G.S. Professional Paper 160.) U.S. Govt. Printing Office, Washington, 1930.

——. *The Incomparable Valley: A Geologic Interpretation of the Yosemite.* 51 photographs. Univ. Calif. Press, Berkeley, 1950.

——. *Sequoia National Park: A Geological Album.* 125 photographs. Univ. Calif. Press, Berkeley, 1950.

McDERMAND, C. *Waters of the Golden Trout Country.* G. P. Putnam's Sons, New York, 1946.

——. *Yosemite and Kings Canyon Trout.* G. P. Putnam's Sons, New York, 1947.

MUENCH, JOSEF AND JOYCE. *Along Sierra Trails: Kings Canyon National Park.* 146 photographs. Hastings House, New York, 1947.

MUENCH, JOSEF. *Along Yosemite Trails.* A collection of photographs. Hastings House, New York, 1948.

MUIR, JOHN. *My First Summer in the Sierra.* Houghton Mifflin Company, Boston, 1911.

——. *The Mountains of California.* The Century Co., New York, 1894.

——. *Yosemite and the Sierra Nevada.* Selected writings of John Muir and 64 photographs by Ansel Adams. Houghton Mifflin Company, Boston, 1948.

PEATTIE, RODERICK (ed.). *The Sierra Nevada: The Range of Light.* Vanguard Press, New York, 1947.

ROPER, STEVE. *A Climber's Guide to Yosemite Valley.* Sierra Club, San Francisco, 1964.

RUSSELL, C. P. *One Hundred Years in Yosemite.* 52 illus. Univ. Calif. Press, Berkeley, 1947.

SCHUMACHER, GENNY. *The Mammoth Lakes Sierra. A Handbook for Roadside and Trail.* Sierra Club, San Francisco, 1959.

——. *Deepest Valley. Guide to Owens Valley and Its Mountain Lakes, Roadsides, and Trails.* Sierra Club, San Francisco, 1962.

STARR, W. A., JR. *Guide to the John Muir Trail and the High Sierra Region.* Rev. ed., Sierra Club, San Francisco, 1963.

WHEELOCK, W., AND CONDON, T. *Climbing Mount Whitney.* La Siesta Press, Glendale, Calif., 1960.

WHITE, J. R., AND S. J. PUSATERI. *Sequoia and Kings Canyon National Parks.* Stanford Univ. Press, Stanford, 1949.

WOLFE, LINNIE MARSH (ed.). *John of the Mountains: Unpublished Journals of John Muir.* Houghton Mifflin Company, Boston, 1938.

WRIGHT, CEDRIC. *Words of the Earth.* Sierra Club, San Francisco, 1960.

Table 1. Geographic Arrangement of the U.S.G.S. 15 Minute Series Maps of the High Sierra.

Sonora Pass	Fales Hot Springs					
Tower Peak	Matterhorn Peak	Bodie				
Hetch Hetchy Reservoir	Tuolumne Meadows	Mono Craters				
	Merced Peak	Devils Postpile	Mount Morrison	Casa Diablo Mountain		
	Shuteye Peak	Kaiser Peak	Mount Abbot	Mount Tom	Bishop	
	Shaver Lake	Huntington Lake	Blackcap Mountain	Mount Goddard	Big Pine	
		Patterson Mountain	Tehipite Dome	Marion Peak	Mount Pinchot	
			Giant Forest	Triple Divide Peak	Mount Whitney	Lone Pine
			Kaweah	Mineral King	Kern Peak	Olancha

Maps

THERE ARE a number of maps of the High Sierra region that show trails and road approaches. Some of these are issued by the National Park Service, some by the U.S. Forest Service, and some by private publishers. The latter are designed primarily for hunters and fishermen. The map in Starr's *Guide* shows trails and some knapsack routes but does not give topographic detail. By far the best maps for the climber are the topographic maps of the U.S. Geological Survey. They may be purchased from a number of bookstores or sporting shops, or from Survey offices in Washington or Denver. The original maps on a scale of 1:125,000 (30 Minute Series) cover the entire High Sierra. The quadrangles, in correct geographical arrangement, are as follows:

Dardanelles	Bridgeport		
Yosemite	Mt. Lyell	Mt. Morrison	
	Kaiser	Mt. Goddard	Bishop
		Tehipite	Mt. Whitney
		Kaweah	Olancha

Larger maps on the same scale are combined for Yosemite National Park, which includes most of Dardenelles, Bridgeport, Yosemite, and Mount Lyell; and for Sequoia and Kings Canyon National Parks, which includes most of Mount Goddard, Bishop, Tehipite, Mount Whitney, and parts of Kaweah and Olancha. These 1:125,000 maps are now obsolete.

A fine new series of photogrammetrically based maps has been published by the U.S. Geological Survey. These maps are much more accurate than the old maps. They are published for the High Sierra region on a scale of 1:62,500 (15 Minute Series). A list of these maps, in correct geographical arrangement, is given in Table 1. A breakdown of the maps required for individual climbing areas will be found in Table 2.

Table 2. Maps for Climbing Areas.

CLIMBING AREA	MAPS OF 15 MINUTE SERIES (1:62,500)
Sawtooth Ridge	Matterhorn Peak
Bond Pass to Tioga Pass	Tower Peak, Matterhorn Peak, Tuolumne Meadows, Mono Craters
Cathedral Range	Tuolumne Meadows, Mono Craters, Merced Peak, Hetch Hetchy Reservoir
Clark Range	Merced Peak
Minarets and Ritter Range	Devil's Postpile
Mammoth Pass to Mono Pass	Mount Morrison, Mount Abbot, Devil's Postpile, Kaiser Peak
Mono Pass to Pine Creek	Mount Abbot, Mount Tom
Mount Humphreys	Mount Tom, Mount Abbot, Mount Goddard
LeConte Divide	Blackcap Mountain, Mount Goddard, Tehipite Dome
Evolution Region	Mount Goddard, Blackcap Mountain, Mount Pinchot
Palisades	Mount Goddard, Big Pine
Kings Canyon Region	Tehipite Dome, Marion Peak
Palisades to Kearsarge	Mount Pinchot, Marion Peak, Big Pine, Mount Goddard
Kings-Kern Divide	Mount Whitney, Mount Pinchot
Whitney Region	Mount Whitney, Lone Pine
Kaweahs	Mineral King, Triple Divide Peak, Mount Whitney, Kern Peak

Index